The CCC Reader

IDCR 151
CREATED AND CALLED
FOR COMMUNITY

MESSIAH COLLEGE.

Copley Custom Textbooks

An imprint of XanEdu Publishing, Inc.

ISBN 13: 978-1-58152-851-0
ISBN 10: 1-58152-851-5

Cover Art: 2011, by David Kasparek, associate professor of graphic design.

Copley Custom Textbooks
An imprint of XanEdu Publishing, Inc.
138 Great Road
Acton, MA 01720
800-562-2147

Contents

Vocation

Afterword

Editors

Mary Holloway
Assistant Professor of Communication

Jim LaGrand
Professor of History

Ben Taylor
Residence Director/Coordinator of the First Year Experience

Cynthia A. Wells
Assistant Professor of Higher Education

With meaningful contributions from Brenna Stewart, Class of 2012, and capable assistance from Tina Keul, Administrative Assistant

Preface

As Christians, we turn to the Scriptures for guidance on life's deepest questions of meaning and purpose. Genesis reminds us that humankind is made in God's image. In turn, we must consider what this means for how we understand ourselves, how we relate to one other, and how we care for God's creation. The Sermon on the Mount, as recorded in the Gospel of Matthew, illustrates the values of the Kingdom of God. We must discern what these ideals require of us as followers of Jesus, both individually and as a community of believers. And in the gospel of Luke, the Parable of the Good Samaritan reminds us not only to love God with all of our heart, soul, mind, and strength but also to love our neighbor as ourselves. We must engage what it means to love God holistically and consider the implications of Jesus's expansive view of neighbor. *Created and Called for Community*—commonly referred to as CCC—beckons students to consider these significant themes of Christian faith and provides a space for shared conversation across the Messiah College community.

In CCC, you will encounter habits of mind, heart, and soul that will enrich the remainder of your college education and your life. CCC is an interdisciplinary course, that is the content and the faculty reflect a breadth of academic disciplines. As a participant, you will be able to connect what you are learning to your major, to other general education courses, and to your life as a whole. The course builds on the skills addressed in the First Year Seminar, such as writing, verbal communication, text engagement, and critical thinking. These abilities will serve you well as you live out your Christian vocation in all its dimensions.

Indeed, in this and all endeavors, may each of our lives be enriched and deepened in our ability to love God and neighbor.

Messiah College

Mission and Identity

Messiah College is a Christian college of the liberal and applied arts and sciences. The College is committed to an embracing evangelical spirit rooted in the Anabaptist, Pietist, and Wesleyan traditions of the Christian Church. Our mission is to educate men and women toward maturity of intellect, character, and Christian faith in preparation for lives of service, leadership, and reconciliation in church and society.

Statements of Faith

Apostles' Creed

I believe in God the Father almighty, Creator of heaven and earth.
I believe in Jesus Christ, God's only Son, our Lord,
who was conceived by the Holy Spirit,
born of the Virgin Mary
suffered under Pontius Pilate,
was crucified, died and was buried.
He descended to the dead.
On the third day he rose again,
ascended into heaven
and is seated at the right hand of the Father.
He will come again to judge the living and the dead.

I believe in the Holy Spirit,
the holy catholic Church,
the communion of saints,
the forgiveness of sins,
the resurrection of the body,
and the life everlasting. Amen.

Confession of Faith

We believe in the triune God—Father, Son and Holy Spirit—who created and sustains the universe, and who desires to redeem us and all creation.

God creates each of us in the very image of God to live in loving relationships: free, responsible and accountable to God and each other for our decisions and our actions.

God speaks to us in many different ways, times, and places but is uniquely revealed to all the world in Jesus of Nazareth who was fully human and fully divine.

God forgives our sins, renews our hearts and minds, and calls us to join in the work of reconciliation by grace through faith in the life, teachings, death and resurrection of Jesus Christ.

God bestows on us the Holy Spirit who leads us to repentance, instructs us in righteousness and empowers us to live joyfully as disciples of Christ, as servants of others and as caretakers of the created order.

God calls us to unite in the Church as a visible community of believers which celebrates God's grace in its worship and bears witness to the truth of the Gospel through its being, doing, and speaking.

God gives us the Bible as the inspired, trustworthy and authoritative Scripture to reveal God's ways and purposes, to nourish our minds and souls, and to instruct us in how we ought to think and to live.

God instructs us to pursue the kingdom of peace, righteousness and justice which ultimately will prevail with the return of Christ and assures us that those judged faithful will share resurrected life with God and all the saints forever.

We praise the one God—our Creator, Redeemer, and Sustainer—who has called us to personal faith and new life in Christ and to so order our lives that they may demonstrate the truth of our confession.

Foundational Values

Since its founding by the Brethren in Christ Church, Messiah College has affirmed a set of values derived from the Anabaptist, Pietist, and Wesleyan traditions of that denomination. These values have guided the school as it has sought to keep Christ preeminent in the total life of the institution. Stated in slightly different ways during the College's history, the following five ideals provide a summary of how Messiah College has defined its distinctive Christian character.

Unity of Faith, Learning, and Life. This principle affirms the wholeness of persons and the unity of every dimension of life as revealed in the incarnation of Jesus Christ. It also emphasizes that all truth is God's truth and thus avoids the creation of false dichotomies in thinking and in living. Messiah College affirms a unified Christian world view and lifestyle that joins revelation with rational inquiry and that integrates believing with doing. Christian "calling" and vocation is accordingly broadly understood. All of our gifts, talents, and interests are to be nurtured as acts of praise towards God while serving humanity and all creation.

Importance of the Person. Every person is to be respected and valued, regardless of gender, race, nationality, status, or position, because each person is created in the image of God. Freedom and responsibility are primary characteristics of being human and we must take care to protect each other's freedom while encouraging responsible living. As free agents, individuals make choices that determine the contours of their lives and they bear responsibility for those choices. Individuals are accountable for their manner of response to God's grace. Similarly, every person must be responsible in their pursuit of truth, and yet be free to develop their own understandings as they integrate their formal studies with their broader experience of faith.

Significance of Community. Our understanding of the Church as the body of Christ and our recognition of humanity's interdependence cause us to value community. In community, we voluntarily share our lives with each other, we care for each other, we rejoice and suffer together, we worship together, and we offer counsel to each other. While every community develops rules, in Christian communities such rules should always be humane, recognizing the impact they have on the lives of those affected, and should help us appreciate each other's gifts and talents. In any community there will be tensions that require mutual give and take, but a Christian spirit of care and support provides the security needed to accept one's own strengths and weaknesses as one also accepts the strengths and weaknesses of others. The ultimate goal of every Christian community should be to help us live more faithfully as disciples of Christ.

Disciplined and Creative Living. The mature Christian life is characterized by a delicate mix of discipline and creativity. We are called to a life of devotion and obedience to the Gospel. Such discipleship demands of us self-control and sacrifice and requires us to examine all our wants and desires in the light of God's holiness. The Gospel also calls us to celebrate the goodness of creation and to live our lives in active engagement with this ever changing world in which God has placed us. In order to fulfill these tasks, we must be both creative interpreters of the world around us and creative actors in that world. Creativity and discipline are complementary characteristics of the mature, joyful Christian life.

Service and Reconciliation. Central to the Gospel is the work of reconciling individuals with God, with each other, and with all of creation. God has called us to be active agents in this work as we are empowered by the Holy Spirit and bear the fruit of the Spirit within us: love, joy, peace, patience, kindness, generosity, faithfulness, gentleness, and self-control. Prepared in this way, we are compelled to share the redeeming Gospel of Jesus with those around us, to build bridges of understanding and peace across the dividing lines of race, class, age, gender, religion, and ethnicity, to demonstrate the love of God in service to others, to open our hearts to the poor and needy, and to work for justice wherever injustice prevails.

College-Wide Educational Objectives

1) **To develop those abilities essential to liberal arts education.** These abilities include:

   a. Thinking logically and creatively, analytically and synthetically, and abstractly and concretely;
   b. Reading, observing, and listening carefully and critically;
   c. Writing and speaking clearly and coherently;
   d. Appreciating the aesthetic dimensions of life;
   e. Functioning effectively in quantitatively- and technologically-oriented cultures;
   f. Accessing, evaluating, and using information effectively and ethically;
   g. Pursuing the process of learning as a life-long pursuit;
   h. Balancing commitment with humility.

2) **To gain knowledge common to liberal arts education.** This includes:

   a. Developing basic understanding of geographical, social, political, and religious realities throughout the world;
   b. Learning significant aspects of the Western social, cultural, political, religious, and philosophical heritage;
   c. Learning significant aspects of at least one non-Western culture;
   d. Becoming aware of how people of different cultures perceive the world, interpret reality, and make meaning;
   e. Learning the methods, philosophies, and basic principles of the mathematical, natural, and social sciences;
   f. Learning the traditions and methods of the arts and the humanities;
   g. Making connections (i.e., probing relationships, including congruencies and contradictions) between learnings acquired in a–f above.

3) **To become biblically literate and theologically reflective.** This includes:

   a. Developing knowledge of and about God as revealed in Jesus Christ;
   b. Gaining knowledge of the Bible's content and themes, including the biblical witness on service, leadership, and reconciliation;

    c.   Learning about historic Christian beliefs, practices, and ecclesiastical expressions, and the particular emphases of the Anabaptist, Pietist, and Wesleyan traditions;

    d.   Becoming familiar with contemporary theological dialogue and biblical scholarship;

    e.   Recognizing the influence of culture upon the Christian faith, and appreciating the insights that other cultures contribute to Christian theology and practice;

    f.   Acquiring the ability to articulate and evaluate one's faith;

    g.   Exploring various connections between faith and learning.

4) To attain specialized knowledge and abilities in at least one area of study. This includes:

    a.   Understanding the foundational content and philosophical assumptions of one's specialized area of study;

    b.   Engaging in scholarship in one's specialized area of study;

    c.   Developing proficiency in one's specialized area of study sufficient to pursue a career and/or continue education at the graduate level;

    d.   Gaining an awareness of options for employment, voluntary service, and/or graduate education in one's specialized area of study;

    e.   Articulating how faith connects to one's specialized area of study and to potential career options in that area of study.

5) To develop an understanding of one's identity and Christian vocation. This includes:

    a.   Developing an awareness of and concern for the whole person, including physical, emotional, and spiritual wellness;

    b.   Acquiring an appreciation for how one's faith, community, and culture impact one's identity and sense of meaning;

    c.   Developing a sense of vocation that includes but transcends career choice;

    d.   Gaining a realistic sense of one's distinctiveness, including one's interests, abilities, and limitations;

    e.   Discerning and reflecting on the role(s) one assumes in groups, including one's faith community.

6) **To develop the intellect and character necessary to express Christian commitments in responsible decisions and actions.** This includes:

   a. Developing individual and corporate spiritual disciplines that nurture personal faith and compassion for others;

   b. Assessing cultural values and ethical traditions in light of the biblical witness;

   c. Applying the insights of Christian theology and ethics to complex social and personal issues;

   d. Understanding the nature and causes of violence in the world and the means for promoting peace;

   e. Recognizing the implications of living in an increasingly interdependent world;

   f. Evaluating institutional policies and social/cultural practices on the basis of whether they promote peace, justice, and reconciliation;

   g. Gaining an appreciation for cultural and ethnic diversity.

7) **To become servants, leaders, and reconcilers in the world.** This includes:

   a. Practicing a lifestyle based on Christian commitments;

   b. Developing a sense of civic responsibility and commitment to work with others for the common good;

   c. Developing the courage to act responsibly and redemptively in a complex world;

   d. Practicing good stewardship of economic and natural resources;

   e. Acting in ways that respect gender, cultural, and ethnic diversity;

   f. Making decisions that reflect an ethic of service, a concern for justice, and a desire for reconciliation;

   g. Recognizing the relevance of Christian faith to all of life.

Community Covenant

All of Life Under the Lordship of Christ

In the motto "Christ Preeminent" the Messiah College community affirms that life draws meaning from submission to Christ and service to others. Our philosophy statement affirms the triune God as the creator of all that is, the source of all truth. As beings created in the image of God, we have special responsibilities and challenges. In our community of believer-scholars we affirm the interrelatedness of what we believe, the way we live, and the way we learn. Our search for truth and commitment to Christ connect us not only to each other but also to God's creation and God's people throughout history.

Freedom and Obligation

Within this community, it is not easy to find the right balance of challenge and support for each individual. Personal freedom and community obligation sometimes seem to be in tension as individuals work to integrate belief and behavior. This growth-producing process benefits from the dynamics of a diverse but concerned community, as well as the sense that the lordship of Christ and a commitment to being part of the body of Christ are key values to guide us.

With the task before us of searching for truth and promoting personal growth, we join together in the hope of achieving more together than we could separately. We agree to pursue the obligations and challenges of community membership with integrity, respecting our institutional heritage and practicing biblical accountability.

Benefits and Responsibilities

Our submission to the lordship of Christ has many implications. Some of the primary implications can be seen in terms of benefits and responsibilities based on our relationship to God, to his creation, and to the group of people who constitute the Messiah College community.

Relationship with God

The benefits and responsibilities of living under the lordship of Christ focus first on our relationship to God. We affirm that there is but one true God and that His Word is our guide for faith and life. Because of the importance of knowing God and His Word, we affirm the importance of the spiritual disciplines in corporate and individual life. Prayer, Bible study, meditation, fellowship, and group worship should be regular activities in the believer's life.

Because God is a faithful keeper of covenants, we affirm the importance of fidelity and covenant-keeping in our relationship with God and in our relationships with each other.

Scripture guides us in knowing how to live out the impact of God's grace in our lives. We are to honor and revere Him in the way that we worship, serve, and enjoy Him. As teachers and learners we see our activities as acts of service and honor to Him. Because of the love which He initiates by grace, we respond in love to Him and to those He has created. His love gives us a sense of meaning and intrinsic worth that goes beyond any earned value or identity.

Relationship to Creation

The benefits and responsibilities of living under the lordship of Christ focus also on our relationship to God's creation. As people created in God's image we are to follow Christ's example in preaching the good news to the poor, binding the brokenhearted, proclaiming freedom to the captives, and restoring sight to the blind. As those committed to living out the teachings of Scripture, we are to act justly, love mercy, and walk humbly. We are to bring peace and unity where there is conflict and discrimination. We are to respect people and to value life above material wealth. Because we see people as having intrinsic worth, we avoid gossip, manipulative behavior, and sexist or racist attitudes or behaviors, stressing instead integrity, commitment, and compassion in relationships with others. This respect for creation also shows itself in our treatment of natural resources. As stewards we are to be faithful in preserving the environment and in maintaining the balances within the creation order. We are to use our intellect and creativity to preserve and enhance the creation, using its resources prudently in light of the uncertain limits to history and life as we know it.

Relationships with People

The benefits and responsibilities of living under the lordship of Christ focus also on our relationship to the group of people who constitute the Messiah College community. We recognize that significant diversity exists within our community, bringing a richness that results from varying ability levels, backgrounds, and interests. That individual diversity, however, must come within the bounds by which the community defines itself. Individuals who join the community must also be willing to live with integrity within those boundaries if the community is to function.

Practical Implications

While acknowledging the difficulty of applying general principles to specific behaviors and contexts, we agree to the following guidelines:

Integrity and Excellence

As a community we commit ourselves to academic integrity and excellence in a cooperative, rather than a competitive, environment. We strive to work together responsibly and honestly in exploring and understanding the world around us, searching for truth within all academic areas.

Christian Values

As a community we commit ourselves to expressing Christian values in responsible decisions and actions. While not all Christians agree about the application of Christian values to specific situations, we expect honesty in dialoguing about and applying Christian values to things such as the use of language, leisure time and entertainment options, observance of the Lord's Day, and personal appearance.

Corporate Guidelines

As a community we commit ourselves to balancing personal freedom with concern for the moral standards of others. In addition, rules are designed to promote a campus atmosphere that is most conducive to personal well-being, corporate service, and the achievement of the College's distinctives, goals, and educational objectives. Prohibitions about the use of alcoholic beverages, tobacco products, and the abuse or unauthorized use of prescription or nonprescription drugs relate most clearly to concerns about personal wellbeing and the scriptural mandate to care for our bodies. Gambling is prohibited because we want to be wise stewards of the resources entrusted to us by God.

Scriptual Guidelines

As a community we believe that certain scriptural teachings apply to us as they have to all people in all cultures. Our lives are to be characterized by love, joy, peace, patience, kindness, goodness, faithfulness, gentleness, and self-control. We are to use our gifts in doing such things as serving, teaching, encouraging, giving, leading, and showing mercy. In contrast, we are to avoid such sinful practices as drunkenness, stealing, dishonesty, profanity, occult practices, sexual intercourse outside of marriage, homosexual behavior, and sexually exploitative or abusive behavior. Although wrong attitudes such as greed, jealousy, pride, lust, prejudice, and factiousness are harder to detect than wrong behaviors, both are prohibited as sinful and destructive of community life and of the body of Christ.

Corporate Covenant

With this understanding of our benefits and responsibilities as members of the Messiah College community, we covenant together as a community of believer scholars to pursue the challenge of living out this document. We commit ourselves to pursuing the distinctives, goals, and educational objectives of the College. We commit ourselves to seeking increased understanding of the Christian faith and applying that faith to specific academic disciplines and world problems. We commit ourselves to encouraging growth in others by living as examples, applying our faith to personal lifestyle issues, confronting inappropriate attitudes or behaviors directly, and affirming the evidence of God's work in others. We will strive to use our talents and time, both in and out of class, for the benefit of the community and the glory of God, working together to bring all of life under the lordship of Christ.

Creation

The account of creation in the beginning of Genesis is one of the most widely read passages in the Bible. While scholars and theologians debate its proper interpretation, there is no doubt that as Christians we are to understand from this passage that God created the world with loving care, and pronounced creation to be "good." The first two chapters of Genesis also raise questions about the implications of being created in God's image, and provide some examples of how humans are to exercise their responsibility over God's creation.

Genesis 1:1–2:25 (NRSV)

Six Days of Creation and the Sabbath

1 In the beginning when God created the heavens and the earth, **2** the earth was a formless void and darkness covered the face of the deep, while a wind from God swept over the face of the waters. **3** Then God said, "Let there be light"; and there was light. **4** And God saw that the light was good; and God separated the light from the darkness. **5** God called the light Day, and the darkness he called Night. And there was evening and there was morning, the first day.

6 And God said, "Let there be a dome in the midst of the waters, and let it separate the waters from the waters." **7** So God made the dome and separated the waters that were under the dome from the waters that were above the dome. And it was so. **8** God called the dome Sky. And there was evening and there was morning, the second day.

9 And God said, "Let the waters under the sky be gathered together into one place, and let the dry land appear." And it was so. **10** God called the dry land Earth, and the waters that were gathered together he called Seas. And God saw that it was good. **11** Then God said, "Let the earth put forth vegetation: plants yielding seed, and fruit trees of every kind on earth that bear fruit with the seed in it." And it was so. **12** The earth brought forth vegetation: plants yielding seed of every kind, and trees of every kind bearing fruit with the seed in it. And God saw that it was good. **13** And there was evening and there was morning, the third day.

14 And God said, "Let there be lights in the dome of the sky to separate the day from the night; and let them be for signs and for seasons and for days and years, **15** and let them be lights in the dome of the sky to give light upon the earth." And it was so. **16** God made the two great lights— the greater light to rule the day and the lesser light to rule the night—and the stars. **17** God set them in the dome of the sky to give light upon the earth, **18** to rule over the day and over the night, and to separate the light from the darkness. And God saw that it was good. **19** And there was evening and there was morning, the fourth day.

20 And God said, "Let the waters bring forth swarms of living creatures, and let birds fly above the earth across the dome of the sky." **21** So God created the great sea monsters and every living creature that moves, of every kind, with which the waters swarm, and every winged bird of every kind. And God saw that it was good. **22** God blessed them, saying, "Be fruitful and multiply and fill the waters in the seas, and let birds multiply on the earth." **23** And there was evening and there was morning, the fifth day.

24 And God said, "Let the earth bring forth living creatures of every kind: cattle and creeping things and wild animals of the earth of every kind." And it was so. **25** God made the wild animals of the earth of every kind, and the cattle of every kind, and everything that creeps upon the ground of every kind. And God saw that it was good.

26 Then God said, "Let us make humankind in our image, according to our likeness; and let them have dominion over the fish of the sea, and over the birds of the air, and over the cattle, and over all the wild animals of the earth, and over every creeping thing that creeps upon the earth."

27 So God created humankind in his
image,
in the image of God he created
them;
male and female he created them.

28 God blessed them, and God said to them, "Be fruitful and multiply, and fill the earth and subdue it; and have dominion over the fish of the sea and over the birds of the air and over every living thing that moves upon the earth." **29** God said, "See, I have given you every plant yielding seed that is upon the face of all the earth, and every tree with seed in its fruit; you shall have them for food. **30** And to every beast of the earth, and to every bird of the air, and to everything that creeps on the earth, everything that has the breath of life, I have given every green plant for food." And it was so. **31** God saw everything that he had made, and indeed, it was very good. And there was evening and there was morning, the sixth day.

2 Thus the heavens and the earth were finished, and all their multitude. **2** And on the seventh day God finished the work that he had done, and he rested on the seventh day from all the work that he had done. **3** So God blessed the seventh day and hallowed it, because on it God rested from all the work that he had done in creation.

4 These are the generations of the heavens and the earth when they were created.

Another Account of the Creation

In the day that the LORD God made the earth and the heavens, **5** when no plant of the field was yet in the earth and no herb of the field had yet sprung up—for the LORD God had not caused it to rain upon the earth, and there was no one to till the ground; **6** but a stream would rise from the earth, and water the whole face of the ground— **7** then the LORD God formed man from the dust of the ground, and breathed into his nostrils the breath of life; and the man became a living being. **8** And the LORD God planted a garden in Eden, in the east; and there he put the man whom he had formed. **9** Out of the ground the LORD God made to grow every tree that is pleasant to the sight and good for food, the tree of life also in the midst of the garden, and the tree of the knowledge of good and evil.

10 A river flows out of Eden to water the garden, and from there it divides and becomes four branches. **11** The name of the first is Pishon; it is the one that flows around the whole land of Havilah, where there is gold; **12** and the gold of that land is good; bdellium and onyx stone are there. **13** The name of the second river is Gihon; it is the one that flows around the whole land of Cush. **14** The name of the third river is Tigris, which flows east of Assyria. And the fourth river is the Euphrates.

15 The LORD God took the man and put him in the garden of Eden to till it and keep it. **16** And the LORD God commanded the man, "You may freely eat of every tree of the garden; **17** but of the tree of the knowledge of good and evil you shall not eat, for in the day that you eat of it you shall die."

18 Then the LORD God said, "It is not good that the man should be alone; I will make him a helper as his partner." **19** So out of the ground the LORD God formed every animal of the field and every bird of the air, and brought them to the man to see what he would call them; and whatever the man called every living creature, that was its name. **20** The man gave names to all cattle, and to the birds of the air, and to every animal of the field; but for the man there was not found a helper as his partner. **21** So the LORD God caused a deep sleep to fall upon the man, and he slept; then he took one of his ribs and closed up its place with flesh. **22** And the rib that the LORD God had taken from the man he made into a woman and brought her to the man. **23** Then the man said,

> "This at last is bone of my bones
> and flesh of my flesh;
> this one shall be called Woman,
> for out of Man this one was taken."

24 Therefore a man leaves his father and his mother and clings to his wife, and they become one flesh. **25** And the man and his wife were both naked, and were not ashamed.

*B*ruce C. Birch (1941–) is dean and professor of Old Testament at Wesley Theological Seminary in Washington, DC. He has published several books on
interpreting the Bible, and has contributed to the production of the New Inter-
preter's Bible *Volume II. In this essay, Birch uses his understanding of the Old
Testament to examine our role as Christians in a broken world. He argues that,
while many people disregard the Old Testament as simply providing a historical
background for the "more relevant" New Testament, the Old Testament actually
provides important insights regarding God's intentions for humanity in general
and Christians in particular. According to Birch, the account of Creation in Genesis reveals to us the personality of a God who created us for a purpose, and gives
us a clue as to what that purpose may be.*

In the Image of God

Bruce C. Birch

1   Many of those in the churches who are most concerned for the witness of the Christian faith in the social order find themselves hard
pressed to describe a significant role for the Bible in that task of social
witness. It is not that they do not honor the scripture, but that it
seems to become a kind of distant historical background rather than
a direct resource in addressing the urgent needs of our broken world.
A socially committed pastor once said to me after I had spoken on
biblical understandings of hunger issues, "That was interesting, but
we really don't have time to be reading the Bible. People are starving
out there."

2   One of the reasons for this is that Christian social witness in our time
has become chiefly identified with the "doing" side of the Christian
moral life. "What shall we do about_____?" You can fill in any issue
of concern: peace, racism, poverty. The emphasis is on decision-making, strategy, and action. Some of the church's finest moments in our
time have come when Christians made decisions of conscience and
courageously acted on those decisions.

3   The Bible, however, does not make decisions for us or plan courses of
    action. Attempts to use the Bible as a rule book are not very success-
    ful. There are, of course, broad moral imperatives, such as the com-
    mand to love our neighbor, which are of central importance, but the
    church is left with the struggle to decide what the loving act toward
    the neighbor might be in a given situation. Many issues our society
    faces— nuclear war, environmental damage—were not anticipated at
    all by the biblical communities. Even when we share a common con-
    cern with those communities, such as feeding the hungry, we must
    make decisions and take actions in a complex global economic sys-
    tem totally unlike anything imagined in the biblical tradition.

4   Does this make the Bible remote or irrelevant to our Christian social
    concern? By no means! Alongside the concern for the ethics of "doing"
    lies an ethics of "being." Christian social concern requires not only that
    we ask what we should *do* in a broken world but also that we ask
    who we are to *be*. The shaping of the decision-makers is as important
    as the shaping of the decision. As we enter and are nurtured by the
    Christian community, we form values, perspectives, and perceptions
    that inform our deciding and acting. The identity we bring with us as
    Christians deeply affects our participation in ministering to a broken
    world.

5   In the shaping of our Christian "being," or identity, the Bible plays a
    central role. We encounter its witness in the preaching, teaching, and
    liturgy of the church, and we are shaped by it. Stories, hymns, histo-
    ries, parables, and visions become as important as commandments
    and ethical teachings in molding the faith perspective through which
    we view our broken world and seek to mediate God's healing.

6   It is for this reason that those who are committed to the task of Christ-
    ian social witness as a natural outgrowth of Christian faith must seek
    the broadest possible understanding of the biblical inheritance that is
    ours. To settle for a narrow acquaintance with our biblical traditions is
    to limit the faith vision we bring with us to the task of discerning God's
    will for a broken world. Unfortunately for many in the church, there is
    an entire portion of scripture that is inadequately known and poorly
    understood. Our use of its resources is highly selective and often pulled
    out of context. The portion of which I speak is the Old Testament.

The Old Testament as Scripture

7   It is not uncommon to run across persons in the church who declare that they are New Testament Christians. The implication is that they can do without the Old Testament entirely, or at best that the Old Testament has less authority than the New. This is a bit like trying to affirm only one person of the Trinity. In every period of its history and in all its major traditions, the church has refused to part with the Old Testament or to reduce its status as fully scripture. Both the Old Testament and the New are considered to be the Word of God, and since we believe in only one God the two portions of our scripture are linked by witness to a single divine reality. The Old Testament was quoted by Jesus and the apostles as scripture. To understand Jesus Christ as the center of our faith is not to reject the God of the Old Testament, but to see that same God acting out in Christ the final and fullest chapter in the great drama of God's salvation which began with the story of Israel.

8   Some of our attitude toward the Old Testament is caused simply by a lack of acquaintance with its contents, but we have also been the victims of some misconceptions.

9   Many believe that the church actually holds the Old Testament to be second-class scripture, or that the church has replaced the Old Testament with the New. Such views are actually versions of a position taken by Marcion in the second century A.D. He utterly rejected the Old Testament as authoritative and accepted only the Pauline epistles and the Gospel of Luke as authentic witness to our faith. He believed that the God of the Old Testament was a God of law who was different from the God of love revealed in Jesus Christ. The purpose of God in Christ was to overthrow the God of law (who was also the creator). Marcion's views were declared heretical and the early church opposed them, claiming the Old Testament to be a witness to the activity of the same God revealed to us fully in Jesus Christ; thus they declared both the Old Testament and the New to be the scripture of the church, the Word of God for God's people. This position was reaffirmed by the theologians of the early church, the Protestant Reformers, and the early preachers of the American religious movements and revivals. It is still the position of all major Christian traditions today.

10 Another misconception takes the form of stereotyping: the Old Testament is law while the New Testament is gospel. This is often meant to characterize the Old Testament as primarily judgment and the New as grace, but it does not do justice to the richness of either the Old or the New Testament. A picture of God's wrath and judgment can certainly be found in the Old Testament, and these pictures of God as warrior or judge are sometimes a problem for us. But the same side of God's nature can also be seen in the New Testament: in the book of Revelation, or in Jesus' cleansing of the temple, or in some of Jesus' harsh words to the Pharisees and others who oppose God's kingdom. On the other hand, the definitive picture of God's grace in Jesus Christ has already been preceded by a rich tapestry of witness to God's grace in the Old Testament: God's creation and blessing of the world, God's presence in history to bring Israel out of bondage in Egypt and to identify with all who suffer and are oppressed, God's call to become the covenant community, and God's forgiveness and comfort offered even to those whose sin takes them into exile. The law is, of course, an important Old Testament theme, but not as an end in itself. Unless law serves God's grace, we can find ourselves in bondage to the law, as the apostle Paul observed. However, when law follows grace it is not opposed to gospel, as Jesus himself proclaimed: "Think not that I have come to abolish the law and the prophets; I have come not to abolish them but to fulfil them" (Matt. 5:17).

11 It is the goal of this book to recover the Old Testament roots of our faith and to highlight the manner in which those roots inform the witness of the church in the modern social order. Spiritual and social dimensions of faith will interrelate in this series as they do in the Old Testament. The constant working assumption will be that the God revealed to us in Israel's story in the Old Testament is the same God who comes to us in Jesus Christ. We cannot fully understand who the New Testament proclaims Jesus to be unless we know the God who comes to us in Jesus as already revealed in the Old Testament story, from creation onward.

12 It is always difficult to choose a starting point when dealing with the Old Testament witness as a whole. Israel as a people come to birth in the events surrounding the deliverance out of Egypt recorded in the book

of Exodus. To start here would be to begin with God's salvation, and, indeed, most of our best materials on the Old Testament have stressed the salvation history of Israel, the mighty acts of God in moments of crisis. Only out of this awareness of its own salvation did Israel later begin to understand that God was also the Creator and giver of the promise to the ancestors in the stories of Israel's early traditions (Genesis). To begin with Israel's birth in Exodus would make sense.

13   We have chosen, however, to begin with the beginning not of Israel but of all beginnings; we speak first of creation. The whole of scripture starts with creation, and by passing on the tradition in this form the ancient biblical community must have intended us first to encounter the God who creates and then to read of the God who saves. It is true that the creation stories that open the book of Genesis received written form later in Israel's history, but we are not concerned here with literary development. We will begin with the picture of what God intended us to be in creation. When our faith story culminates in Jesus Christ, it is to return to a picture of what we are intended to be—new creation.

In the Beginning

14   The materials that witness to Israel's faith in God as Creator are scattered throughout the Old Testament. The Psalms, several of the Prophets (especially Deutero-Isaiah), and the Wisdom literature (e.g., Proverbs, Job) all contain rich and important creation passages. In the limited space available here, however, we will look primarily at the two creation accounts that open the book of Genesis. They touch on all major elements of the Old Testament witness to Creator and creation.

15   The whole of scripture opens with the well-known creation story in Genesis 1:1–2:4a. This is the story that follows the formal, almost liturgical, seven-day pattern. In the beginning is a formless, watery chaos out of which God brings order by the mere command of divine word, "'Let there be light'; and there was light" (Gen. 1:3). Creation begins with the great elements of the cosmos: light, waters, firmament, dry land. It then moves to the various life forms on the earth: plants, animals, and finally humanity itself. The seventh day is the day of God's rest, establishing the Sabbath as a memorial to God's creative work (cf. Ex. 20:8–11).

16   The creation story of Genesis 1 is immediately followed and in many
ways balanced by the creation account in Genesis 2:4b–25. It is the
human creature, created by God at the very beginning of the account,
who occupies the center of attention throughout the story. Things do
not seem to be created as separate orders; rather, humans, plants, and
animals are all created for harmonious relationship. The Garden of
Eden is the symbol of total and idyllic harmony. Even the earth itself
is a part of this picture. Humanity is created from the dust of the
ground. The Hebrew words themselves indicate closeness: *'adam*
(humanity), *'adamab* (soil). In this account God is the creator, but not
in the remote and sovereign sense of Genesis 1. God creates almost as
a loving craftsman, intimately shaping the first human creature and
breathing life into it. God then responds to the needs of this human
creature in subsequent acts of creation. God is concerned for harmonious balance in this creation even to the point of dividing the first
human creation into male and female to make the full relationship of
sexual union and unity possible.

The God Who Creates and Blesses

17   Although these two creation stories are quite different in emphasis and
details, they are marvelously complementary. This is especially clear in
the pictures of God as Creator. Each account shows a different side of
our faith understanding of God as Creator, and a lack of either would
leave us with an impoverished and incomplete theology of creation

18   In Genesis 1 the stress is on the absolute *sovereignty* of God. God's
word alone calls the world into existence. Unlike the other ancient
Near Eastern religions, God vanquishes no other primeval powers to
create the world. In Babylonian mythology the god Marduk had to
defeat the monster Tiamat in order to create. As a result, Babylonian
religion lived constantly with the need to reenact that battle lest the
order of creation fail. The Hebrews by contrast knew a God who is
declared in Genesis 1 to be unrivaled, and who creates as an act of
divine grace and freedom. Nothing compels the creation except God's
own creative will. "The Lord by wisdom founded the earth; by understanding he established the heavens; by his knowledge the deeps
broke forth, and the clouds drop down the dew" (Prov. 3:19–20). Confidence in the absolute sovereignty of God is reflected in a sense of
the reliability of the creation which is God's work.

19 A picture of the Creator only in terms of divine sovereignty could leave us with a remote and transcendent God. Fortunately, Genesis 2:4b–9 balances the picture with a stress on the *relatedness* of God. Here God fashions the first creature like a loving craftsman, breathes the very breath of life into it, and relates caringly to the needs of this human creature. God walks and talks in the garden and is anguished when sin breaks the harmonious relationship (Genesis 3). In this story we come to know our Creator God as a caring, intimately related God, involved with the creation from the very beginning. It will not surprise us to find such a God involved once again in our redemption.

20 The combination of these two pictures of God the Creator points us to a unique dimension of the God of our faith. The sovereign yet related Creator foreshadows a constant biblical picture of a God whose power is expressed in vulnerability to the world's suffering, whose mysterious otherness comes close to us in intimate relationship. For those who know such a God, the exercise of power must always be tempered by caring relationship.

21 In these creation stories God not only creates, God also blesses. The verb itself appears in 1:28: "And God blessed them." The concept of a blessing from God appears in the constant divine concern for the well-being of the creation. God pronounces each element of the creation good (Genesis 1); God provides for the care of creation (Gen. 1:28–30 and 2:15), sees to the provision of needs (Gen. 2:9, 18), and continues to sustain all creatures, human and nonhuman ("These all look to thee," Ps. 104:27).

22 We know the God of blessing not only as the Creator who called the world into being but in the ongoing reliability of the created order and in the divine presence that sustains life in all its week-to-week rhythms. This aspect of God is present with us in all moments and is universally known by all humanity. God's intention in creation is for all to experience *shalom*, a Hebrew word meaning wholeness.

23 In the Old Testament, the God who creates and blesses helps to balance the tradition of a God who saves. The church in its use of the Bible has usually stressed the God who saves, for that is where we as a particular community of faith come into relationship to God. The mighty acts of salvation from Exodus to Resurrection stress the particular moments of crisis where we have known God's redeeming power. To acknowledge and serve this God who saves compels the

church to respond in the midst of the crises of our time by bringing aid and hope, both spiritual and material.

24 But God is not found in the crises alone. God acts not only to deliver but to sustain us in all of life. To begin as we have with creation is to be reminded of God's relationship to all creation and not simply to our Judeo-Christian tradition. We are called not only to crisis intervention in a broken world but to the creation and maintenance of faithful systems of order that mediate the blessings of full life to all creation, persons and environment. To know God as Creator will force the church not only to interventions of the moment but to the building of *shalom*.

The Creation and the Creatures

25 The opening chapters of Genesis reveal to us something of the Creator and speak also of the creation itself. It is here that we begin to discover what it means to be given life as a creature and to live that life in relationship to God and the rest of the created order.

26 One of the most important themes in the creation material appears in Genesis 1:26–27 with the statement that *humanity is created in the image of God.* Here scripture affirms the unique and precious quality of every person, male and female, as a bearer of the image of God. This is a clear and unambiguous affirmation of the coequal status of men and women as creatures of God. It is also a witness to the divine character as encompassing both maleness and femaleness, if indeed both men and women bear the image of God.

27 Creation in the image of God is not just a gift, it is also a responsibility. To be created in the image of God brings with it the commission to care for the earth, which follows in Genesis 1:28–30 (cf. 2:15). It was the practice of ancient kings to erect images of themselves to represent their sovereignty in the far-flung corners of their empires. The biblical writer has transferred this metaphor to the divine realm. In Genesis 1, God, who is truly sovereign over all creation, has chosen to place the divine image into human beings as the representatives not of some inherent human right of our own to exploit the creation for our own needs but as the representatives or trustees of God. So the commission to have dominion over the earth (v. 28) is a trusteeship of divine right, a trusteeship of God's own care for the creation and an entrusting to our stewardship of that care. Except for Genesis 1, this theme of

human dominion is found explicitly only in Psalm 8. In both instances, exercise of dominion is accountable to God; it is not license for human indulgence. Thus, to have the gift of God's image is to have also the responsibility to show that image forth in relation to the whole of creation.

28   Another important theme in this material is *the affirmation of the goodness of creation*. At the end of the sixth day, "God saw everything that he had made, and behold, it was very good" (1:31). In biblical times this was a remarkable statement. Ancient cultures spoke of divine powers inhabiting all the realms of nature; hence, one often stood in fear and apprehension of the world and needed magic or incantations to protect oneself and appease the gods. In contrast, the Hebrews express the assurance that God's sovereign power has been used to create a world that is benevolent and trustworthy. Further, it is clear that God's intention is that the goodness of creation be experienced by all its parts, all persons and all nature. It was not to be good for some and bad for others and that's the breaks. Those who know the vision of God's good creation, therefore, cannot settle for a world where the desire of some for an excess of creation's good gifts begins to deny enough for others. To ensure that all participate in creation's goodness is a fundamental concern of Christian discipleship.

29   A third important theme is *the interrelatedness of creation*. Human beings are not self-sufficient. We are created for relationship to God, to others, and to nature. Genesis 2:18 tells us that God saw it was not good for the human creature to be alone. The story then goes on to express relationship with nature (garden, animals), as well as with other humans. Human relationship includes the possibility of sexual relationship as a part of God's creation. The first creature (called *'adam*, the general Hebrew word for humanity) is divided to make maleness and femaleness possible. There is no new creative forming-from-the-dust to make woman. Neither man nor woman exists until this point of sexual differentiation in the *'adam*. The Hebrew word often translated as helper (*'ezer*) in 2:18 does not imply subordination. After all, the Bible often refers to God as our *'ezer*. It is better translated here as companion.

30   The Hebrew concept of creation is relational. Not only are we created as trustees of God to experience the goodness of creation, we are created to be in community with all creation. Only in this way can we

experience God's intended wholeness (*shalom*). Each part of God's creation finds its fulfillment in interrelatedness with all. If some are denied wholeness, we all are diminished.

31   Opposed to this concept of creation as relational is a common and dangerous distortion of the biblical understanding of creation. It is *the distortion of hierarchical thinking about creation.* Over the centuries, in the church, the misuse of God's commission giving humanity dominion over the earth led to a hierarchical understanding that divided the relationship of the human to God and to nature. Hierarchical understanding operates something like this. Picture a ladder of categories. At the top is God, whose nature is pure spirit. At the bottom is the earth, whose nature is material. Already you have a polarity between the spiritual and the material, the divine and the bodily. Ranged in between are the other "orders" of creation: humans, animals, plants. The closer you get up the ladder to God, the higher is the moral worth attributed to that order of creation. Thus, the earth itself is far from God and of little worth. This is hardly in keeping with the pronouncement of God that the creation was all very good.

32   Early in the history of the Christian church a subdivided hierarchy became the standard: God, males, females, other races than white, Jews, animals, plants, and the earth itself. This hierarchical understanding of creation became the foundation for entire superstructures of racism, sexism, and anti-Semitism. It was the custom in the medieval law codes to list the killing of a Jew in the same section and with the same penalty as poaching the king's deer. Jews were thought guilty of deicide and therefore worth little more than animals. We all know that women and members of the nonwhite races have been slandered in the history of the church by defining their nature as closer to the bodily and animal orders of creation and therefore farther from God's spirit. They were said to occupy lower orders of creation, and this understanding in turn was used to justify slavery and the denial of ordination to women as well as a host of other racist and sexist actions. It has been suggested that in our century the poor have been added to the hierarchical list among those who are farther from God, while those who have been blessed with prosperity elevate themselves on the ladder to a position of greater closeness to God. The mere fact of being poor is treated by some as evidence of lower moral worth in the eyes of God.

33   If we had really understood the wholeness of the relational creation pictured in scripture, we could not have created that insidious hierarchical ladder. We would have understood that the welfare and the fullness of life for every part of creation is dependent on interrelationship and full participation of every other part. Creation is relational, not hierarchical.

The Brokenness of Creation

34   The Hebrew writers knew that the wholeness of creation which God intended was not a reality in human history. Thus, alongside the pictures of creation stands a story of the broken creation (Genesis 3). This story is closely attached to and flows from the garden creation story in Genesis 2. It is our first encounter with the biblical understanding of the nature and reality of sin.

35   Along with the other gifts of creation already discussed came the gift of human freedom. The man and the woman are given the capacity to make choices for themselves, and the choices are for either obedience or disobedience. It is the motif of the tree of knowledge in the midst of the garden (the tree of life does not figure in the story of chapter 3 until the end) which gives the possibility of human freedom. To eat of it is forbidden by God (Gen. 2:16–17). To have such freedom is a great gift, but with it comes human responsibility to live with the consequences of our choices. The consequence of eating from the tree of knowledge is said to be death.

36   What unfolds in the story of Genesis 3 is a drama that speaks to all of human existence concerning the meaning of our choices, the nature of sin, and the consequences of broken creation. It is important at the outset to note that this chapter does not exhaust the biblical perspective of sin. Sin is the word we use to describe how *shalom*, wholeness, gets broken. This story speaks of that brokenness in one important way, but we will see other aspects of sin later in Israel's story (e.g., covenant-breaking).

37   Since this is a story of human freedom and responsibility, it is important to note that the biblical text is quite clear that the serpent is simply one of the "wild creature[s] that the Lord God had made" (3:1). There is no coercive outside power of evil to take the man and the woman off the hook of responsibility for their own disobedience. We might think

of the serpent as the tempting occasion for disobedience that comes into every human life.

38 In this case the temptation is to "be like God, knowing good and evil" (3:5). The aspect of sin highlighted in this story is the sin of overreach, attempting to go beyond the limits of our humanness to try for the prerogatives of God. Some theologians refer to this as the sin of pride. Pride is involved, but sin here is more than the attitude we associate with the word *pride*. It is the attempt to take destiny into one's own control as if we had no limits we must acknowledge.

39 Knowledge of good and evil does not refer to the ability to make moral choices. After all, in being given the capacity to choose obedience or disobedience, humanity already has that capacity by virtue of God's creation. In Hebrew literature, pairs of opposites are used to bracket a whole category. East and west means everywhere; day and night means all the time; good and evil probably means everything. The temptation is to want to know everything that God knows. In Hebrew the verb *to know* does not mean just cognitive knowledge. To know something is to be related to the reality of what is known. It can almost mean "to experience" something. Thus, the man and the woman want to experience all that God does.

40 We must be careful in our interpretation here. This account does not imply that faithful life is against knowledge. It instead asks whether there are boundaries to human knowing that must be honored. How do we live in God's creation in a way that acknowledges the limits of our humanness and refuses to play God by reaching beyond those boundaries in ways that threaten to bring death? There may be forms of knowing that we attempt for our own human pride and self-centeredness which exact death-bringing penalties. One wonders if nuclear technology and some forms of genetic research are not flirting with these boundaries in ways that affect the entire human race. But apart from these dramatic issues, the biblical story speaks of the thousands of temptations to make choices that try to rearrange creation for our own benefit, only to bring death; biological, social, or spiritual.

41 The consequences of sin in this story are many. Death in the Old Testament is not simply biological. For *shalom* to be broken, for humans to be denied wholeness, is to experience death already. In this story the disobedient act immediately creates brokenness in the harmony

of creation, as indicated by the appearance of shame and fear and guilt. In the creation story the man and woman were naked and not ashamed (2:25). Now they are ashamed of their nakedness and attempt to cover themselves (3:7). *Shame* is here the sign of brokenness in the openness of relationship between the man and the woman. When God finds the couple hiding from the divine presence, the man says he was afraid (3:10). *Fear* is here the sign of brokenness in the trustful relationship with God. Finally, there is a great buck-passing ceremony where the man and the woman try to pass responsibility on to others rather than face their own choice and its consequences (3:12–13). This is *guilt*, and it is here the sign of brokenness within one's own self.

42   In the penalties pronounced and the exile from the garden, the biblical writers are communicating to us their knowledge that we live in a broken world, far from the harmony of the garden. Many aspects of the reality of our lives remind us of what brokenness we have settled for when we were created for wholeness. One element of these verses on the consequences of sinful choice needs special comment. A part of the brokenness that the woman experiences is said to be her subservience to her husband ("he shall rule over you," 3:16). We must note carefully that scripture understands such subordination of women to be a sign of sin and not the intention of God in creation. Those of us whose story now includes the event of Jesus Christ, the new creation, must ask more seriously than in the past whether the church is in the business of enforcing the curses of sin in the old creation or of demonstrating the wholeness of relationship between men and women which God intended by acting as the community of new creation.

Toward the Promise

43   We have spent a good deal of time on the opening chapters of the Old Testament. From these chapters we know much of the nature of God as Creator and ourselves as creatures, but as the story moves forward, Creator and creatures are alienated from one another. In the chapters that follow, the alienation seems to grow. Sin abounds and its consequences grow more violent. In the Cain and Abel story, violence is directed toward an innocent brother (Genesis 4). In the story of the flood, sin and violence have reached universal proportions and God is sorry that the world was created (Gen. 6:5–7). At the tower of

Babel, humanity attempts to assault the heavens themselves for their own glory ("let us make a name for ourselves," Gen. 11:4). The gulf between God and humanity seems to grow greater, as does the brokenness in humanity itself. In each story there are consequences of sin: Cain's exile, the flood, the scattering and confusion of language. But in each story there is a sign that in spite of sin God continues to care and to act with grace: God marks Cain for protection, saves Noah, guarantees the natural order with the rainbow.

44 After the tower of Babel story, there is no immediate sign of God's care. We are dramatically suspended for a moment. Where can this escalation of sin and alienation end? It is then that we are shifted from stories that speak of all humanity to the story of a single man and woman and the people who spring from them. Genesis 12 begins the story of Abraham and Sarah. Significantly, their story begins with a promise, and it becomes clear that the story of this people of promise is the sign of God's grace. God acts to bridge the gap through relationship to a particular people. The story of God's relationship to this people is now the subject of the rest of the Old Testament. By beginning with creation and broken creation, the scripture reminds us that this people is not to be an end in itself but a means of God's grace to "all the families of the earth" (Gen. 12:3).

*J*ames Weldon Johnson (1871–1938) was one of the most influential African Americans of the late nineteenth and early twentieth century. His writing is merely one way in which he has influenced American history; others include his political activism, diplomacy, and educational leadership. In this poem, Johnson describes the creation as he imagines it may have happened, and succeeds in ascribing great personality to a God who sometimes seems distant in his creation of earth. God is described by Johnson as having great power to create the earth, but also great care and concern for his creation of humans, whom he wanted as his companions. This contrast is often considered the most touching aspect of the poem, because it is difficult to imagine such a powerful God desiring us so deeply. "The Creation" is one of Johnson's most renowned poems and is widely used to help people connect to the creative God of Genesis.

The Creation

James Weldon Johnson

And God stepped out on space,
And he looked around and said:
I'm lonely—
I'll make me a world.

5   And far as the eye of God could see
Darkness covered everything,
Blacker than a hundred midnights
Down in a cypress swamp.

Then God smiled,
10   And the light broke,
And the darkness rolled up on one side,
And the light stood shining on the other,
And God said: That's good!

Then God reached out and took the light in his hands,
15   And God rolled the light around in his hands
Until he made the sun;
And he set that sun a-blazing in the heavens.

And the light that was left from making the sun
God gathered it up in a shining ball
20 And flung it against the darkness,
Spangling the night with the moon and stars.
Then down between
The darkness and the light.
He hurled the world;
25 And God said: That's good!

Then God himself stepped down—
And the sun was on his right hand,
And the moon was on his left;
The stars were clustered about his head,
30 And the earth was under his feet.
And God walked, and where he trod
His footsteps hollowed the valleys out
And bulged the mountains up.

Then he stopped and looked and saw
35 That the earth was hot and barren.
So God stepped over to the edge of the world
And he spat out the seven seas—
He batted his eyes, and the lightnings flashed—
He clapped his hands, and the thunders rolled—
40 And the waters above the earth came down,
The cooling waters came down.

Then the green grass sprouted,
And the little red flowers blossomed,
The pine tree pointed his finger to the sky,
45 And the oak spread out his arms,
The lakes cuddled down in the hollows of the ground,
And the rivers ran down to the sea;
And God smiled again,
And the rainbow appeared,
50 And curled itself around his shoulder.

Then God raised his arm and he waved his hand
Over the sea and over the land,
And he said: Bring forth! Bring forth!
And quicker than God could drop his hand,

55   Fishes and fowls
     And beasts and birds
     Swam the rivers and the seas,
     Roamed the forests and the woods,
     And split the air with their wings.
60   And God said: That's good!

     Then God walked around,
     And God looked around
     On all that he had made.
     He looked at his sun,
65   And he looked at his moon,
     And he looked at his little stars;
     He looked on his world
     With all its living things,
     And God said: I'm lonely still.

70   Then God sat down—
     On the side of a hill where he could think;
     By a deep, wide river he sat down;
     With his head in his hands,
     God thought and thought,
75   Till he thought: I'll make me a man!

     Up from the bed of the river
     God scooped the clay;
     And by the bank of the river
     He kneeled him down;
80   And there the great God Almighty
     Who lit the sun and fixed it in the sky,
     Who flung the stars to the most far corner of the night,
     Who rounded the earth in the middle of his hand;
     This Great God,
85   Like a mammy bending over her baby,
     Kneeled down in the dust
     Toiling over a lump of clay
     Till he shaped it in his own image;

     Then into it he blew the breath of life,
90   And man became a living soul.
     Amen. Amen.

*A*lice Walker (1944–) is a famous American author and poet, best known for her Pulitzer Prize–winning novel The Color Purple. Walker's writing deals mostly with issues of race in the South, where she was raised as the daughter of a sharecropper during the rule of Jim Crow laws. "In Search of Our Mothers' Gardens" describes the deep imprint of creativity on humanity, so strong as to be evident in the will of oppressed people to fulfill acts of creation even when most methods of expressing their creative urges are prohibited.

In Search of Our Mothers' Gardens

Alice Walker

I described her own nature and temperament. Told how they needed a larger life for their expression. . . . I pointed out that in lieu of proper channels, her emotions had overflowed into paths that dissipated them. I talked, beautifully I thought, about an art that would be born, an art that would open the way for women the likes of her, I asked her to hope, and build up an inner life against the coming of that day. . . . I sang, with a strange quiver in my voice, a promise song.

—Jean Toomer, "Avey,"
cane

The poet speaking to a prostitute who falls asleep while he's talking —

1   When the poet Jean Toomer walked through the South in the early twenties, he discovered a curious thing: black women whose spirituality was so intense, so deep, so unconscious, that they were themselves unaware of the richness they held. They stumbled blindly through their lives: creatures so abused and mutilated in body, so dimmed and confused by pain, that they considered themselves unworthy even of hope. In the selfless abstractions their bodies became to the men who used them, they became more than "sexual objects," more even than mere women: they became "Saints." Instead of being perceived as whole persons, their bodies became shrines: what was thought to be their minds became temples suitable for worship. These crazy Saints stared out at the world, wildly, like lunatics—or quietly, like suicides; and the "God" that was in their gaze was as mute as a great stone.

23

2 Who were these Saints? These crazy, loony, pitiful women?

3 Some of them, without a doubt, were our mothers and grandmothers.

4 In the still heat of the post-Reconstruction South, this is how they seemed to Jean Toomer: exquisite butterflies trapped in an evil honey, toiling away their lives in an era, a century, that did not acknowledge them, except as "the mule of the world." They dreamed dreams that no one knew—not even themselves, in any coherent fashion—and saw visions no one could understand. They wandered or sat about the countryside crooning lullabies to ghosts, and drawing the mother of Christ in charcoal on courthouse walls.

5 They forced their minds to desert their bodies and their striving spirits sought to rise, like frail whirlwinds from the hard red clay. And when those frail whirlwinds fell, in scattered particles, upon the ground, no one mourned. Instead, men lit candles to celebrate the emptiness that remained, as people do who enter a beautiful but vacant space to resurrect a God.

6 Our mothers and grandmothers, some of them: moving to music not yet written. And they waited.

7 They waited for a day when the unknown thing that was in them would be made known; but guessed, somehow in their darkness, that on the day of their revelation they would be long dead. Therefore to Toomer they walked, and even ran, in slow motion. For they were going nowhere immediate, and the future was not yet within their grasp. And men took our mothers and grandmothers, "but got no pleasure from it." So complex was their passion and their calm.

8 To Toomer, they lay vacant and fallow as autumn fields, with harvest time never in sight: and he saw them enter loveless marriages, without joy; and become prostitutes, without resistance; and become mothers of children, without fulfillment.

9 For these grandmothers and mothers of ours were not Saints, but Artists; driven to a numb and bleeding madness by the springs of creativity in them for which there was no release. They were Creators, who lived lives of spiritual waste, because they were so rich in spirituality—which is the basis of Art—that the strain of enduring their unused and unwanted talent drove them insane. Throwing away this spirituality was their pathetic attempt to lighten the soul to a weight their work-worn, sexually abused bodies could bear.

10   What did it mean for a black woman to be an artist in our grand-mothers' time? In our great-grandmothers' day? It is a question with an answer cruel enough to stop the blood.

11   Did you have a genius of a great-great-grandmother who died under some ignorant and depraved white overseer's lash? Or was she required to bake biscuits for a lazy backwater tramp, when she cried out in her soul to paint watercolors of sunsets, or the rain falling on the green and peaceful pasturelands? Or was her body broken and forced to bear children (who were more often than not sold away from her)—eight, ten, fifteen, twenty children—when her one joy was the thought of modeling heroic figures of rebellion, in stone or clay?

12   How was the creativity of the black woman kept alive, year after year and century after century, when for most of the years black people have been in America, it was a punishable crime for a black person to read or write? And the freedom to paint, to sculpt, to expand the mind with action did not exist. Consider, if you can bear to imagine it, what might have been the result if singing, too, had been forbid-den by law. Listen to the voices of Bessie Smith, Billie Holiday, Nina Simone, Roberta Flack, and Aretha Franklin, among others, and imagine those voices muzzled for life. Then you may begin to com-prehend the lives of our "crazy," "Sainted" mothers and grandmoth-ers. The agony of the lives of women who might have been Poets, Novelists, Essayists, and Short-Story Writers (over a period of cen-turies), who died with their real gifts stifled within them.

13   And, if this were the end of the story, we would have cause to cry out in my paraphrase of Okot p'Bitek's great poem:

> *O, my clanswomen*
> *Let us all cry together!*
> *Come,*
> *Let us mourn the death of our mother,*
> *The death of a Queen*
> *The ash that was produced*
> *By a great fire!*
> *O, this homestead is utterly dead*
> *Close the gates*
> *With lacari thorns,*
> *For our mother*
> *The creator of the Stool is lost!*
> *And all the young women*
> *Have perished in the wilderness!*

14 But this is not the end of the story, for all the young women—our mothers and grandmothers, ourselves—have not perished in the wilderness. And if we ask ourselves why, and search for and find the answer, we will know beyond all efforts to erase it from our minds, just exactly who, and of what, we black American women are.

15 One example, perhaps the most pathetic, most misunderstood one, can provide a backdrop for our mothers' work: Phillis Wheatley, a slave in the 1700s.

16 Virginia Woolf, in her book *A Room of One's Own*, wrote that in order for a woman to write fiction she must have two things, certainly: a room of her own (with key and lock) and enough money to support herself.

17 What then are we to make of Phillis Wheatley, a slave, who owned not even herself? This sickly, frail black girl who required a servant of her own at times—her health was so precarious—and who, had she been white, would have been easily considered the intellectual superior of all the women and most of the men in the society of her day.

18 Virginia Woolf wrote further, speaking of course not of our Phillis, that "any woman born with a great gift in the sixteenth century [insert "eighteenth century," insert "black woman," insert "born or made a slave"] would certainly have gone crazed, shot herself, or ended her days in some lonely cottage outside the village, half witch, half wizard [insert "Saint"], feared and mocked at. For it needs little skill and psychology to be sure that a highly gifted girl who had tried to use her gift for poetry would have been so thwarted and hindered by contrary instincts [add "chains, guns, the lash, the ownership of one's body by someone else, submission to an alien religion"], that she must have lost her health and sanity to a certainty."

19 The key words, as they relate to Phillis, are "contrary instincts." For when we read the poetry of Phillis Wheatley—as when we read the novels of Nella Larsen or the oddly false-sounding autobiography of that freest of all black women writers, Zora Hurston—evidence of "contrary instincts" is everywhere. Her loyalties were completely divided, as was, without question, her mind.

20 But how could this be otherwise? Captured at seven, a slave of wealthy, doting whites who instilled in her the "savagery" of the

Africa they "rescued" her from . . . one wonders if she was even able to remember her homeland as she had known it, or as it really was.

21   Yet, because she did try to use her gift for poetry in a world that made her a slave, she was "so thwarted and hindered by . . . contrary instincts, that she . . . lost her health. . . ." In the last years of her brief life, burdened not only with the need to express her gift but also with a penniless, friendless "freedom" and several small children for whom she was forced to do strenuous work to feed, she lost her health, certainly. Suffering from malnutrition and neglect and who knows what mental agonies, Phillis Wheatley died.

22   So torn by "contrary instincts" was black, kidnapped, enslaved Phillis that her description of "the Goddess"—as she poetically called the Liberty she did not have—is ironically, cruelly humorous. And, in fact, has held Phillis up to ridicule for more than a century. It is usually read prior to hanging Phillis's memory as that of a fool. She wrote:

The Goddess comes, she moves divinely fair,

Olive and laurel binds her *golden* hair.

Wherever shines this native of the skies,

Unnumber'd charms and recent graces rise. [My Italics]

23   It is obvious that Phillis, the slave, combed the "Goddess's" hair every morning; prior, perhaps, to bringing in the milk, or fixing her mistress's lunch. She took her imagery from the one thing she saw elevated above all others.

24   With the benefit of hindsight we ask, "How could she?"

25   But at last, Phillis, we understand. No more snickering when your stiff, struggling, ambivalent lines are forced on us. We know now that you were not an idiot or a traitor; only a sickly little black girl, snatched from your home and country and made a slave; a woman who still struggled to sing the song that was your gift, although in a land of barbarians who praised you for your bewildered tongue. It is not so much what you sang, as that you kept alive, in so many of our ancestors, the notion of song.

26   Black women are called, in the folklore that so aptly identifies one's status in society, "the *mule* of the world," because we have been

handed the burdens that everyone else—*everyone else*—refused to carry. We have also been called "Matriarchs," "Superwomen," and "Mean and Evil Bitches." Not to mention "Castraters" and "Sapphire's Mama." When we have pleaded for understanding, our character has been distorted; when we have asked for simple caring, we have been handed empty inspirational appellations, then stuck in the farthest corner. When we have asked for love, we have been given children. In short, even our plainer gifts, our labors of fidelity and love, have been knocked down our throats. To be an artist and a black woman, even today, lowers our status in many respects, rather than raises it: and yet, artists we will be.

27   Therefore we must fearlessly pull out of ourselves and look at and identify with our lives the living creativity some of our great-grandmothers were not allowed to know. I stress *some* of them because it is well known that the majority of our great-grandmothers knew, even without "knowing" it, the reality of their spirituality, even if they didn't recognize it beyond what happened in the singing at church—and they never had any intention of giving it up.

28   How they did it—those millions of black women who were not Phillis Wheatley, or Lucy Terry or Frances Harper or Zora Hurston or Nella Larsen or Bessie Smith; or Elizabeth Catlett, or Katherine Dunham, either—brings me to the title of this essay, "In Search of Our Mothers' Gardens," which is a personal account that is yet shared, in its theme and its meaning, by all of us. I found, while thinking about the far-reaching world of the creative black woman, that often the truest answer to a question that really matters can be found very close.

29   In the late 1920s my mother ran away from home to marry my father. Marriage, if not running away, was expected of seventeen-year-old girls. By the time she was twenty, she had two children and was pregnant with a third. Five children later, I was born. And this is how I came to know my mother: she seemed a large, soft, loving-eyed woman who was rarely impatient in our home. Her quick, violent temper was on view only a few times a year, when she battled with the white landlord who had the misfortune to suggest to her that her children did not need to go to school.

30   She made all the clothes we wore, even my brothers' overalls. She made all the towels and sheets we used. She spent the summers

canning vegetables and fruits. She spent the winter evenings making quilts enough to cover all our beds.

31 During the "working" day, she labored beside—not behind—my father in the fields. Her day began before sunup, and did not end until late at night. There was never a moment for her to sit down, undisturbed, to unravel her own private thoughts; never a time free from interruption—by work or the noisy inquiries of her many children. And yet, it is to my mother—and all our mothers who were not famous—that I went in search of the secret of what has fed that muzzled and often mutilated, but vibrant, creative spirit that the black woman has inherited, and that pops out in wild and unlikely places to this day.

32 But when, you will ask, did my overworked mother have time to know or care about feeding the creative spirit?

33 The answer is so simple that many of us have spent years discovering it. We have constantly looked high, when we should have looked high—and low.

34 For example: in the Smithsonian Institution in Washington, D.C., there hangs a quilt unlike any other in the world. In fanciful, inspired, and yet simple and identifiable figures, it portrays the story of the Crucifixion. It is considered rare, beyond price. Though it follows no known pattern of quilt-making, and though it is made of bits and pieces of worthless rags, it is obviously the work of a person of powerful imagination and deep spiritual feeling. Below this quilt I saw a note that says it was made by "an anonymous Black woman in Alabama, a hundred years ago."

35 If we could locate this "anonymous" black woman from Alabama, she would turn out to be one of our grandmothers—an artist who left her mark in the only materials she could afford, and in the only medium her position in society allowed her to use.

36 As Virginia Woolf wrote further, in *A Room of One's Own*:

> Yet genius of a sort must have existed among women as it must have existed among the working class. [Change this to "slaves" and "the wives and daughters of sharecroppers."] Now and again an Emily Brontë or a Robert Burns [change this to "a Zora Hurston or a Richard Wright"] blazes out and proves its presence. But certainly it never got itself on to

paper. When, however, one reads of a witch being ducked, of a woman possessed by devils [or "Sainthood"], of a wise woman selling herbs [our root workers], or even a very remarkable man who had a mother, then I think we are on the track of a lost novelist, a suppressed poet, of some mute and inglorious Jane Austen. . . . Indeed, I would venture to guess that Anon, who wrote so many poems without signing them, was often a woman. . . .

37   And so our mothers and grandmothers have, more often than not anonymously, handed on the creative spark, the seed of the flower they themselves never hoped to see: or like a sealed letter they could not plainly read.

38   And so it is, certainly, with my own mother. Unlike "Ma" Rainey's songs, which retained their creator's name even while blasting forth from Bessie Smith's mouth, no song or poem will bear my mother's name. Yet so many of the stories that I write, that we all write, are my mother's stories. Only recently did I fully realize this: that through years of listening to my mother's stories of her life, I have absorbed not only the stories themselves, but something of the manner in which she spoke, something of the urgency that involves the knowledge that her stories—like her life—must be recorded. It is probably for this reason that so much of what I have written is about characters whose counterparts in real life are so much older than I am.

39   But the telling of these stories, which came from my mother's lips as naturally as breathing, was not the only way my mother showed herself as an artist. For stories, too, were subject to being distracted, to dying without conclusion. Dinners must be started, and cotton must be gathered before the big rains. The artist that was and is my mother showed itself to me only after many years. This is what I finally noticed:

40   Like Mem, a character in *The Third Life of Grange Copeland*, my mother adorned with flowers whatever shabby house we were forced to live in. And not just your typical straggly country stand of zinnias, either. She planted ambitious gardens—and still does—with over fifty different varieties of plants that bloom profusely from early March until late November. Before she left home for the fields, she watered her flowers, chopped up the grass, and laid out new beds. When she returned from the fields she might divide clumps of bulbs, dig a cold pit, uproot and replant roses, or prune branches from her taller bushes or trees—until night came and it was too dark to see.

41   Whatever she planted grew as if by magic, and her fame as a grower of flowers spread over three counties. Because of her creativity with her flowers, even my memories of poverty are seen through a screen of blooms—sunflowers, petunias, roses, dahlias, forsythia, spirea, delphiniums, verbena . . . and on and on.

42   And I remember people coming to my mother's yard to be given cuttings from her flowers; I hear again the praise showered on her because whatever rocky soil she landed on, she turned into a garden. A garden so brilliant with colors, so original in its design, so magnificent with life and creativity, that to this day people drive by our house in Georgia—perfect strangers and imperfect strangers—and ask to stand or walk among my mother's art.

43   I notice that it is only when my mother is working in her flowers that she is radiant, almost to the point of being invisible—except as Creator: hand and eye. She is involved in work her soul must have. Ordering the universe in the image of her personal conception of Beauty.

44   Her face, as she prepares the Art that is her gift, is a legacy of respect she leaves to me, for all that illuminates and cherishes life. She has handed down respect for the possibilities—and the will to grasp them.

45   For her, so hindered and intruded upon in so many ways, being an artist has still been a daily part of her life. This ability to hold on, even in very simple ways, is work black women have done for a very long time.

46   This poem is not enough, but it is something, for the woman who literally covered the holes in our walls with sunflowers:

> *They were women then*
> *My mama's generation*
> *Husky of voice—Stout of*
> *Step*
> *With fists as well as*
> *Hands*
> *How they battered down*
> *Doors*
> *And ironed*
> *Starched white*
> *Shirts*
> *How they led*
> *Armies*

Headragged Generals
Across mined
Fields
Booby-trapped
Kitchens
To discover books
Desks
A place for us
How they knew what we
Must know
Without knowing a page
Of it
Themselves.

47 Guided by my heritage of a love of beauty and a respect for strength—in search of my mother's garden, I found my own.

48 And perhaps in Africa over two hundred years ago, there was just such a mother; perhaps she painted vivid and daring decorations in oranges and yellows and greens on the walls of her hut; perhaps she sang—in a voice like Roberta Flack's—sweetly over the compounds of her village; perhaps she wove the most stunning mats or told the most ingenious stories of all the village storytellers. Perhaps she was herself a poet—though only her daughter's name is signed to the poems that we know.

49 Perhaps Phillis Wheatley's mother was also an artist.

50 Perhaps in more than Phillis Wheatley's biological life is her mother's signature made clear.

est known for authoring the Lord of the Rings *trilogy, J. R. R. Tolkien (1892–1973) was also a well-known Christian writer who produced many other works. While known to have professed a hatred for allegory, he nonetheless composed this allegory, "Leaf by Niggle," relating to creation. The story addresses the human impulse to create as well as the struggle to be creative in a society that does not value creation.*

Leaf by Niggle

J. R. R. Tolkien

1 There was once a little man called Niggle, who had a long journey to make. He did not want to go, indeed the whole idea was distasteful to him; but he could not get out of it. He knew he would have to start some time, but he did not hurry with his preparations.

2 Niggle was a painter. Not a very successful one, partly because he had many other things to do. Most of these things he thought were a nuisance; but he did them fairly well, when he could not get out of them: which (in his opinion) was far too often. The laws in his country were rather strict. There were other hindrances, too. For one thing, he was sometimes just idle, and did nothing at all. For another, he was kindhearted, in a way. You know the sort of kind heart: it made him uncomfortable more often than it made him do anything; and even when he did anything, it did not prevent him from grumbling, losing his temper, and swearing (mostly to himself). All the same, it did land him in a good many odd jobs for his neighbour, Mr. Parish, a man with a lame leg. Occasionally he even helped other people from further off, if they came and asked him to. Also, now and again, he remembered his journey, and began to pack a few things in an ineffectual way: at such times he did not paint very much.

3 He had a number of pictures on hand; most of them were too large and ambitious for his skill. He was the sort of painter who can paint leaves better than trees. He used to spend a long time on a single leaf,

trying to catch its shape, and its sheen, and the glistening of dew-drops on its edges. Yet he wanted to paint a whole tree, with all of its leaves in the same style, and all of them different.

4   There was one picture in particular which bothered him. It had begun with a leaf caught in the wind, and it became a tree; and the tree grew, sending out innumerable branches, and thrusting out the most fantastic roots. Strange birds came and settled on the twigs and had to be attended to. Then all round the Tree, and behind it, through the gaps in the leaves and boughs, a country began to open out; and there were glimpses of a forest marching over the land, and of mountains tipped with snow. Niggle lost interest in his other pictures; or else he took them and tacked them on to the edges of his great picture. Soon the canvas became so large that he had to get a ladder; and he ran up and down it, putting in a touch here, and rubbing out a patch there. When people came to call, he seemed polite enough, though he fiddled a little with the pencils on his desk. He listened to what they said, but underneath he was thinking all the time about his big canvas, in the tall shed that had been built for it out in his garden (on a plot where once he had grown potatoes).

5   He could not get rid of his kind heart. "I wish I was more strong-minded!" he sometimes said to himself, meaning that he wished other people's troubles did not make him feel uncomfortable. But for a long time he was not seriously perturbed. "At any rate, I shall get this one picture done, my real picture, before I have to go on that wretched journey," he used to say. Yet he was beginning to see that he could not put off his start indefinitely. The picture would have to stop just growing and get finished.

6   One day, Niggle stood a little way off from his picture and considered it with unusual attention and detachment. He could not make up his mind what he thought about it, and wished he had some friend who would tell him what to think. Actually it seemed to him wholly unsatisfactory, and yet very lovely, the only really beautiful picture in the world. What he would have liked at that moment would have been to see himself walk in, and slap him on the back, and say (with obvious sincerity): "Absolutely magnificent! I see exactly what you are getting at. Do get on with it, and don't bother about anything else! We will arrange for a public pension, so that you need not."

7   However, there was no public pension. And one thing he could see: it would need some concentration, some *work*, hard uninterrupted work, to finish the picture, even at its present size. He rolled up his sleeves, and began to concentrate. He tried for several days not to bother about other things. But there came a tremendous crop of interruptions. Things went wrong in his house; he had to go and serve on a jury in the town; a distant friend fell ill; Mr. Parish was laid up with lumbago; and visitors kept on coming. It was springtime, and they wanted a free tea in the country: Niggle lived in a pleasant little house, miles away from the town. He cursed them in his heart, but he could not deny that he had invited them himself, away back in the winter, when he had not thought it an "interruption" to visit the shops and have tea with acquaintances in the town. He tried to harden his heart; but it was not a success. There were many things that he had not the face to say *no* to, whether he thought them duties or not; and there were some things he was compelled to do, whatever he thought. Some of his visitors hinted that his garden was rather neglected, and that he might get a visit from an Inspector. Very few of them knew about his picture, of course; but if they had known, it would not have made much difference. I doubt if they would have thought that it mattered much. I dare say it was not really a very good picture, though it may have had some good passages. The Tree, at any rate, was curious. Quite unique in its way. So was Niggle; though he was also a very ordinary and rather silly little man.

8   At length Niggle's time became really precious. His acquaintances in the distant town began to remember that the little man had got to make a troublesome journey, and some began to calculate how long at the latest he could put off starting. They wondered who would take his house, and if the garden would be better kept.

9   The autumn came, very wet and windy. The little painter was in his shed. He was up on the ladder, trying to catch the gleam of the westering sun on the peak of a snow-mountain, which he had glimpsed just to the left of the leafy tip of one of the Tree's branches. He knew that he would have to be leaving soon: perhaps early next year. He could only just get the picture finished, and only so so, at that: there were some corners where he would not have time now to do more than hint at what he wanted.

10 There was a knock on the door. "Come in!" he said sharply, and climbed down the ladder. He stood on the floor twiddling his brush. It was his neighbour, Parish: his only real neighbour, all other folk lived a long way off. Still, he did not like the man very much: partly because he was so often in trouble and in need of help; and also because he did not care about painting, but was very critical about gardening. When Parish looked at Niggle's garden (which was often) he saw mostly weeds; and when he looked at Niggle's pictures (which was seldom) he saw only green and grey patches and black lines, which seemed to him nonsensical. He did not mind mentioning the weeds (a neighbourly duty), but he refrained from giving any opinion of the pictures. He thought this was very kind, and he did not realize that, even if it was kind, it was not kind enough. Help with the weeds (and perhaps praise for the pictures) would have been better.

11 "Well, Parish, what is it?" said Niggle.

12 "I oughtn't to interrupt you, I know," said Parish (without a glance at the picture). "You are very busy, I'm sure."

13 Niggle had meant to say something like that himself, but he had missed his chance. All he said was: "Yes." "But I have no one else to turn to," said Parish.

14 "Quite so," said Niggle with a sigh: one of those sighs that are a private comment, but which are not made quite inaudible. "What can I do for you?"

15 "My wife has been ill for some days, and I am getting worried," said Parish. "And the wind has blown half the tiles off my roof, and water is pouring into the bedroom. I think I ought to get the doctor. And the builders, too, only they take so long to come. I was wondering if you had any wood and canvas you could spare, just to patch me up and see me through for a day or two." Now he did look at the picture.

16 "Dear, dear!" said Niggle. "You *are* unlucky. I hope it is no more than a cold that your wife has got. I'll come round presently, and help you move the patient downstairs."

17 "Thank you very much," said Parish, rather coolly. "But it is not a cold, it is a fever. I should not have bothered you for a cold. And my wife is in bed downstairs already. I can't get up and down with trays,

not with my leg. But I see you are busy. Sorry to have troubled you. I had rather hoped you might have been able to spare the time to go for the doctor, seeing how I'm placed; and the builder too, if you really have no canvas you can spare.

18 "Of course," said Niggle; though other words were in his heart, which at the moment was merely soft without feeling at all kind. "I could go. I'll go, if you are really worried."

19 "I am worried, very worried. I wish I was not lame," said Parish.

20 So Niggle went. You see, it was awkward. Parish was his neighbour, and everyone else a long way off. Niggle had a bicycle, and Parish had not, and could not ride one. Parish had a lame leg, a genuine lame leg which gave him a good deal of pain: that had to be remembered, as well as his sour expression and whining voice. Of course, Niggle had a picture and barely time to finish it. But it seemed that this was a thing that Parish had to reckon with and not Niggle. Parish, however, did not reckon with pictures; and Niggle could not alter that. "Curse it!" he said to himself, as he got out his bicycle.

21 It was wet and windy, and daylight was waning. "No more work for me today!" thought Niggle, and all the time that he was riding, he was either swearing to himself, or imagining the strokes of his brush on the mountain, and on the spray of leaves beside it, that he had first imagined in the spring. His fingers twitched on the handlebars. Now he was out of the shed, he saw exactly the way in which to treat that shining spray which framed the distant vision of the mountain. But he had a sinking feeling in his heart, a sort of fear that he would never now get a chance to try it out.

22 Niggle found the doctor, and he left a note at the builder's. The office was shut, and the builder had gone home to his fireside. Niggle got soaked to the skin, and caught a chill himself. The doctor did not set out as promptly as Niggle had done. He arrived next day, which was quite convenient for him, as by that time there were two patients to deal with, in neighbouring houses. Niggle was in bed, with a high temperature, and marvellous patterns of leaves and involved branches forming in his head and on the ceiling. It did not comfort him to learn that Mrs. Parish had only had a cold, and was getting up. He turned his face to the wall and buried himself in leaves.

23   He remained in bed some time. The wind went on blowing. It took away a good many more of Parish's tiles, and some of Niggle's as well: his own roof began to leak. The builder did not come. Niggle did not care; not for a day or two. Then he crawled out to look for some food (Niggle had no wife). Parish did not come round: the rain had got into his leg and made it ache; and his wife was busy mopping up water, and wondering if "that Mr. Niggle" had forgotten to call at the builder's. Had she seen any chance of borrowing anything useful, she would have sent Parish round, leg or no leg; but she did not, so Niggle was left to himself.

24   At the end of a week or so Niggle tottered out to his shed again. He tried to climb the ladder, but it made his head giddy. He sat and looked at the picture, but there were no patterns of leaves or visions of mountains in his mind that day. He could have painted a far-off view of a sandy desert, but he had not the energy.

25   Next day he felt a good deal better. He climbed the ladder, and began to paint. He had just begun to get into it again, when there came a knock on the door.

26   "Damn!" said Niggle. But he might just as well have said "Come in!" politely, for the door opened all the same. This time a very tall man came in, a total stranger.

27   "This is a private studio," said Niggle. "I am busy. Go away!"

28   "I am an Inspector of Houses," said the man, holding up his appointment-card, so that Niggle on his ladder could see it.

29   "Oh!" he said.

30   "Your neighbour's house is not satisfactory at all," said the Inspector.

31   "I know," said Niggle. "I took a note to the builders a long time ago, but they have never come. Then I have been ill."

32   "I see," said the Inspector. "But you are not ill now."

33   "But I'm not a builder. Parish ought to make a complaint to the Town Council, and get help from the Emergency Service."

34   "They are busy with worse damage than any up here," said the Inspector. "There has been a flood in the valley, and many families are homeless. You should have helped your neighbour to make temporary repairs and prevent the damage from getting more costly to

mend than necessary. That is the law. There is plenty of material here: canvas, wood, waterproof paint."

35 "Where?" asked Niggle indignantly.

36 "There!" said the Inspector, pointing to the picture.

37 "My picture!" exclaimed Niggle.

38 "I dare say it is," said the Inspector. "But houses come first. That is the law."

39 "But I can't . . ." Niggle said no more, for at that moment another man came in. Very much like the Inspector he was, almost his double: tall, dressed all in black.

40 "Come along!" he said. "I am the Driver."

41 Niggle stumbled down from the ladder. His fever seemed to have come on again, and his head was swimming; he felt cold all over.

42 "Driver? Driver?" he chattered. "Driver of what?"

43 "You, and your carriage," said the man. "The carriage was ordered long ago. It has come at last. It's waiting. You start today on your journey, you know."

44 "There now!" said the Inspector. "You'll have to go; but it's a bad way to start on your journey, leaving your jobs undone. Still, we can at least make some use of this canvas now.

45 "Oh, dear!" said poor Niggle, beginning to weep. "And it's not, not even finished!"

46 "Not finished?" said the Driver. "Well, it's finished with, as far as you're concerned, at any rate. Come along!"

47 Niggle went, quite quietly. The Driver gave him no time to pack, saying that he ought to have done that before, and they would miss the train; so all Niggle could do was is to grab a little bag in the hall. He found that it contained only a paint-box and a small book of his own sketches: neither food nor clothes. They caught the train all right. Niggle was feeling very tired and sleepy; he was hardly aware of what was going on when they bundled him into his compartment. He did not care much: he had forgotten where he was supposed to be going or what he was going for. The train ran almost at once into a dark tunnel.

48   Niggle woke up in a very large, dim railway station. A Porter went along the platform shouting, but he was not shouting the name of the place; he was shouting *Niggle!*

49   Niggle got out in a hurry, and found that he had left his little bag behind. He turned back, but the train had gone away.

50   "Ah, there you are!" said the Porter. "This way! What! No luggage? You will have to go to the Workhouse."

51   Niggle felt very ill, and fainted on the platform. They put him in an ambulance and took him to the Workhouse Infirmary.

52   He did not like the treatment at all. The medicine they gave him was bitter. The officials and attendants were unfriendly, silent, and strict; and he never saw anyone else, except a very severe doctor, who visited him occasionally. It was more like being in a prison than in a hospital. He had to work hard, at stated hours: at digging, carpentry, and painting bare boards all one plain colour. He was never allowed outside, and the windows all looked inwards. They kept him in the dark for hours at a stretch, "to do some thinking," they said. He lost count of time. He did not even begin to feel better, not if that could be judged by whether he felt any pleasure in doing anything. He did not, not even in getting into bed.

53   At first, during the first century or so (I am merely giving his impressions), he used to worry aimlessly about the past. One thing he kept on repeating to himself, as he lay in the dark: "I wish I had called on Parish the first morning after the high winds began. I meant to. The first loose tiles would have been easy to fix. Then Mrs. Parish might never have caught cold. Then I should not have caught cold either. Then I should have had a week longer." But in time he forgot what it was that he had wanted a week longer for. If he worried at all after that, it was about his jobs in the hospital. He planned them out, thinking how quickly he could stop that board creaking, or rehang that door, or mend that table-leg. Probably he really became rather useful, though no one ever told him so. But that, of course, cannot have been the reason why they kept the poor little man so long. They may have been waiting for him to get better, and judging "better" by some odd medical standard of their own.

54   At any rate, poor Niggle got no pleasure out of life, not what he had been used to call pleasure. He was certainly not amused. But it could

not be denied that he began to have a feeling of—well, satisfaction: bread rather than jam. He could take up a task the moment one bell rang, and lay it aside promptly the moment the next one went, all tidy and ready to be continued at the right time. He got through quite a lot in a day, now; he finished small things off neatly. He had no "time of his own" (except alone in his bed-cell), and yet he was becoming master of his time; he began to know just what he could do with it. There was no sense of rush. He was quieter inside now, and at resting-time he could really rest.

55 Then suddenly they changed all his hours; they hardly let him go to bed at all; they took him off carpentry altogether and kept him at plain digging, day after day. He took it fairly well. It was a long while before he even began to grope in the back of his mind for the curses that he had practically forgotten. He went on digging, till his back seemed broken, his hands were raw, and he felt that he could not manage another spadeful. Nobody thanked him. But the doctor came and looked at him.

56 "Knock off!" he said. "Complete rest—in the dark."

57 Niggle was lying in the dark, resting completely; so that, as he had not been either feeling or thinking at all, he might have been lying there for hours or for years, as far as he could tell. But now he heard Voices: not voices that he had ever heard before. There seemed to be a Medical Board, or perhaps a Court of Inquiry, going on close at hand, in an adjoining room with the door open, possibly, though he could not see any light.

58 "Now the Niggle case," said a Voice, a severe voice, more severe than the doctor's.

59 "What was the matter with him?" said a Second Voice, a voice that you might have called gentle, though it was not soft—it was a voice of authority, and sounded at once hopeful and sad. "What was the matter with Niggle? His heart was in the right place."

60 "Yes, but it did not function properly," said the First Voice. "And his head was not screwed on tight enough: he hardly ever thought at all. Look at the time he wasted, not even amusing himself! He never got ready for his journey. He was moderately well-off, and yet he arrived

here almost destitute, and had to be put in the paupers' wing. A bad case, I am afraid. I think he should stay some time yet."

61   "It would not do him any harm, perhaps," said the Second Voice. "But, of course, he is only a little man. He was never meant to be anything very much; and he was never very strong. Let us look at the Records. Yes. There are some favourable points, you know."

62   "Perhaps," said the First Voice; "but very few that will really bear examination."

63   "Well," said the Second Voice, "there are these. He was a painter by nature. In a minor way, of course; still, a Leaf by Niggle has a charm of its own. He took a great deal of pains with leaves, just for their own sake. But he never thought that that made him important. There is no note in the Records of his pretending, even to himself, that it excused his neglect of things ordered by the law."

64   "Then he should not have neglected so many," said the First Voice.

65   "All the same, he did answer a good many Calls."

66   "A small percentage, mostly of the easier sort, and he called those Interruptions. The Records are full of the word, together with a lot of complaints and silly imprecations.

67   "True; but they looked like interruptions to him, of course, poor little man. And there is this: he never expected any Return, as so many of his sort call it. There is the Parish case, the one that came in later. He was Niggle's neighbour, never did a stroke for him, and seldom showed any gratitude at all. But there is no note in the Records that Niggle expected Parish's gratitude; he does not seem to have thought about it."

68   "Yes, that is a point," said the First Voice; "but rather small. I think you will find Niggle often merely forgot. Things he had to do for Parish he put out of his mind as a nuisance he had done with."

69   "Still, there is this last report," said the Second Voice, "that wet bicycle-ride. I rather lay stress on that. It seems plain that this was a genuine sacrifice: Niggle guessed that he was throwing away his last chance with his picture, and he guessed, too, that Parish was worrying unnecessarily."

70   "I think you put it too strongly," said the First Voice. "But you have the last word. It is your task, of course, to put the best interpretation on the facts. Sometimes they will bear it. What do you propose?"

71   "I think it is a case for a little gentle treatment now," said the Second Voice.

72   Niggle thought that he had never heard anything so generous as that Voice. It made Gentle Treatment sound like a load of rich gifts, and the summons to a King's feast. Then suddenly Niggle felt ashamed. To hear that he was considered a case for Gentle Treatment overwhelmed him, and made him blush in the dark. It was like being publicly praised, when you and all the audience knew that the praise was not deserved. Niggle hid his blushes in the rough blanket.

73   There was a silence. Then the First Voice spoke to Niggle, quite close. "You have been listening," it said.

74   "Yes," said Niggle.

75   "Well, what have you to say?"

76   "Could you tell me about Parish?" said Niggle. "I should like to see him again. I hope he is not very ill? Can you cure his leg? It used to give him a wretched time. And please don't worry about him and me. He was a very good neighbour, and let me have excellent potatoes very cheap, which saved me a lot of time."

77   "Did he?" said the First Voice. "I am glad to hear it."

78   There was another silence. Niggle heard the Voices receding. "Well, I agree," he heard the First Voice say in the distance. "Let him go on to the next stage. Tomorrow, if you like."

79   Niggle woke up to find that his blinds were drawn, and his little cell was full of sunshine. He got up, and found that some comfortable clothes had been put out for him, not hospital uniform. After breakfast the doctor treated his sore hands, putting some salve on them that healed them at once. He gave Niggle some good advice, and a bottle of tonic (in case he needed it). In the middle of the morning they gave Niggle a biscuit and a glass of wine; and then they gave him a ticket.

80   "You can go to the railway station now," said the doctor. "The Porter
     will look after you. Good-bye."

81   Niggle slipped out of the main door, and blinked a little. The sun was
     very bright. Also he had expected to walk out into a large town, to
     match the size of the station; but he did not. He was on the top of a hill,
     green, bare, swept by a keen invigorating wind. Nobody else was
     about. Away down under the hill he could see the roof of the station
     shining.

82   He walked downhill to the station briskly, but without hurry. The
     Porter spotted him at once.

83   "This way!" he said, and led Niggle to a bay, in which there was a
     very pleasant little local train standing: one coach, and a small
     engine, both very bright, clean, and newly painted. It looked as if this
     was their first run. Even the track that lay in front of the engine
     looked new: the rails shone, the chairs were painted green, and the
     sleepers gave off a delicious smell of fresh tar in the warm sunshine.
     The coach was empty.

84   "Where does this train go, Porter?" asked Niggle.

85   "I don't think they have fixed its name yet," said the Porter. "But
     you'll find it all right." He shut the door.

86   The train moved off at once. Niggle lay back in his seat. The little
     engine puffed along in a deep cutting with high green banks, roofed
     with blue sky. It did not seem very long before the engine gave a
     whistle, the brakes were put on, and the train stopped. There was no
     station, and no signboard, only a flight of steps up the green embank-
     ment. At the top of the steps there was a wicket-gate in a trim hedge.
     By the gate stood his bicycle; at least, it looked like his, and there was
     a yellow label tied to the bars with NIGGLE written on it in large
     black letters.

87   Niggle pushed open the gate, jumped on the bicycle, and went bowl-
     ing downhill in the spring sunshine. Before long he found that the
     path on which he had started had disappeared, and the bicycle was
     rolling along over a marvellous turf. It was green and close; and yet
     he could see every blade distinctly. He seemed to remember having
     seen or dreamed of that sweep of grass somewhere or other. The

curves of the land were familiar somehow. Yes: the ground was becoming level, as it should, and now, of course, it was beginning to rise again. A great green shadow came between him and the sun. Niggle looked up, and fell off his bicycle.

88   Before him stood the Tree, his Tree, finished. If you could say that of a Tree that was alive, its leaves opening, its branches growing and bending in the wind that Niggle had so often felt or guessed, and had so often failed to catch. He gazed at the Tree, and slowly he lifted his arms and opened them wide.

89   "It's a gift!" he said. He was referring to his art, and also to the result; but he was using the word quite literally.

90   He went on looking at the Tree. All the leaves he had ever laboured at were there, as he had imagined them rather than as he had made them; and there were others that had only budded in his mind, and many that might have budded, if only he had had time. Nothing was written on them, they were just exquisite leaves, yet they were dated as clear as a calendar. Some of the most beautiful—and the most characteristic, the most perfect examples of the Niggle style—were seen to have been produced in collaboration with Mr. Parish: there was no other way of putting it.

91   The birds were building in the Tree. Astonishing birds: how they sang! They were mating, hatching, growing wings, and flying away singing into the Forest, even while he looked at them. For now he saw that the Forest was there too, opening out on either side, and marching away into the distance. The Mountains were glimmering far away.

92   After a time Niggle turned towards the Forest. Not because he was tired of the Tree, but he seemed to have got it all clear in his mind now, and was aware of it, and of its growth, even when he was not looking at it. As he walked away, he discovered an odd thing: the Forest, of course, was a distant Forest, yet he could approach it, even enter it, without its losing that particular charm. He had never before been able to walk into the distance without turning it into mere surroundings. It really added a considerable attraction to walking in the country, because, as you walked, new distances opened out; so that you now had doubled, treble, and quadruple distances, doubly, trebly, and quadruply enchanting. You could go on and on, and have a

whole country in a garden, or in a picture (if you preferred to call it that). You could go on and on, but not perhaps for ever. There were the Mountains in the background. They did get nearer, very slowly. They did not seem to belong to the picture, or only as a link to something else, a glimpse through the trees of something different, a further stage: another picture.

93   Niggle walked about, but he was not merely pottering. He was looking round carefully. The Tree was finished, though not finished with—"Just the other way about to what it used to be," he thought—but in the Forest there were a number of inconclusive regions, that still needed work and thought. Nothing needed altering any longer, nothing was wrong, as far as it had gone, but it needed continuing up to a definite point. Niggle saw the point precisely, in each case.

94   He sat down under a very beautiful distant tree—a variation of the Great Tree, but quite individual, or it would be with a little more attention—and he considered where to begin work, and where to end it, and how much time was required. He could not quite work out his scheme.

95   "Of course!" he said. "What I need is Parish. There are lots of things about earth, plants, and trees that he knows and I don't. This place cannot be left just as my private park. I need help and advice: I ought to have got it sooner."

96   He got up and walked to the place where he had decided to begin work. He took off his coat. Then, down in a little sheltered hollow hidden from a further view, he saw a man looking round rather bewildered. He was leaning on a spade, but plainly did not know what to do. Niggle hailed him. "Parish!" he called.

97   Parish shouldered his spade and came up to him. He still limped a little. They did not speak, just nodded as they used to do, passing in the lane; but now they walked about together, arm in arm. Without talking, Niggle and Parish agreed exactly where to make the small house and garden, which seemed to be required.

98   As they worked together, it became plain that Niggle was now the better of the two at ordering his time and getting things done. Oddly enough, it was Niggle who became most absorbed in building and gardening, while Parish often wandered about looking at trees, and especially at the Tree.

99 One day Niggle was busy planting a quickset hedge, and Parish was lying on the grass near by, looking attentively at a beautiful and shapely little yellow flower growing in the green turf. Niggle had put a lot of them among the roots of his Tree long ago. Suddenly Parish looked up: his face was glistening in the sun, and he was smiling.

100 "This is grand!" he said. "I oughtn't to be here, really. Thank you for putting in a word for me."

101 "Nonsense," said Niggle. "I don't remember what I said, but anyway it was not nearly enough."

102 "Oh yes, it was," said Parish. "It got me out a lot sooner. That Second Voice, you know: he had me sent here; he said you had asked to see me. I owe it to you."

103 "No. You owe it to the Second Voice," said Niggle. "We both do."

104 They went on living and working together: I do not know how long. It is no use denying that at first they occasionally disagreed, especially when they got tired. For at first they did sometimes get tired. They found that they had both been provided with tonics. Each bottle had the same label: *A few drops to be taken in water from the Spring, before resting.*

105 They found the Spring in the heart of the Forest; only once long ago had Niggle imagined it, but he had never drawn it. Now he perceived that it was the source of the lake that glimmered, far away and the nourishment of all that grew in the country. The few drops made the water astringent, rather bitter, but invigorating; and it cleared the head. After drinking they rested alone; and then they got up again and things went on merrily. At such times Niggle would think of wonderful new flowers and plants, and Parish always knew exactly how to set them and where they would do best. Long before the tonics were finished they had ceased to need them. Parish lost his limp.

106 As their work drew to an end they allowed themselves more and more time for walking about, looking at the trees, and the flowers, and the lights and shapes, and the lie of the land. Sometimes they sang together; but Niggle found that he was now beginning to turn his eyes, more and more often, towards the Mountains.

107   The time came when the house in the hollow, the garden, the grass, the forest, the lake, and all the country was nearly complete, in its own proper fashion. The Great Tree was in full blossom.

108   "We shall finish this evening," said Parish one day. "After that we will go for a really long walk."

109   They set out next day, and they walked until they came right through the distances to the Edge. It was not visible, of course: there was no line, or fence, or wall; but they knew that they had come to the margin of that country. They saw a man, he looked like a shepherd; he was walking towards them, down the grass slopes that led up into the Mountains.

110   "Do you want a guide?" he asked. "Do you want to go on?"

111   For a moment a shadow fell between Niggle and Parish, for Niggle knew that he did now want to go on, and (in a sense) ought to go on; but Parish did not want to go on, and was not yet ready to go.

112   "I must wait for my wife," said Parish to Niggle. "She'd be lonely. I rather gathered that they would send her after me, some time or other, when she was ready, and when I had got things ready for her. The house is finished now, as well as we could make it; but I should like to show it to her. She'll be able to make it better, I expect: more homely. I hope she'll like this country, too." He turned to the shepherd. "Are you a guide?" be asked. "Could you tell me the name of this country?"

113   "Don't you know?" said the man. "It is Niggle's Country. It is Niggle's Picture, or most of it: a little of it is now Parish's Garden."

114   "Niggle's Picture!" said Parish in astonishment. "Did *you* think of all this, Niggle? I never knew you were so clever. Why didn't you tell me?"

115   "He tried to tell you long ago," said the man; "but you would not look. He had only got canvas and paint in those days, and you wanted to mend your roof with them. This is what you and your wife used to call Niggle's Nonsense, or That Daubing."

116   "But it did not look like this then, not *real*," said Parish.

117   "No, it was only a glimpse then," said the man; "but you might have caught the glimpse, if you had ever thought it worth while to try."

118 "I did not give you much chance," said Niggle. "I never tried to explain. I used to call you Old Earthgrubber. But what does it matter? We have lived and worked together now. Things might have been different, but they could not have been better. All the same, I am afraid I shall have to be going on. We shall meet again, I expect: there must be many more things we can do together. Good-bye!" He shook Parish's hand warmly: a good, firm, honest hand it seemed. He turned and looked back for a moment. The blossom on the Great Tree was shining like flame. All the birds were flying in the air and singing. Then he smiled, and nodded to Parish, and went off with the shepherd.

119 He was going to learn about sheep, and the high pasturages, and look at a wider sky, and walk ever further and further towards the Mountains, always uphill. Beyond that I cannot guess what became of him. Even little Niggle in his old home could glimpse the Mountains far away, and they got into the borders of his picture; but what they are really like, and what lies beyond them, only those can say who have climbed them.

120 "I think he was a silly little man," said Councillor Tompkins. "Worth less, in fact; no use to Society at all."

121 "Oh, I don't know," said Atkins, who was nobody of importance, just a schoolmaster. "I am not so sure: it depends on what you mean by *use*."

122 "No practical or economic use," said Tompkins. "I dare say he could have been made into a serviceable cog of some sort, if you schoolmasters knew your business. But you don't, and so we get useless people of his sort. If I ran this country I should put him and his like to some job that they're fit for, washing dishes in a communal kitchen or something, and I should see that they did it properly. Or I would put them away. I should have put *him* away long ago."

123 "Put him away? You mean you'd have made him start on the journey before his time?"

124 "Yes, if you must use that meaningless old expression. Push him through the tunnel into the great Rubbish Heap: that's what I mean."

125 "Then you don't think painting is worth anything, not worth preserving, or improving, or even making use of?"

126   "Of course, painting has uses," said Tompkins. "But you couldn't make use of his painting. There is plenty of scope for bold young men not afraid of new ideas and new methods. None for this old-fashioned stuff. Private day-dreaming. He could not have designed a telling poster, to save his life. Always fiddling with leaves and flowers. I asked him why, once. He said he thought they were pretty! Can you believe it? He said *pretty!* "What, digestive and genital organs of plants?" I said to him; and he had nothing to answer. Silly footler."

127   "Footler," sighed Atkins. "Yes, poor little man, he never finished anything. Ah well, his canvases have been put to 'better uses,' since he went. But I am not sure, Tompkins. You remember that large one, the one they used to patch the damaged house next door to his, after the gales and floods? I found a corner of it torn off, lying in a field. It was damaged, but legible: a mountain-peak and a spray of leaves. I can't get it out of my mind."

128   "Out of your what?" said Tompkins.

129   "Who are you two talking about?" said Perkins, intervening in the cause of peace: Atkins had flushed rather red.

130   "The name's not worth repeating," said Tompkins. "I don't know why we are talking about him at all. He did not live in town."

131   "No," said Atkins; "but you had your eye on his house, all the same. That is why you used to go and call, and sneer at him while drinking his tea. Well, you've got his house now, as well as the one in town, so you need not grudge him his name. We were talking about Niggle, if you want to know, Perkins."

132   "Oh, poor little Niggle!" said Perkins. "Never knew he painted."

133   That was probably the last time Niggle's name ever came up in conversation. However, Atkins preserved the odd corner. Most of it crumbled; but one beautiful leaf remained intact. Atkins had it framed. Later he left it to the Town Museum, and for a long while "Leaf: by Niggle" hung there in a recess, and was noticed by a few eyes. But eventually the Museum was burnt down, and the leaf, and Niggle, were entirely forgotten in his old country.

134   "It is proving very useful indeed," said the Second Voice. "As a holiday, and a refreshment. It is splendid for convalescence; and not only

for that, for many it is the best introduction to the Mountains. It works wonders in some cases. I am sending more and more there. They seldom have to come back."

135 "No, that is so," said the First Voice. "I think we shall have to give the region a name. What do you propose?"

136 "The Porter settled that some time ago," said the Second Voice. *"Train for Niggle's Parish in the bay*: he has shouted that for a long while now. Niggle's Parish. I sent a message to both of them to tell them."

137 "What did they say?"

138 "They both laughed. Laughed—the Mountains rang with it!"

Madeleine L'Engle's (1918–2007) most famous work is the Wrinkle in Time *trilogy, which won multiple awards and has been hugely popular among both Christian and secular readers since its publication. L'Engle was a prolific Christian writer who believed that Christians who create cannot help but show their love for God in their work, and therefore are glorifying him without overtly labeling the work as Christian. She asserted that writing fictional stories, myths, and other works of the imagination is just as much an act of worship to God as writing a psalm or a sermon. In "Story as a Creative Act," she encourages Christians to accept and appreciate not only "Christian" writing, but all other forms of imaginative writing that are glorifying to God.*

Story as a Creative Act

Madeleine L'Engle

1 The power of love that called forth the universe, calls on us to create, too—not out of nothing, for only God can do that—but with what the Creator has given us.

2 All art, good, bad, indifferent, reflects its culture. Great art transcends its culture and touches on that which is eternal. Two writers may write the same story about the same man and woman and their relationship with each other. One writer will come up with art and the other with pornography. There is no subject that is not appropriate for the artist, but the way in which it is handled can sometimes be totally inappropriate. True art has a mythic quality in that it speaks of that which was true, is true, and will be true.

3 Too much concern about *Christian* art can be destructive both to art and to Christianity. I cannot consciously try to write a *Christian* story. My own life and my own faith will determine whether or not my stories are Christian. Too much Christian art relies so heavily on being Christian that the artist forgets that it also must be good art.

4 When we write a story, we must write to the absolute best of our ability. That is the job, first and foremost. If we are truly Christian, that will be evident, no matter what the topic. If we are not truly Christian,

that will also be evident, no matter how pious the tale. When I am working on a book I move into an area of faith that is beyond the conscious control of my intellect. I do not mean that I discard my intellect—that I am an anti-intellectual gung-ho for intuition. Like it or not, I am an intellectual. The struggle is to let my intellect work *for* what I am working on, not against it. And this means, first of all, that I must have more faith in the work than I have in myself.

5 Scientists are now discovering that the cognitive part of the brain is not necessarily the most used part. Ideas, be they scientific or artistic, come when the cognitive mind is at rest, and suddenly it will awaken to an idea that has been given it by the interior, creative, often unrecognized area of the brain. When the storyteller insists on being in control of the story, then the story has no chance to take off and take the writer with it into strange and unexpected places.

6 I do not always choose what I am going to write. Sometimes I feel called to write on subjects I really don't want to tackle. That's when I most need to listen to the story with humility and virtue, virtue in the ancient sense of the word, which has little to do with moral rectitude. True virtue means strength. And in one etymological dictionary, virtue is defined as *that which is necessary.* So let us spell it *vertue*, to differentiate it from self-conscious virtue. In biblical language it means creative power creative power vs. that dominant power that Lord Acton warns us will corrupt us. When the woman with the issue of blood touches the hem of Jesus' garment, he knows someone has touched him, because he feels the *vertue* drain from him. So, indeed the act of creation is virtuous, as the Word shouting the galaxies into being was virtuous. Indeed, our *vertue* may involve a sudden acknowledgment of our wrongdoings. Indeed, our sin.

7 I was upset at the Bible college's statement of faith that emphasized God's wrath at my sin and depravity, not because I think I am sinless, or because I am never "crooked or wrong" (my etymological dictionary's definition of depraved), but because I believe that God is calling me away from sin and depravity, both of which kill the creative element in us, and towards creativity, humility, and vertue.

8 If I dwell constantly on my sin and depravity, and am thereby constantly fearful of God's wrath and indignation, I make it impossible for myself to move out of sin and depravity into joy and creativity.

This does not mean that I forget what I have done that is wrong. Adam, in *The Arm of the Starfish*, must live the rest of his life knowing that he was at least partially responsible for Joshua's death. But his calling is not to dwell on this terrible awareness, but to move on and to live the rest of his life as creatively as possible.

9   King David's life was changed forever because he succumbed to temptation with Bathsheba, and then tried to get out of the mess by having her husband killed.

10 He confessed in an anguish of repentance, and Nathan the prophet told him:

> The LORD has taken away your sin. You are not going to die. But because by doing this you have made the enemies of the LORD show utter contempt, the son born to you will die.

11 So it wasn't just what David had done; it was the example he had set. People who have accepted positions of public trust are particularly responsible not to give occasion to the enemies of the Lord to say it's okay to dump your wife, to sleep around, to evade income tax. Fulfill yourself, that's what the world says is important.

12 But the people I know, in literature and in life, whose chief concern is fulfilling themselves, are always empty.

13 The rules are not the same for all of us; we'd like them to be, but they are not. I am free to have a glass of wine at a dinner party. My surgeon friend who is on call and may have to operate on someone that night is not. I have committed myself very publicly in my writing about marriage and marriage vows. Hugh and I used to laugh and agree that it was a good thing that we didn't want to get divorced, because we couldn't. I believe that those who are ordained to the ministry are also called to set an example in their daily living.

14 A man in a position of public trust said to me that he was unhappy with his marriage, that he could not stay in it and keep his integrity. This may sometimes be true. Too often it means, "I cannot stay in this marriage and have my own way."

15 Someone else told me of a monk who, after ten years in a monastery, had recognized his homosexuality, and left the monastery because he felt he could not stay there and keep his integrity. I asked, "Why was it harder for him to be a celibate monk as a homosexual than as

a heterosexual?" Didn't keeping his integrity once again mean, "I cannot stay here and have my own way"?

16   If the public persona and the inner man (or woman) are not close together, there is trouble, and there is certainly loss of integrity. It is only as we recognize our sin and depravity and turn to God for healing (not wrath) that we are enabled to sin less frequently. If we set ourselves up as models of rectitude and make ourselves believe that we have perfect morality, we are apt to fall on our faces, as have some televangelists and many politicians. Moral rectitude may come naturally to angels, but not to us human beings.

17   King David's public and private selves were close together, despite his adultery, and that is why his repentance was real. Ultimately he truly became a king, but not until after he knew himself a sinner, after he had suffered civil war with his son Absalom, and grieved for the death of those closest to his heart. Then, at last, he became "royal David," a true king. *We went through fire and water*, David, the psalmist sings. *But you brought us out into a wide place.*

18   *"My God, my God!"* David cried. *"Why have you forsaken me?"*

19   And Jesus, on the cross, echoed King David's words.

20   Story is seldom true if we try to control it, manipulate it, make it go where we want it to go, rather than where the story itself wants to go. I do not control my stories, and most of the writers with whom I have talked agree with me. We listen to the story, and must be willing to grow with it. But how do we know that the story is right?

21   We've lost much of the richness of that word *know*. Nowadays "to know" means to know with the intellect. But it has much deeper meaning than that. Adam *knew* Eve. To know deeply is far more than to know consciously. My husband *knew* me. Sometimes he knew me far better than I know myself. In the realm of faith I *know* far more than I can believe with my finite mind. I *know* that a loving God will not abandon what has been created. I *know* that the human calling is co-creation with this power of love. I *know* that *neither death nor life, neither angels nor demons, neither the present nor the future, nor any powers, neither height nor depth, nor anything else in all creation, will be able to separate us from the love of God that is in Christ Jesus our Lord.*

22   The powers of darkness would like to keep us from this knowing, and
     it is possible that we can permit them to blind us, because we are mor-
     tal and flawed. But Love is always more powerful than hate, creativity
     than destruction. When I falter and fear I turn to story to return me
     to light. God's story, God's wonderful, impossible, glorious story of
     the mystery of the Word made flesh.

                              •   •   •

23   After President Coolidge retired, he and Mrs. Coolidge lived a quiet
     life together, away from politics and political problems. One rainy Sun-
     day Mrs. Coolidge had a cold, and decided to stay home from church.
     When President Coolidge returned, she asked him what the preacher's
     sermon had been about.

24   "Sin."

25   "What did he have to say about it?"

26   President Coolidge, ever laconic, replied, "He was agin it."

27   We're all "agin" sin, and yet we're all deep in it, because it is an
     intrinsic part of human nature, and until we are aware that we're sin-
     ners, it isn't really possible for us to be "agin" it.

28   And what is sin?

30   As I read and reread the great stories in the Bible it seems more and
     more clear that sin is separation from God, and one way to separate
     ourselves from God is to over-define God. If Jesus was like us, but
     sinless, it wasn't that he never did anything the moral majority of his
     day considered wrong. Indeed, he did many things that they consid-
     ered sin, such as breaking the law by healing people on the Sabbath.
     But he was never separate from the Source, while we, of our essence,
     separate ourselves over and over.

31   The first great story in the Bible, after the wonderful paean of praise
     to Creation, is a story of separation from God, the story of Adam and
     Eve in the Garden. It doesn't really matter who was the first to eat of
     the fruit of the tree of the knowledge of good and evil. What is impor-
     tant is that in going against God's wishes, they separated themselves
     from their Maker. Both of them.

32   Like many of the tales in Scripture, the story of the expulsion of the
     human beings from the Garden is an ambiguous one. It is a story not

of punishment, but of separation, the two human beings' separation from God, and separation from their own natures. Suddenly Adam and Eve became aware of knowledge—intellectual knowledge, and they weren't yet ready for all that they learned. It was out of chronology and inconsistent with God's time. Perhaps, in God's time, when Adam and Eve were ready, God would have called them to the tree and said, "Eat." But they took matters into their own hands and ate too soon. Their intellectual and spiritual development was sundered.

33   We are still paying for that sundering. We know with our intellects far more than we know with our spirits. We know how to make war and to kill; how to build factories and make slaves of those who work in them; how to allow immense wealth and terrible poverty side by side; how to be judgmental and intolerant and exclusive and unforgiving.

34   And so Adam and Eve were prematurely expelled from the Garden. I suspect that sooner or later they would have had to leave, that God would have gently shoved them out, as the mother bird pushes the fledgling from the nest. But the timing would have been right. They would have been ready to fly.

35   But, prodded by the serpent, they took time into their own hands and broke it. When we look for a way to heal this brokenness, God offers us story, and sometimes the story is so extraordinary that it is difficult for us to understand, especially if we try to understand, as Adam and Eve did after they had left the Garden, with mind alone, and not with heart and spirit.

36   After the first separation from God in the Garden, the next story is of an even more terrible separation: murder. Cain killed Abel. And this kind of separation has gone on ever since. At its worst this sin of separation is murder, literal murder; occasionally it is hysterical folly. Last summer before going to Oxford for a conference I re-read Elizabeth Goudge's *Towers in the Mist*, set in Oxford at the time of Queen Elizabeth, and I had forgotten the terrible things Protestants and Catholics did to each other, each group as brutal as the other, depending on which was politically in power.

37   The story of Romeo and Juliet is a story about this kind of irrational separation, as are the Narnia Chronicles, as is *The Brothers Karamazov*. As we read of the pain caused by separation, we are offered healing. And that is why I love the stories in Scripture, for they are prescriptions for

healing, even when they are incomprehensible, such as this marvelous passage from Ezekiel:

> I looked, and I saw beside the cherubim four wheels, one beside each of the cheru-
> bim . . . the four of them looked alike; each was like a wheel intersecting a wheel.
> As they moved, they would go in any one of the four directions the cherubim
> faced. . . . Their entire bodies, including their backs, their hands and their wings,
> were completely full of eyes, as were their four wheels. . . . Each of the cherubim
> had four faces: One face was that of a cherub, the second the face of a man, the
> third the face of a lion, and the fourth the face of an eagle.

38   This is from the tenth chapter of Ezekiel, and the cherubim, man, lion,
and eagle are reprised in John's Revelation. What are we to make of
these extraordinary wheels? of the glorious cherubim? There are
many marvels in this book as well as terrible prophecies of doom and
destruction and, ultimately, God's promise of love, forgiveness, and
regeneration. In Chapter 37 the Lord says to Ezekiel, "Son of man, can
these bones live?" Dry, dead bones, with no life in them. Ezekiel
answers, "O Sovereign LORD, you alone know." Then the Lord says to
Ezekiel,

> Prophesy to these bones and say to them, "Dry bones, hear the word of the
> LORD! This is what the Sovereign LORD says to these bones: I will make breath
> enter you, and you will come to life."

39   And the Lord God lays sinews upon the bones, and flesh, and skin,
and they live again.

40   This is strong stuff. This is mythic stuff, great creative story that
moves beyond fact into the redemptive truth of myth.

41   Elijah, like Ezekiel, is a mythic figure, larger than life. He challenges
the gods of Baal, laughing their prophets to scorn when Baal cannot
kindle a fire, whereas Elijah's God ignites wood over which buckets
of water have been poured until it is soaked, saturated. And Elijah's
fire blazes and burns brilliantly. Then Elijah slays, single-handedly,
all the prophets of Baal.

42   Later, the Lord God tells Elijah to

> "Go out and stand on the mountain in the presence of the LORD, for the LORD
> is about to pass by." Then a great and powerful wind tore the mountains apart
> and shattered the rocks before the LORD, but the LORD was not in the wind.
> After the wind there was an earthquake, but the LORD was not in the earth-
> quake. After the earthquake came a fire, but the LORD was not in the fire. And
> after the fire came a gentle whisper.

43   Or, as the *King James Version* has it: "*a still small voice.*" We have to listen
      if we want to hear God, to listen through all the noise and the storm
      and the turmoil, to hear that still small voice.

44   At the end of Elijah's life, a chariot of fire appears, and horses of fire,
      and *Elijah went up to heaven in a whirlwind.* What a wonder!

45   Strong stuff. Mythic stuff.

46   It is all through both Testaments, this wondrous creative wildness of
      God, this strong stuff not to be understood in the pale language of
      provable fact. Jesus, like Elijah, stands *on the mountain in the presence of
      the* LORD and takes with him Peter and James and John, and extraordi-
      nary things, incomprehensible things, come to pass. Jesus' clothing
      becomes shining, and Elijah himself appears to Jesus in the brilliance,
      and so does Moses, and the three talk together, breaking ordinary
      chronology into a million fragments. And then a cloud over-shadows
      them, as it over-shadowed Moses on the mount, and the voice of God
      thunders out of the cloud.

47   Strong stuff. Mythic stuff. Story. True story.

48   A misinterpretation of Peter's Epistle sees him as warning us against
      myth, or what he calls *cleverly invented stories,* and he tells us that he
      saw what happened on the Mount of Transfiguration; he was an eye-
      witness, and he himself heard the voice of God coming out of the
      cloud. True. But he didn't have the faintest idea what was going on,
      as Mark reminds us: *He did not know what to say, they were so frightened.*
      And in his bewilderment he wanted to build three tabernacles, to put
      Jesus, Elijah, and Moses into boxes where they would be safe. But
      safety was not the reality of the Transfiguration. Glory was.

49   Yea, verily! Those who are terrified of story jump on that one line of
      Peter, out of context, and cry out: "Beware! Stories are lies! If you
      can't prove it, literally, don't believe it."

50   But faith is *the substance of things hoped for, the evidence of things not
      seen.* The language of proof is needed for knowing how much money
      we need to buy our food for the week or what our rent is. It is neces-
      sary, but it is not for our faith, for the wondrous joy we live by. Most
      of what makes life worth living lies beyond the world of provable
      fact. God can be neither proved nor disproved. Did God make the
      universe? While in the language of provable fact we have neither

proof nor disproof, in the promise of Scripture we can cry out a resounding *Yes!*

51   Yes, indeed, let us beware of the *cleverly invented stories* that we see in television commercials every day, and let us look for that truth that will make us free, and that is frequently expressed in myth—true myth, not the *cunningly devised fables* (KJV) of floor waxes that are better than other floor waxes, or pain killers that will deaden all our physical aches, or all the other false promises that are constantly being offered a gullible public, and that the public (including Christians) far too often swallows wholesale. Why do we swallow those false promises given us by the media and yet boggle at the truth of Ezekiel, or Elijah, or the unreasonable, overwhelming Love of God in Christ Jesus?

52   Just as we are losing vocabulary in these last years of the twentieth century, we are losing myth and the creativity of myth—myth as truth, not lie; myth as that truth promised by Jesus to make us free.

53   Rollo May in his book *The Cry for Myth* tells us that it is myths that give us our sense of identity. They make possible our sense of community. They undergird our moral values (and this is particularly important if we truly want to understand what moral values mean). And they are our way of dealing with the inscrutable mystery of Creation.

54   May continues,

> Our powerful hunger for myth is a hunger for community. The person without a myth is a person without a home. . . . To be a member of one's community is to share in its myths. . . . [In church, our] rituals and myths supply fixed points in a world of bewildering change and disappointment.

55   Conversely, the current "clinging to cults and our neurotic passion to make money is a flight from our anxiety, which comes in part from our mythlessness."

56   We have a deep need for heroes in this anxious age where drug use has increased to epidemic proportions. Rollo May points out that we have confused celebrities with heroes, and that is disastrous. David was a hero, not a celebrity.

57   And what about Jesus? He was certainly not a celebrity! He shunned everything that would have marked him as a celebrity. Satan offered to make Jesus a celebrity. But Jesus showed us true heroism. And how did he teach? Yes, once again: Jesus taught by telling stories, parables, myths, and his stories were true, though not everybody could hear

them. Jesus came to show us through his stories what it is to be human and what it is to be heroic and to understand heroes. He told stories to show us how to counteract our sins and imperfections with love, rather than anger; to show us how to rejoice, to laugh, to heal; and the world couldn't stand true humanness, and tried to kill it.

58 If Jesus came today, would we be any braver, any more open, any more willing to give ourselves to his love, than were those who cried out, "Crucify him! Crucify him!" Would we be any more willing today to allow him to love all kinds of people, even those we don't much care about?

59 That, of course, was part of the problem—Jesus' friends. They were not the right people. He went to the wrong dinner parties (his first miracle took place at a big party). He loved children, and let them climb all over him with their sticky little hands and dirty little feet. He even told us that we had to be like little children ourselves if we wanted to understand God, and yet the world (and too often the church) taught then, and still teaches, that we have to outgrow our childhood love of story, of imagination, of creativity, of fun, and so we blunder into the grown up world of literalism.

60 Literalism kills the stories of Jesus, and comes close to killing us. Literalism makes no demands of us, asks of us no faith, does not cause us to grow. Story pushes and shoves us and then helps us out of the mud puddle. Sometimes I remind myself of the little boy who was going to be late for school for the third day in a row, and he set off in a total panic, running as fast as he could, and panting out, "God help me! God help me!" He stumbled and fell into a mud puddle, and he looked up to heaven and said, "I didn't say push!"

61 God pushes, and often pushes through story.

62 God also pushes through our prayers, and for me the disciplines of writing and praying are ever closer and closer together, each a letting go of our own will and an opening up to the power of God's will. We pray that our own will may reflect God's will and that we will be given the discernment to know when it does not.

63 When I listen to a story, trying to set it down faithfully, the two disparate parts of myself, the mind and the heart, the intellect and the intuition, the conscious and the subconscious mind, stop fighting each other and begin to collaborate. They know each other, as two

people who love each other know each other. And as the love of two people is a gift—a totally unmerited, incomprehensible gift—so is the union of mind and heart.

64   The storyteller knows complete dependence on listening to the story. One of the current buzz words today is *codependence* which means, as far as I can tell, that you have to get your sense of self from someone else, rather than from God's image within you.

65   Codependence is certainly to be avoided, but sometimes fear of it leads people to be wary of any kind of dependence. Once again I remember Dean Inge of Saint Paul's saying, "God promised to make you free. He never promised to make you independent." The freer I am, the more I am aware of my interdependence, with my family, my friends, the people I sit near in church, or even those I pass on the street. And I am dependent on faith in God, who pushes me in my work, sends me to places I am not at all sure I want to go.

66   I listen to my stories; they are given to me, but they don't come without a price. We do have to pay, with hours of work that ends up in the wastepaper basket, with intense loneliness, with a vulnerability that often causes us to be hurt. And I'm not sure that it's a choice. If we're given a gift—and the size of the gift, small or great, does not matter—then we are required to serve it, like it or not, ready or not. Most of us, that is, because I have seen people of great talent who have done nothing with their talent, who mutter about "When there's time. . . ," or who bury their talent because it's too risky to use.

67   Yes, it is risky. We may not hear the story well. We may be like faulty radios, transmitting only static and words out of context. But I believe that it is a risk we have to take. And it is worth it, because the story knows more than the artist knows.

68   It is nothing short of miraculous that I am so often given, during the composition of a story, just what I need at the very moment that I need it. When I was roughing out *A Swiftly Tilting Planet*, trying to find a structure for the family, home for Thanksgiving and facing a nuclear war, I opened the mail one day and there was a card from the holy island of Iona, in Scotland, with the words of Patrick's Rune, that glorious rune that became the structure of the book. It led me to a lot of research I hadn't expected, and it was hard work, but it was also exhilarating, a lot of fun.

69　I can't explain how these gifts come to me—at least not in the language of provable fact, but that is the language of human control, not the language of faith. And acceptance of the wonder of such gifts helps me to understand what Ezekiel is saying, or Daniel, or Matthew, Mark, Luke, and John! I read their stories with sublime wonder, with rapturous joy, acknowledging that reality cannot be organized by us human creatures. It can only be lived. Indifference goes along with perfectionism and literalism as a great killer of story, and perhaps indifference is nothing more than a buffer against fear.

70　When I was in Egypt I asked the guide why there were so many cobras, crocodiles, vultures, in the temples. The reply was, "The people worshiped what they feared."

71　This same kind of fear is behind much bibliolatry today. Many fundamentalists—not all, thank God, but some—worship the Bible, which is largely terrifying, and so they try to tame it by putting it into their temple, as the Egyptians did with the cobras, crocodiles, vultures. How are we to understand Elijah's ascending into heaven in chariots of fire drawn by horses of fire? Has anyone ever seen such a thing? How is it to be believed? What are we to make of Jesus in a blaze of blinding glory on the Mount of Transfiguration? Or Moses with his face shining so brilliantly after he has talked with God on another mount that the people can't bear to look at him? These marvelous mysteries cannot be understood in the language of literalism or inerrancy, and all such attempts to tame and restrict the glory are deadly. Deadly indeed.

72　How can we understand in terms of literalism the glory of the Creation of the universe, Jonah in the belly of the large fish, Daniel in the lions' den, or angels coming to unsuspecting, ordinary people and crying out, "Fear not!"

73　Literalism is a vain attempt to cope with fear by quelling Scripture, attempting to make it more palatable, less wild and wonderful. Would the angels cry out "Fear not!" if there were nothing to fear?

74　Story makes us more alive, more human, more courageous, more loving. Why does anybody tell a story? It does indeed have something to do with faith, faith that the universe has meaning, that our little human lives are not irrelevant, that what we choose or say or do matters, matters cosmically. It is we humans who either help bring about, or hinder the coming of the kingdom. We look at the world around us, and it is a complex world, full of incomprehensible greed (why are we continuing to cut down our great forests that supply our planet with so much of its oxygen?), irrationality, brutality, war, terrorism—but also self-sacrifice, honor, dignity—and in all of this we look for, and usually find, pattern, structure, meaning. Our truest response to the irrationality of the world is to paint or sing or write, for only in such response do we find truth.

75   In a recent article in a medical journal (given me by my friend, Pat, the physician), Dr. Richard F. Ott writes that "throughout time, myths have provided meaning for the life of the individual and his society. They have also provided the ability for people to experience the mystery of life by participating in the rituals of myth." How marvelous is the ritual of the Holy Mysteries, the Eucharist, where we joyfully eat Love! For me, one of the most potent phrases in the Episcopal *Book of Common Prayer* is "in the mystery of the Word made flesh . . ." It is a mystery that cannot be understood in terms of provable fact or the jargon of the media. Mystery, unlike magic, can be understood only mythically.

76   When we lose our myths we lose our place in the universe. Dr. Ott points out that "our sense of self-worth has become based on what we possess, and our language has evolved to reflect this. We not only have material possessions, we have children. When we cannot sleep, we have insomnia. We have even replaced 'my head hurts' with 'I have a headache.'" We have sex rather than making love. We even "have" the Bible.

77   How do we get rid of this "have, have, have" mentality and return to "I am, I will be, I am hopeful, I love, I am joyful?" The "I have" complex has led to a litigious society in which malpractice suits are crippling medicine. Why was it necessary for my family to employ a lawyer in San Diego before the insurance company of the truck driver who ran the red light was willing to pay even the minimum he was insured for? Dr. Ott says that—

> the Japanese have a fraction of the numbers of lawyers that we have because the myths behind their culture have meaning to them. We need not contrast their [scientific] successes in the last 20 years, as it is common knowledge. Yet the Western mind seems incapable of understanding what lies behind these successes.

78   Jesus was not a Westerner. He did not have a Western mind, which is perhaps why he is so frequently misunderstood by the Western mind today. He was not interested in the righteous and morally upright people whom he saw to be also hard of heart and judgmental; he devoted himself to those who knew they were sinners and broken, and who came to him for healing. His birth was heralded by angels and visited by adoring shepherds, and it horrifically resulted in the slaughter of all Jewish infants under the age of two.

79   If Jesus was a threat to Herod two thousand years ago, he is still a threat today, because he demands that we see ourselves as we really are, that we drop our smug, self-protective devices, that we become willing to live the abundant life he calls us to live. It's too strong, so we react by trying to turn him into a wimp come to protect us from an angry Father God who wants us punished for our sins: not forgiven, but punished. And our response of fear hasn't worked, and we're left even more frightened and even more grasping and even more judgmental.

80   Let's recover our story because we'll die without it. It's a life-giving story—this magnificent narrative we find, in Scripture—if we are willing to read openly and to read all of Scripture, not just passages selected to help us prove our point. The God of Scripture can sometimes seem brutal, seen through the eyes of the early biblical narrator, who is looking at the Creator through crudely primitive eyes. But the God of Scripture is also the God who refused to nuke Nineveh, even though that's what Jonah wanted, who forgave David for a really staggering list of wrongdoings; who wants only for us stiff-necked people to repent and come home; who goes out into the stormy night for the one lost black sheep; who throws a party when the Prodigal Son returns; who loves us so much that God did indeed send his only begotten son to come live with us, as one of us, to help us understand our stories—each one unique, infinitely valuable, irreplaceable.

81   Jesus. The God who came to us as one of us and told us stories. How marvelous! The life of Jesus has been called the greatest story ever told, and that is true, but one of Satan's cleverest successes has been to make us distrust story. But God's stories are great gifts to us, gifts to help us understand what it is that the Creator wants of us.

82   God wants a lot. Satan is much more easily pleased, or that's what he'd have us believe. God wants everything, and calls us to have faith in what, if we are truly Christian, is impossible—at least in terms of morals or perfectionism or qualifications. It is not only secular humanists who have trouble believing in the Incarnation. Honest struggle with the truth of the Incarnation is more creative than taking it for granted. How can we smugly accept, without feeling wondrous awe, the infinitely small seed within Mary that grew, as all of us grow in our mother's wombs, until it was ready to be born as a human baby?

83   In the fascinating study of modern physics we learn that energy and matter are interchangeable. So the sheer energy of Christ, for love of us, put on the matter of Jesus—ordinary human matter. What love! It is beyond all our puny efforts in clay, or stone, or music, or paint, or ink, but that love is behind our artistic endeavors, no matter how insignificant.

84   The Incarnation hallows our human lives. We've heard the story of Jesus so often that our ears have become blunted. Story reawakens us to truth, the truth that will set us free. Jesus, the Story, taught by telling stories, quite a few of which on the surface would appear to be pretty secular, but all of which lead us, if we will listen, to a deeper truth than we have been willing to hear before.

85   I suspect that the story about President Coolidge and sin is factual as well as true; I think it probably really happened. But it's the truth of the story that matters. Yes, we're "agin" sin, and we know ourselves to be sinners, but forgiven sinners, sinners loved by God. John writes in his first Epistle,

> How great is the love the Father has lavished on us, that we should be called children of God! And that is what we are! . . . Dear friends, now we are children of God, and what we will be has not yet been made known. But we know that when he appears, we shall be like him, for we shall see him as he is.

86   What a wonderful story! What wonderful good news! Let us respond by looking fearlessly at our own stories, so that we may, with God's help, create a story that will be pleasing to our Maker.

87   Once upon a time . . . And it came to pass . . . Yes! We are about to hear a story; we are about to be part of the great creative action of the universe.

*F*red Van Dyke is chair of the Department of Biology and director of the Environmental Studies Program at Wheaton College in Illinois. In this chapter of his book Between Heaven and Earth: Christian Perspectives on Environmental Protection, *Van Dyke argues that Christians must recognize the intrinsic, aesthetic, and instrumental value of nature as God created it. Based on this recognition, he advocates for a Christian ethic of servanthood toward nature, rather than the popular attitude of stewardship which implies that humans are placed atop the rest of creation. In Van Dyke's view, humans were created to serve creation rather than use it to serve their own purposes.*

A Comprehensive Christian Environmental Ethic

Fred Van Dyke

What if thou make us able to make like thee—
To light with moons, to clothe with greenery,
To hang gold sunsets o'er a rose and purple sea!
George MacDonald[1]

The Great Questions Revisited—Is There a Genuinely Christian Ethic of the Environment?

1   Any ethic of the environment must answer the great questions of environmental ethics with which we began. A comprehensive environmental ethic should be able to explain the basis of the environment's value and our appropriate response. It must be able to explain what gives humans the authority to care for, manage, or use nature differently than other kinds of creatures. All non-human creatures use nature for their own interests. Humans have the power to self-consciously advance the interests of other species, but should they? Further, an effective environmental ethic must answer the question of whether non-human entities can be treated as moral subjects. This is a question related to but distinct from the value of these entities, for it raises the issue of whether or not they can be the subjects of protective contract, covenant, or law, and whether they can, in any

meaningful sense, be imbued with rights that humans can recognize and respect. Finally, a comprehensive environmental ethic must address nature's future. Specifically, what is that future, and do present actions toward the environment make sense in light of it? Altogether, the moral theory that underlies the ethic must, in the words of Willis Jenkins, "show how nature's moral status can bear upon a variety of environmental issues" and "link nature's moral standing with practical obligations and motivations for human agents."[2]

The World Is a Good Creation

The Intrinsic Value of Nature

2   A Christian ethic of the environment begins with the affirmation of nature's value: "God saw that it was good." The six-times repeated phrase of Genesis 1:1–25 should be understood in its context to affirm that all things God created are good in and of themselves. We can know this to be a correct interpretation of the statement because God needs nothing and thus can have no instrumental use for anything that he has made, and because human beings, at the time the valuation is declared, do not exist, nor will they be asked for their assessment of the creation after God creates them. This intrinsic value is located in the object itself. There it can be perceived by humans, but it exists whether humans perceive it or not. When they do not, they are burdened with an anthropocentric worldview that distorts their understanding of God, nature, and themselves. "Behold now, Behemoth," God says to Job, "which I made as well as you. He eats grass like an ox. Behold now, his strength in his loins and his power in the muscles of his belly. . . . His bones are tubes of bronze; his limbs are like bars of iron. He is the first of the ways of God. . . ."[3]

3   In answer to Job's repeated complaint that God has treated him unjustly, God's repeated response is to make Job understand that his own view of the world and God's work in it is too self-centered to understand the truth about God or nature. Speaking of the great beast Leviathan, God taunts Job by exposing his ignorance about how to value the world and its creatures as God does. He does so by contrasting Job's market-based valuations with God's estimation of worth. "Can you draw out Leviathan with a hook?" asks God. "Can you put a rope in his nose or pierce his jaw with a hook? . . . Will you play with him as with a bird, or will you bind him for your maidens?

Will the traders bargain over him? Will they divide him among the merchants? . . . Lay your hand on him; you will not do it again! Behold, your expectation is false . . . No one is so fierce that he dares arouse him; Who then is he that can stand before Me?"[4] In the end, Job learns his lesson: The creation is to be viewed theocentrically, not anthropocentrically. "Therefore, I retract," says Job of his past statements and viewpoints, "and I repent in dust and ashes"[5]

The Aesthetic Value of Nature

4 In current strategies of environmental ethics, many ethicists stress the importance of intrinsic value over all others. The goal, as previously noted, is to "protect" creation from a one-dimensional instrumental analysis that can easily turn into an anthropocentric assessment of human welfare maximization. This strategy is well-intentioned, but a Christian environmental ethic cannot fully endorse it. In contrast, a Christian environmental ethic requires a more multi-dimensional valuation of nature that begins with intrinsic value but does not end there.

5 It is significant that the text of Genesis 1 does not say of any created thing that "It was good," but rather "God *saw* that is was good." The divine Valuer possesses an appreciation of *aesthetic* as well as *intrinsic* value. An appreciation of nature's aesthetic value is aroused by *seeing* the beauty of God's creatures and the created world. That appreciation grows through in-depth study of non-human creatures and their environments. For example, Saint Basil expresses the joy he finds in his study of the behavior of cranes when he speaks to his congregation in Homily 8 on the works of God in creation:

> How could I possibly make an accurate review of the peculiarities in the lives of birds? How the cranes in turn accept the responsibility of outposts at night, and while some sleep, others, making the rounds, provide every safety for those asleep . . . [how] in their flight, a different one takes up the task of guiding at different times and, having led the flight for a certain appointed time, goes round to the rear, transferring the leadership of the journey to the one behind him.[6]

6 The cognitive appreciation of the harmonious functioning of creatures in nature deepens an understanding of nature's aesthetic value still further. Aquinas captures an understanding of this dimension of aesthetic value well in words we have read before:

> For God brought things into being in order to communicate the divine goodness to creatures and this be represented by them. And because God's goodness could not be represented by any single creature, God produced many and diverse creatures, that what one lacked in representing divine goodness might be supplied by another. For goodness, which exists in God simply and uniformly, exists in creatures multiply and distributively.[7]

7   Appreciation of aesthetic value also emerges from the contemplation of the nature of the universe, even when such contemplation is beyond human cognition and understanding. "When I consider your heavens," wrote David, "the work of your fingers, the moon and the stars which you have ordained, what is man that you take thought of him, and the son of man that you care for him?"[8] The world is to be understood as intrinsically valuable, but it is also to be enjoyed, studied, and contemplated to better apprehend its aesthetic value, an experience uniquely available to the human being as a way of sharing God's own pleasure it, what he has made.[9]

The Instrumental Value of Nature

8   The goodness of the world is not only intrinsic and aesthetic, but instrumental, for each part of the created order serves the needs of others, including humans. Human need, however, is never to usurp the needs of other elements of creation. All species on Earth are not here to serve just one species. Rather the reverse. The one is to serve all, working, as only it can, to understand and nurture the proper function of all creation in its entirety. God finds pleasure in how his creation sustains the needs of every creature, and humans are to do the same. Aquinas' understanding of this instrumental value is summarized by Catholic ethicist James Schaefer:

> God values the entire universe most as a functioning whole of intrinsically valuable beings that achieve their purposes for existing by acting or being acted upon according to their natures. Concurrently, God values all types of entities as instruments of others progressively up the hierarchical chain by which the universe maintains itself. For Aquinas, the universe is God's instrument for achieving God's purposes for it.[10]

9   A Christian environmental ethic affirms and celebrates nature's instrumental value. But instrumental value must not be limited by an anthropocentric perspective. The needs of all creatures are met instrumentally through the right functioning of the good creation, and humans are not unique in finding their needs met by God in this way. Again the point

is clarified in God's discourse with Job. "Can you hunt the prey for the lion, or satisfy the appetite of the young lions, when they crouch in their dens and lie in wait in their lair? Who prepares for the raven its nourishment when its young cry to God and wander about without food?"[11] God's answer to his rhetorical question is, "I do." Human beings are particularly important objects of God's care and provision, but they are not the only objects of God's care and provision.

10   When value is understood within the context of an ethic that affirms its multi-dimensional nature, and asserts that such value, in every dimension, is manifested only in the full and complete functioning of the natural world, we have an ethical position that at once establishes the primacy of intrinsic value of the non-human world, provides motivation for humans to devote themselves to the study and contemplation of that world (aesthetic value), and affirms the goodness of the provision that world creates for every living creature (instrumental value). We are spared from, and can categorically reject, the false dichotomy of "us or them" in our ethical decisions about the environment. We are to learn to celebrate the good gifts we receive from nature, but to all the more study and appreciate what other creatures receive from nature and how we might help provide it. Because we are now in an ethical position that rejects the premise that our good cannot be met without nature's loss, we are committed to finding a way forward to understand and provide the instrumental needs of all creation, neither excluding humans from nature nor destroying nature's functioning capacities for other creatures. This *position* of valuing is the first step on the path of reconciliation between humans and nature. In a Christian environmental ethic, we believe that path must exist, for we believe that this is the very essence of the way the world has been made.

Humanity's First Environmental Responsibility Is to Serve and Protect the Good Creation

11   Critics of the "strategy of nature's moral standing" have had much to say on the failure of this approach to identify or imagine proper human *behaviors* toward nature, whatever they may think of its value. Some, as we have seen, dismiss the strategy altogether as useless in real debates about real choices. Recall the sarcastic assessment of environmentalist Lynn McGuire and philosopher James Justus.

"Although intrinsic value may get conservationists out of bed in the morning and into the field or up to the bargaining table, it does not serve them well once they get there. Conservation requires decision-making, and here intrinsic value falls short."[12] Yes, left to itself, it does. A Christian environmental ethic, however, is not guided solely, or even primarily, by its recognition of nature's intrinsic, aesthetic, and instrumental value. It is directed by specific instruction regarding the human task toward nature: "Then the Lord God took the man and put him into the Garden of Eden to cultivate it and keep it."[13]

12   We have noted earlier that the Hebrew verbs used here are better and, in other contexts, more often translated as "serve and protect." They are consistent with the injunction to "rule over the fish of the sea, and the birds of the air, and over every living creature that moves on the face of the earth"[14] when viewed in the Christian understanding of rulers as servants of God and of those they govern. "For it [the ruling authority]," wrote Paul, "is a minister of God to you for good. . . . For because of this you also pay taxes, for rulers are servants of God, devoting themselves to this very thing [governing]."[15] If Paul teaches clearly that rulers are servants of God, Jesus is even more plainspoken that those who rule must see themselves as servants of their subjects, and he is explicit in contrasting this understanding with the world's perspective on ruling. "You know that the rulers of the Gentiles lord it over them, and their great men exercise authority over them. It is not this way among you, but whoever wishes to become great among you shall be your servant, and whoever wishes to be first among you shall be your slave."[16]

13   Here we must make the point, and sharply, that in a Christian ethic of the environment, the proper model and metaphor is that of humans as *servants* of creation, not *stewards* of creation. The concept of *creation stewardship* has been the most popular and widely used image of the human relationship to nature in Christian teaching on the environment for the last 30 years, and, to this point, we have used it repeatedly. It has not been without good effect in communicating the importance of the human responsibility to care for creation. The image is understandably appealing as a picture of one given authority over the household, possessions, and resources of another. However, the image is rarely used biblically or historically in the church's teachings. When it is, it is almost always employed in the context of

safeguarding a truth, teaching, or spiritual gift (for example, Matthew 13:52, I Corinthians 4:1–2, I Peter 4:10), not a physical resource or environment. Further, the Bible typically uses the function or image of a steward and his stewardship to describe a situation where the real landlord is *absent* (for example, Matthew 25:14–30, Luke 12:42). This is not an accurate way of describing God's relationship to creation.

14 The stewardship metaphor also becomes problematic because it emphasizes human control *over* creation rather [than] human service *toward* creation. The former is a dangerous and potentially idolatrous illusion. The latter is an accurate and practical posture toward developing a humble and other-centered way for humans to act with the non-human world. Although a stewardship motif captures the concept of human accountability toward God, it is deficient in representing the equally important concept of humans being "other-directed" in giving primary attention to meeting needs other than their own, in this case, the needs of nature. As theologian Norman Wirzba notes, "Servanthood . . . shifts the orientation of our action away from ourselves to the well-being of others. . . ."[17] In creating, God "makes room," in the homely words of John of Damascus, for life that is other than himself."[18] God, in his act of creation, performs a service to that which he creates by "giving it a place" without which it could not exist. So, humans, made in the image of God and designed to carry out his intentions toward creation, are to direct their activities first and foremost to "making room" for non-human life. It is this strong concept of service toward creation that enables the creation of parks and wilderness areas to make sense as part of the human vocation toward nature, just as it is this same concept of service that validates the work of saving species, even those whom we have no instrumental motive to "steward." This was the case when Francis Orpen Morris and his fellow pastors established the Association for the Protection of Sea Birds. . . . A model of "serving" the interests of these seabirds makes much better sense of Morris's actions than a model of "stewardship." In fact, it does so in most examples of genuine and effective conservation effort.

15 If, according to Genesis 2:15, human beings are created to serve and protect creation, then humanity's prime concern must be to understand the needs of others, including others that represent non-human species. The provision of the U.S. Endangered Species Act that mandates the

designation of critical habitat is a first, if still relatively weak, attempt to manifest this principle in practice. Similarly, the requirement of the U.S. National Environmental Policy Act to identify, through the mechanism of an Environmental Impact Statement, the potentially irrevocable consequences of a planned action by humans also expresses this principle in the opposite way, by identifying in advance the effects of human actions that create *adverse impacts* upon other creatures.

16   Unquestionably, modern human culture destroys the natural world. Holmes Rolston III explained our present condition eloquently:

> It is a sad truth that life preys on life, that culture does have to eat nature, but that is not the only truth; there is a glad truth that culture can be satisfied, can only be satisfactory, if its destiny is entwined with nature. I do not say that there is no further cultural development needed, only that we do not need further cultural development that sacrifices nature for culture, that enlarges the sphere of culture at the price of diminishing the sphere of nature. Nor will culture be harmed if we do not get it.[19]

17   It was not so long ago that humans believed that they could not power cars without gasoline, make electricity without mining coal or building dams, or construct a factory that did not produce solid or chemical waste. Today we have cars that do not need gas. We can make electricity without building dams or mining coal. We have designed factories with a closed-loop waste production stream such that everything used in the production process, even what was once considered waste, can now be transformed to re-enter that process at various stages (that is, recycled) or sold to another buyer who sees one market's waste as another market's good. And it was not so long ago that people believed that they could not burn lamps without killing whales, farm without using pesticides, and or cut timber without destroying forests. But history, recent and otherwise, has shown these assertions to be false.

18   Are we smart enough to see the trend? Perhaps our problem was not that we lacked the *ability* to serve and care for the Earth, but that we lacked the *intention* to do so. No human technology is without environmental effect. But is it possible that a defined and, dare we say, relentless intention to serve and protect the Earth in all human activity could be the greatest spark to technological innovation history has ever seen? And could such a determined intention also be the stimulus for the most effective effort yet made to curb the sins of affluence, materialism, and greed that are consuming the western world? Again it is

Rolston who puts it well, "Few persons would need to go without 'enough' if we could use, justly and charitably, the produce of the already domesticated landscape. If such redistribution does not take place, people will be hurt. But it is better to try to fix this problem where it arises, within society, than to try to enlarge the sphere of society by the sacrifice of remnant natural values."[20] Who is willing to find out if these things could be?

19   A Christian ethic of the environment insists that right rewards are the fruit of right objectives. The right objective for humans in their inter-action with nature is that they should learn and practice how to serve and care for it. Similarly, there are wrong rewards that are nothing but bribes because they are not the normal or "natural" fruit of right behavior. Affluence, an unending increase in material goods and eco-nomic production, and ever-increasing disconnection from the natural world in order to increase human levels of ease and comfort are the wrong objectives, and they will always generate the wrong rewards. Wisdom consists of choosing the right goal, desiring the rewards that are the natural fruit of that goal, and living in a manner consistent with obtaining it.

20   Jesus spells out this strategy as the fundamental cure for anxiety, for anxiety is invariably produced by trying to satisfy legitimate needs and wants in inappropriate and ineffective ways. Therefore, "Seek first the kingdom of God, and all these things will be added to you."[21] Jesus never disregarded the human desire for reward and signifi-cance. Nurturing a creation that glorifies God is one of the deepest of human desires, and its attainment is one of humanity's most satisfy-ing rewards. But the glory of God is the thing to be pursued, and the service and care of his creation is an act of obedience to that pursuit.

Humans Possess Unique Ability and Authority to Serve and Protect Nature

21   Recently, in preparing a new textbook on conservation biology,[22] my editor allowed me to select the cover photo. I chose a picture showing three individuals, Betty, Sirius, and Wiwik, engaged in a common task related to a particular conservation study, the problem of extracting termites from a termite mound. All three individuals are Indonesian, but from there differences emerge. Betty and Sirius are much like one another. Wiwik is different from both. You see, Betty and Sirius are

three- to four-year-old female orangutans. Wiwik is an Indonesian woman who works with them and other orangutans at an orangutan orphanage. The orphanage was created to address the growing problem of orangutan orphans, infant orangs whose mothers are killed by hunters so that the infants can be captured and sold as pets. This practice is against the law in Indonesia but nevertheless is widespread. If the perpetrator is caught, he might pay a fine or go to jail, but that does not solve the orangutan's side of the problem. The orphaned infant cannot survive in the forest without training. Orangutan orphanages, sponsored by various conservation organizations, attempt to provide that training.

22   What makes the picture of Wiwik, Betty, and Sirius enlightening to a discussion of a Christian environmental ethic is the fundamental differences it reveals among the three individuals. All are working on the same problem (getting the termites out of the termite mound), and all are employing considerable dexterity, determination, and intelligence to solve it. The difference is that, in engaging the problem and its solution, only Wiwik is taking the role of what a psychologist would call a *reflective interactant*. Betty and Sirius are approaching the problem from the perspective of orangutans. Ironically, so is Wiwik. In this effort, it is Wiwik who is serving as teacher. Betty and Sirius, although highly gifted and intelligent creatures, are her students.

23   This is an asymmetrical relationship. Betty and Sirius, for all their skill and intelligence, can only see the problem from their own viewpoint. Wiwik, on the other hand, can consciously choose to set aside her human perspective and intentionally place herself into their perspective. To accomplish this, Wiwik must see the world as an orangutan would see it. She must not consider her own needs in that world, but the needs perceived by an orangutan. And then Wiwik must determine not how she would meet those needs, but how those needs would be met *if she were an orangutan*.

24   Betty and Sirius are engaged in this exercise because they are hungry. Wiwik, on the other hand, is engaged in the problem because she thinks it is "the right thing to do." To make this work, Wiwik must consciously advance Betty's and Sirius's ends, rather than her own. Perhaps Wiwik would rather be home doing some gardening, reading a book, watching TV, or eating something that isn't trying to crawl off the plate. It is self-evident that Wiwik has the capacity to

adopt the perspective and advance the interests of others, even if the others are not even members of her own species. The question is, where did Wiwik get this capacity and what is its function in an environmental ethic?

25 Wiwik illustrates a premise that is fundamental to a Christian understanding of the human relationship to nature. Human beings, alone made in the image of God, possess unique qualities and capacities that equip them for their role as servants and protector of nature. Humans alone possess the ability to consider themselves, to evaluate their own thoughts and their own desires. They can, in a real sense, separate themselves from themselves, not only having an awareness of their own thoughts and perspectives but a capacity to judge whether the thoughts they are thinking are the thoughts they *ought to be thinking*, whether the desires they are experiencing are the *right desires to pursue*, and whether those "others" they interact with have the same or different perspectives and needs in this world as they do. Only in so far as they are in possession of and aware of how to use these qualities can humans serve and protect creation.

26 When we understand these things, we see why humans, as rulers of creation, *must* approach their duties from the perspective of a servant, just as Jesus taught and as Wiwik is doing. Ruling over creation requires an other-centeredness that identifies and assesses the needs of non-human entities, judges their relative importance and urgency, and creates, from its own intellectual resources, a plan to meet them, to serve the needs of the other.

27 Ruling through service requires more than good intentions. Jesus makes clear it also requires a capacity for self-examination and self-correction. "Why do you look," he said, "at the speck which is in your brother's eye, but do not notice the log that is in your own eye? Or, how can you say to your brother, let me take the speck out of your eye, and behold, the log is in your own eye? You hypocrite! First, take the log out of your own eye, and then you will see clearly to take the speck out of your brother's eye."[23]

28 Humans not only have the capacity for self-reflection and critical self-evaluation, they must use it. God expects them to. Using this capacity is essential when dealing with environmental problems. As economist Peter J. Hill writes, "Every call to save the environment is predicated

upon human action. We are asked to respond to stories of environmental disaster, to evidence that nature is being altered in unfortunate ways, and to appeals to reverse the damage that humans inflict
upon the natural order. But every one of these is a call to change, and
it is humans who are being asked to change."[24] In other words,
humans cannot, if we may use the language of Saint Francis, criticize
Brother Sun (or Brother Climate) by telling him that he is making the
world too hot. They must begin every inquiry that touches their rule
of nature with the question, "What have I done to contribute to this
problem?" When the human ruler has answered this question honestly, then, says Jesus, he not only can see clearly to fix what may be
wrong in the other (in this case, nature) but can do so with compassion instead of self-centeredness.

29   Finally, we must add that the service and protection of nature
requires not only intention, but skill. It is a *task* which requires us to
be able to *do* specific things. A Christian ethic, therefore, teaches that
the practice of stewardship requires learning the skills of stewardship
and taking responsibility to use those skills charitably for human and
non-human neighbors alike. As Wendell Berry puts it, "How do you
love your neighbor if you don't know how to build or mend a fence,
how to keep your filth out of his water supply and your poison out
of his air; or if you do not produce anything and so have nothing to
offer, or do not take care of yourself and so become a burden? . . .
How will you practice virtue without skill?"[25] For this reason, a Christian environmental ethic affirms that what institutions of higher education should teach about stewardship is not merely its *concepts* but its
skills, just as such institutions should teach the value of what the
Amish would call "merited occupations," work that is truly charitable
to human and non-human neighbors alike because of what it produces for both, as well as for what it does not produce. Again to
quote Berry, "You cannot affirm the powerplant and condemn the
smokestack, or affirm the smoke and condemn the cough."[26] A Christian environmental ethic affirms that humans are, among all creatures,
uniquely capable of making responsible choices and *must* do so
through the application [of] human skill and intellect that is directed
to benefit the creation around them.

30   If we would affirm and practice a Christian environmental ethic, we
must neither deny nor denigrate the uniqueness of being human. To

deny human uniqueness is a lie, although one which modern culture is endlessly congratulating itself for having discovered as an important "truth." To denigrate the uniqueness of being human is a futile exercise in species' self-flagellation. When we spend our best energies imagining the world without us, which is what Eric Pianka and the producers of *After People* and *The Day the Earth Stood Still* are guilty of, we accomplish nothing for humanity or the non-human world. There is no empowerment in continually saying, "If only humans weren't here." We are here. We are here for a purpose. That purpose is to use for good the unique capacities that belong to us, as creatures made in the image of God. Aquinas clarified this critical perspective in his own teaching, that the natural dominion exercised by humans is based on their ability to know and to will good ends. In doing this, humans are subservient to God's dominion when exercising their dominion, which is never an absolute, but subordinate to the plans and purposes of God. Thus, the goal of human dominion is to cooperate with God in carrying out God's plan for his creation.[27] Informed by the careful study of nature and the regenerative work of the Holy Spirit in the experience of life, human beings can rule creation as God intended, by serving and protecting its interests and its functional integrity.

Non-Human Entities in Nature Should Be Treated As Moral Subjects

31 At first, it might seem that focusing on the question of moral subjects is the same as addressing the question of nature's value. These questions are related but different. Establishing the basis of nature's value tells us what sorts of things ought to be given moral consideration, but it does not tell us precisely how such consideration should be expressed. A Christian environmental ethic can be more specific. Non-human entities are appropriate moral subjects. They are, in the language of ethics, "morally considerable." Further, Christian teaching shows that such entities, living and nonliving, can be the appropriate objects of law and covenant. They can receive and hold legal rights, and humans can and should be punished when those rights are abused.

32 Perhaps the closest we have in modern law to this concept is the U.S. Endangered Species Act (ESA). In this law, as environmental historian

Joseph Petulla noted, "a listed non-human resident of the United States is guaranteed, in a special sense, life and liberty."[28] Therefore, it is not inappropriate for such listed species to have their interests represented in court, as was the case in *Palila v. Hawaii Department of Land and Natural Resources*, in which the Sierra Club Legal Defense Fund represented the palila, a bird that is an endangered species of Hawaiian honey-creeper, against the Hawaii Department of Land and Resources, charging the agency with violation of the Endangered Species Act by permitting the presence of feral goats and sheep within the palila's habitat, thereby contributing to the destruction of that habitat. The Ninth Circuit Court of Appeals found in favor of the palila, concluding that the state had indeed violated the ESA through these actions. A Christian environmental ethic would affirm that this kind of legal protection, as well as legal action on behalf of protected creatures, is ethically appropriate. Both have precedent in God's covenant with the creatures of the ark (Genesis 9:8–17) as well as in the inclusion of Sabbath rest for animals (Exodus 23:12) and the land (Exodus 23:10–11, Leviticus 25:1–22). Further, the failure of humans to observe such laws is a prosecutable offense, and the punishment of the violator shall include relief that runs to the benefit of the injured party, even if the party is the land itself (II Chronicles 36:21).

33   A Christian environmental ethic, then, advocates the full development of environmental laws that recognize non-human creatures and other environmental entities as moral subjects and gives such entities legal standing in court, in effect, a "standing right to sue" if their interests are violated. Thus, the answer to Christopher Stone's famous rhetorical question, "Should trees have standing ?"[29] is yes, if they are trees that have been deemed necessary to protect. A Christian environmental ethic affirms that, because these entities should be viewed as moral subjects, they also are appropriate objects of legal protection that recognizes rights and interests appropriate to them.

34   Although a Christian ethic affirms that interests and rights of non-human entities really exist, it also affirms that not every kind of right or interest is appropriate or attributable to non-human creatures or nonliving environmental entities. This is because, to repeat a point made earlier, there is a difference between moral consideration and moral significance. Although non-human creatures deserve moral consideration, humans possess greater moral significance, and this is

a factor in making ethical decisions. This fact, however, is never to he used as a reason to abuse nature. One of the things that give humans added moral significance is that they have the capacity for reflective decision-making, and their decisions are morally significant because they can affect nature powerfully. Thus, the recognition of greater moral significance its human beings is not to be used as a warrant for humans to assert privileges over other kinds of life, but as a reason to recognize that all human actions must be carefully considered in light of their effects on such life, indeed on all of nature. Laws such as the U.S. National Environmental Policy Act are an expression, albeit still a relatively weak one, of the principle that, because human actions can have powerful effects on the environment, the significance of those actions and their effects must be considered in advance of the action itself. When humans affirm their own moral significance relative to other species, they begin to understand why their decisions are important to other species.

35 This realization guards against two errors. The first is treating all morally considerable entities as beings of equal moral significance. This position easily and naturally leads, in humans, to a species-specific self-loathing, an "I wish my species had never evolved" attitude in those who hold it. If we are indeed no better than bacteria, then it's time to stop using disinfectants. This is a posture of environmental defeatism. It poses as ecological humility. It is really moral ignorance. Unless humans recognize that their own species is uniquely equipped to perceive, serve, and protect the interests of other creatures, they will never use that capacity for those purposes.

36 The second error is the opposite and equally dangerous mistake of assuming that greater moral significance equals greater license and privilege in things environmental and becomes a justification for irresponsible behavior toward nature. The human who recognizes her own moral significance toward God must at the same time recognize that one of the most basic expressions of that significance is the power of her actions on the natural world. Humans can never assume that any action of their own is without importance to the world in which they live. Therefore, no actions that humans propose toward nature can ever be exempted from moral scrutiny.

The Present Care of Nature Must Consider Its Future Destiny

37   Sustainability is one of the most commonly invoked principles for constructing environmental ethics. "Sustainable development" was defined in the Bruntland Report (*Our Common Future*) as "meeting the needs of the present generation without compromising the ability of future generations to meet their own needs."[30] But if sustainability simply refers to an endless iteration of things as they are now from one generation to the next, it hardly inspires enthusiasm. A concept of sustainability that naively sees the global human population always and forever living on a trajectory of ever-increasing wealth (with an attendant attitude of ever-increasing greed) is not a picture of heaven, but of hell. Sustainability, in its best clothes, is an admirable, if limited concept, but it does not begin to encompass a transforming moral of redemption.

38   A Christian environmental ethic does not aim merely at maintaining the status quo or of offering unquestioned assent to every aspiration of modern material consumption. The Bible provides snapshots of redemption, brief and cryptic visions of what redeemed communities and people would look like, and they look very different from their counterparts in the modern world. A redeemed world is, first of all, one in which God is explicitly acknowledged as Creator and Sustainer of life. In a redeemed environment, this understanding permeates everything. Such knowledge is the foundational requisite to the prophecy of the lion and the lamb given in Isaiah 11. The lion and the lamb only lie down together where "They will neither hurt nor destroy in all my holy mountain, for the Earth will be full of the knowledge of the Lord as the waters cover the sea."[31]

39   It is a redemptive future that gives significance to present effort, no matter how small, if that effort is oriented to the same end as the future redemption. This is what Simon Stuart and his colleagues meant when they wrote, "Every time we celebrate a conservation success story such as the recovery of the white rhinoceros in southern Africa, we are strengthened in this present hope that God is working with us to redeem his creation; furthermore, these present successes are a very real foretaste of even greater things to come on that day when God will fully restore all that He has made."[32]

40 Redemption, more than any other ethical element, requires a change of *intent* and not merely a change of *technique*. The current wave of "going green" is a superficial example of a shift in cultural intention. The phrase is used to describe all kinds of efforts, radically diverse in their forms and applications, but united in their common effort to minimize harm to the Earth. This is a good trend, but a shallow one, and its shallowness is betrayed by its approach. Driving a more efficient car, building a more efficient power plant, and screwing in more efficient light bulbs can be beneficial changes, but they all address the problem of the environment as a problem of *technology*. The right (read "new") technology is good. The wrong (read "old") technology is bad. In some cases this is correct, as far as it goes. But technological innovation is not the same as moral redemption. Some cultures that have been most beneficent to the Earth and the land, like the Amish, achieve their effects not by improving on modern technology but by renouncing it. But such renunciation is only possible when there is a change of human *intention*, not merely a change in human *technique*.

41 Current culture treats technological innovation as an imperative. We *must* change to the newest technology because we *can*, and because, like Mount Everest, it is there. A redemptive approach *chooses* an appropriate technology because the user has already made a more fundamental choice. Instead of taking human appetite and desire as givens, a redeemed mind steps back and asks, "What should I *choose to want*? What should I *choose to value*?" In the end, these are the choices that determine what kind of people we shall be, as well as the kind of world in which we shall live.

42 This approach to an environmental ethic requires humility, a particularly unpopular trait in modern societies. A Christian environmental ethic declares that the right action is to sublimate desires based on personal welfare to choose ends that reflect God's purposes and intentions for his creation that will increase the manifestation of his own glory. In a culture whose food and drink is self-actualization and personal autonomy, the idea of redirecting human effort to glorify God doesn't find much support, but such a change in intention must be the beginning of a redemptive ethic and the plans that arise from it. To a watching world, the concept of redemption is certain to be the single most repulsive idea contained in a Christian environmental ethic. Redemption is by its very nature subversive. If we would purchase a

man who is a slave in order to bring him out of slavery, we condemn the practice of slavery in setting him free. And if he has known no other condition but slavery all his life, we will also have to teach him to live as a free man. This will require more than a change in his condition. It will require a change in who he is, and in what he aspires to become.

43   The effort I describe in this example would today be considered heroic. In times past it would have been considered criminal. And one such act, though aiming at the right end, would not bring an end to the institution of slavery. In the United States, that required a civil war. Redemption is costly and painful and always brings with it an element of judgment. Some things in this present world can, with care and nurture, be made part of the redemptive world. Some things must be cast aside. Some things must be destroyed altogether.

44   A Christian environmental ethic looks to a redemptive future. Ironically, this is the element which humans have the least ability to self-initiate, not only because of the limits of their own resources, but because, at any given historical moment, they are immersed in current cultural attitudes that make it difficult to see anything differently. Thus, the Bible teaches that redemption must be God-initiated, because only God possesses the ultimate redemptive vision for the world. And such redemption will come, in the end, as a painful event that takes ordinary life by surprise. So Jesus explained to his disciples, "As it was in the days of Noah, so it will be at the coming of the Son of Man. For in the days before the flood, they were eating, they were drinking. They were marrying, and they were being given in marriage, until the day that Noah entered the ark, and they did not understand until the flood came and took them all away. . . ."[33]

45   Redemptive living looks stupid until redemption arrives. Redemptive efforts appear futile. On their own, they are. But redemptive effort is like the mustard seed in Jesus' parable about the kingdom of heaven. It is not the size or scope of the effort that matters as much as its alignment with an ultimate end that God will bring to pass.

46   Because a Christian environmental ethic is ultimately an ethic of redemption, it necessarily evaluates the means we use in our dealings with the environment in light of the ends they will produce, not only in the environment, but in ourselves. Thus, a redemptive orientation declares that we must change our current thoughts, practices,

and objectives, no matter how rational or successful they appeal under present circumstances, to conform to a greater ultimate reality that is on the way, but not yet here. To do so requires not only hope, but faith, which is defined biblically as "the assurance of things hoped for, the conviction of things not seen."[34] In an age of sensuality, materialism, and empiricism, this word is blasphemy. Nevertheless, it is the final and definitive element of a Christian environmental ethic.

Serving and Protecting Creation Should Be a Normative Experience of Christian Life

47 The gospel of Mark records that Jesus began his public ministry with a simple and direct message, "The time is fulfilled, and the kingdom of God is at hand; repent and believe in the gospel."[35] In more contemporary language, the best restatement of "The kingdom of God is at hand" is "Here's the kingdom of God." As Christian philosopher Dallas Willard makes clear in *The Divine Conspiracy*, Jesus is not announcing that the kingdom of God has just come into existence, for it has always existed. What has changed is that, through Jesus Christ, the kingdom has become *accessible* to human beings, even in this fallen world.[36] It is the confident trust in and use of this access that has given Christians through the ages the ability to do things that no one would have thought possible.

48 Today the kingdom of God remains "at hand" through Christ, and its access remains one of the greatest privileges of faith. Christians who understand and appropriate this privilege can expect redemptive effects over the entire array of broken relationships they face in a fallen world. They can redeem their relationship to God. They can redeem their relationship to one another. They can redeem their own relationship to themselves and their secret but debilitating inner conflicts. And they can redeem their relationship to creation.

49 It is a good idea to start practicing what you are going to be doing for a long time, and the care of the Earth is one of those things. As Willard puts it, "God himself loves the earth dearly and never takes his hands off it. And because he loves it and it is good, our care of it is also eternal work and part of our eternal life."[37] The practice of serving and protecting the Earth was humanity's first vocation. It will remain an eternal one, but, in a redeemed world, such work will

be empowered by abilities now beyond the limits of human imagination. Christian poet and novelist George MacDonald painted the
possibilities of this new life and work in one of his poems.

> And in the perfect time, O perfect God,
> When we are in our home, our natal home,
> When joy shall carry every sacred load,
> And from its life and peace no heart shall roam,
> What if thou make us able to make like thee—
> To light with moons, to clothe with greenery,
> To hang gold sunsets o'er a rose and purple sea![38]

50   Today, in this fallen world, the church should teach the faithful that
the practice of serving and protecting creation is both normative experience in and fundamental preparation for an eternal life in which the
now broken relationship between humanity and nature will be
restored. In other words, it can prepare people to practice a meaningful environmental ethic now and for eternity. The church can move
toward this goal by its attention to three foundational principles.

51   First, the church should nurture an *accurate understanding* of nature
and of the problems that face the environment today. Only when
people possess a common, shared, and accurate vision of the natural
world can they begin to cooperatively approach solutions to it. I do
not mean that it is the task of the church to teach courses on ecology
and environmental science. It is not. But it is the task of the church,
when it addresses these concerns with its considerable theological
and moral resources, to speak of them accurately.

52   Second, the church should provide and facilitate *deliberate contact*
between people and nature. It can choose to do so in the images it dis-
plays in worship, the settings of the worship itself, the locations of its
congregational retreats, and the places to which it directs its members
for practicing the disciplines of solitude and silence, both of which
are essential to growth in Christian discipleship. It can go further, and
plan times for its members to *be in nature* and *learn from nature* by planning retreats, long or short in duration, in which nature is not merely
the backdrop or setting for a gathering but the subject of it. I recently led
a half-day retreat like this for members of my own congregation, using
a forest preserve within a mile of our church building. Simple teachings
about how to tell different kinds of trees, flowers, and grasses from each
other, how to distinguish one bird's song from another's, and how to
read the shape of a landscape and predict what you might find on

hilltops, slopes, and depressions profoundly affect human perception of nature, and human enjoyment of it.

53 Recognizing that things have names, that they are different, and that their differences are important is best learned by experience. When the church shows its saints how to make real contact with God's creation and how to look at it with discernment, such contact becomes the channel through which an accurate understanding of nature develops, as well as an affection for nature that makes it something that would be missed if absent, something to be sought if present, and something to be healed if it has been hurt.

54 Finally, the church should teach its members how to practice the *sacrificial concern* required to serve and protect non-human creation. One can have concern without sacrifice, but the Bible condemns this kind of concern as hypocrisy. "If a brother or sister is without clothing and in need of daily food," wrote James, leader of the first-century Jerusalem church, "and one of you says to them, 'Go in peace, be warmed and be filled, and yet you do not give them what is necessary for their body, what use is that?'"[39] James's rhetorical question expects the answer, "None." In the same way, concern for non-human creation and non-human creatures that knows only sympathy and never sacrifice is of exactly the same value. A wistful attitude toward nature dominated by an abundance of "If only . . ." statements changes nothing. Setting aside a portion of a newly planned church site for a restored prairie or a grove of large, old trees manifests the work of God in creation to everyone who looks at the church, but it costs parking slots and building space. To "make room" for nature requires sacrifice. Conservation organizations need money to do their work. Changing local zoning ordinances to permit parks and open space takes time. Participating in an active restoration effort that requires planting native species takes physical exertion. These efforts, however, are illustrations of how inactive sympathy can be transformed into sacrificial concern, concern that changes things. It has always been the role of the church to teach people how to manifest faith in work. It is no different in teaching how to serve and protect creation.

55 Implementing these practices in a contemporary church culture which largely ignores then requires a redeemed imagination. But making disciples of Jesus Christ, the fundamental mission of the

church, also requires the experience and practice of work and habits that will be the expected norm in a redeemed world. Better to get started now. . . .

Notes

[1] George MacDonald, *Diary of an Old Soul* (Minneapolis: Augsburg Fortress Press, 1994), p. 30.

[2] Willis Jenkins, *Ecologies of Grace: Environmental Ethics and Christian Theology* (Oxford, UK: Oxford University Press, 2008), pp. 44–45.

[3] Job 40:15–16, 18–19, NASB.

[4] Job 4:1–2, 5–6, 8–10, NASB.

[5] Job 42:6.

[6] Saint Basil, *Exegetic Homilies*, translated by Sister Agnes Clare Way (Washington, DC: Catholic University of America Press, 1963), p. 125.

[7] Quoted in Jenkins, p. 125.

[8] Psalm 8:3–4, NASB.

[9] For a well-framed discussion of the various dimensions of aesthetic value that can be understood within a Christian environmental ethic, see Jame Schaefer, *Theological Foundations for Environmental Ethics: Reconstructing Patristic and Medieval Concepts* (Washington, DC: Georgetown University Press, 2009), p. 44ff.

[10] Schaefer, p. 25.

[11] Job 38:39–41, NASB.

[12] Lynn A. Macguire and James Justus,"Why intrinsic value is a poor basis for conservation decisions," *BioScience* 58 (2008). pp. 910–911.

[13] Genesis 2:15, NASB.

[14] Genesis 1:28, NASB.

[15] Romans 13:4, 6, NASB.

[16] Matthew 20:25–27, NASB.

[17] Norman Wizba, *The Paradise of God: Renewing Religion in an Ecological Age* (Oxford, UK: Oxford University Press, 2003), p. 135.

[18] The idea of John of Damascus about creation as being an act of God "making room" for life other than his own is captured in the paraphrase of John's ideas by Robert Jensen. "For God to create is for him to open a place in his triune life for others than the three whose mutual life he is." Quoted in Wizba, p.19.

[19] Holmes Rolston III, "Winning and Losing in Environmental Ethics," in *Ethics and Environmental Policy: Theory Meets Practice*, eds. Frederick Ferré and Peter Hartel (Athens: University of Georgia Press, 1994), p. 231.

[20] Ibid., p. 233.

[21] Matthew 6:33, NASB.

22 Fred Van Dyke, *Conservation Biology: Foundations, Concepts, Applications* (Dordrecht, The Netherlands: Springer: 2008).

23 Matthew 7:2–3, NASB.

24 Peter J. Hill, "Environmental Theology: A Judeo-Christian Defense," *Journal of Markets and Morality* 3(2000): pp. 158–172.

25 Wendell Berry, "The Gift of Good Land." In *The Gift of Good Land: Further Essays Cultural and Agricultural* by Wendell Berry (New York: North Point Press, 1982), p. 275.

26 Ibid., p. 281.

27 Summarized in Schaefer, p. 26.

28 Joseph Petulla, *American Environmental History* (San Francisco: Boyd and Fraser, 1977).

29 Christopher Stone, *Should Trees Have Standing? Toward Legal Rights for Natural Objects* (Los Altos, CA: Kaufman, 1974).

30 World Commission on Environment and Development, *Report of the World Commission on Environment and Development: Our Common Future* (New York: Oxford University Press, 1987).

31 Isaiah 11:9, NASB.

32 Simon Stuart and others, "Conservation Theology for Conservation Biologists— An Open Letter to David Orr," *Conservation Biology* 19(2005): pp. 1689–1692, pp. 1690–1691.

33 Matthew 24:37–39, NASB.

34 Hebrews 11:1, NASB.

35 Mark 1:15, NASB.

36 Dallas Willard, *The Divine Conspiracy* (San Francisco: HarperCollins, 1997).

37 Ibid., p. 205.

38 MacDonald, p. 30.

39 James 2:15, 16.

*R*onald J. Sider is the president of Evangelicals for Social Action, as well as a professor of theology and culture at the Eastern Baptist Theological Seminary in Pennsylvania. In his essay "Biblical Foundations for Creation Care," Sider argues not only that Christians who claim to follow the Bible will be compelled to protect the environment but also that people who are searching for spiritual grounds on which to rest their environmental beliefs may find such support in the Bible. Sider's views provide a middle ground between those who seek to eradicate distinctions between humans and other species and those who claim that there is no obligation whatsoever for Christians to care for the environment.

Biblical Foundations for Creation Care

Ronald J. Sider

1   In March 1990, in Seoul, South Korea, I attended an international conference on Justice, Peace and the Integrity of Creation sponsored by the World Council of Churches. I heard many persuasive claims about the way Christians had distorted humanity's mandate to have dominion over the Earth—the consequence of these distortions being a ravaged creation. I became concerned, however, when I noticed that no-one had mentioned the fact that human beings have an exalted status within creation, in that they alone are created in the image of God.

2   So I proposed a one-sentence addition to the document we were debating. From the floor, I asked that we add a sentence affirming that, as we confess these misunderstandings, we nonetheless 'accept the biblical teaching that people alone have been created in the image of God'.

3   The drafting committee promptly accepted the addition but dropped the word 'alone'. I pointed out that this undercut the basic point. Are trees and toads also created in God's image? When the drafting committee remained adamant, I called for a vote. And the motion lost! At that moment, a majority of attendees at this important convocation were unwilling to say what historical, biblical theology has always affirmed: that human beings alone are created in the image of God.

4   As my experience illustrates, in today's environmental movement
    there is a lot of theological confusion. Actress Shirley MacLaine says
    we must declare that we are all gods. Disciplined but unchastened
    Catholic theologian Matthew Fox says we should turn from a theology
    centred on sin and redemption and develop a creation spirituality,
    with nature as our primary revelation and sin a distant memory. Aus-
    tralian philosopher Peter Singer says any claim that persons have a
    status different from monkeys and moles is 'speciesism'. Several
    decades ago historian Lynn White argued that it is precisely the
    Christian view of persons and nature that created the whole ecologi-
    cal mess. . . . Meanwhile, many evangelicals come close to celebrating
    the demise of the Earth, enthusiastically citing the decay as proof that
    the return of Christ is very near.

5   These and other factors will tempt evangelicals to ignore or denounce
    environmental concerns. But that would be a tragic mistake—for at
    least three reasons. First, because the danger is massive and urgent.
    Second, because there are evangelistic opportunities that arise out of
    environmental concern. And third, because if we do not offer biblical
    foundations for environmental action, we will have only ourselves to
    blame if environmental activists turn to other, finally inadequate,
    worldviews and religions. With wisdom and a renewed appreciation
    of the wholeness of God's plan for redemption, we can lead the way
    forward in the healing of our Earth.

6   Increasingly, people who care deeply about the environment are
    searching for deeper spiritual foundations to ground their crusade to
    save the planet.

7   The pilgrimage proceeds in many directions. Some environmentalists
    are exploring the spirituality of nature people and ancient Druidism;
    others are trying New Age religion or ancient Eastern monism. There is
    a growing consensus, expressed by Maurice Strong, Secretary General
    of the International Earth Summit in 1992, that some spiritual founda-
    tion is essential. Strong said the Rio decisions require 'deep moral, spir
    itual, and ethical roots if they are to be successfully implemented'.

8   In 1990, a group of renowned scientists signed an 'Open Letter to the
    Religious Community', urging religious people to join the movement
    to save the environment. . . . In their statement, the scientists
    acknowledged that the ecological threat is so great that we cannot
    avoid disaster unless the religious community joins the struggle.

9   That is beginning to happen in important ways. On Earth Day 1994, Christians and Jews in the United States mailed out environmental kits to 53,800 congregations all across the country. A wide range of activities followed in the next five years. This effort, and a wide range of related activities, are the work of the National Religious Partnership for the Environment. The Partnership is a coalition of four groups: the US Catholic Conference, the National Council of Churches, the Evangelical Environment Network, and the Coalition on Jewish Life and the Environment.

10 The major religious communities in this country have joined the battle. As a leader in the Evangelical Environmental Network (which publishes the quarterly *Creation Care* magazine) and chairperson of a two-day event that finalized the *Evangelical Declaration on the Care of Creation*, I can say that American Christians are committed to environmental concerns for the long haul.

11 But that does not mean that all Christians are environmentalists. Nor does it mean that the environmental movement has found the spiritual foundations it seeks. One central task for environmentalists in the next decade will be to listen carefully to each other in order to search further for ethical and spiritual foundations solid enough to sustain an enduring movement to save the planet. In that dialogue, we must respectfully share our deepest convictions, even when our viewpoints differ. An open, tolerant discussion of the major alternatives will help us more than will silent avoidance of religious differences or vacuous generalities. In that spirit, I share my own perspective as a contribution to the developing dialogue.

12 I want to put forward two theses. First, people who ground their faith in the Bible will, if they are consistent, be passionate environmentalists. Second, environmentalists searching eagerly for religious foundations might discover unexpected help in biblical faith.

13 Both claims may sound strange. Is not Christianity, as Lynn White suggested decades ago, the problem rather than the solution? Are not Christians who claim to be biblical the worst offenders? Is it not evangelical Christians who tell us that the world will end soon, and therefore we might as well use up our resources before God blows them to bits?

14 How then can today's Christians offer any hope? Many, I confess, including some of the most visible and vocal, do not. But the reason

is not that a biblical framework is destructive to the environment. Rather, it is that many Christians who are not environmentalists, and many environmentalists who are not Christians, have not carefully attended to what the Bible says about the creation and the Creator.

15 Probably nothing is more important for the future of the environmental movement than a proper understanding of the material world and the relationship of people to the non-human creation.

16 Christians have sometimes ignored the significance of the body and the material world, focusing all their energy on preparing the soul for some future, immaterial, invisible existence in a spiritual heaven. Interestingly, there are striking parallels between such Christians and Eastern monists who tell us that the material world is an illusion to be escaped, so that we can discover the divine spark within and eventually merge with the All and lose all individual identity. It is hard to see how either view would be of much help to environmentalists. If the material world is evil or an illusion, why worry about it?

17 Biblical faith, however, is radically different. Every part of the material world comes from the loving hand of the Creator who calls it into being out of nothing and declares it very good. Unlike the Creator, the creation is finite and limited, but it is not an illusion. Nor is it the result of blind, materialistic chance, although the Creator lovingly nurtured it into existence over the course of a long evolutionary history.

18 In biblical faith, the material world is so good that the Creator of the galaxies actually became flesh once in the time of Caesar Augustus. Indeed, the material world is so good that not only did Jesus devote much time to restoring broken bodies, he also arose bodily from death and promised to return to complete his victory over every form of brokenness in persons, nature and civilization.

19 According to biblical faith, God's cosmic plan of restoration includes the whole creation not just individual 'souls'. The apostle Paul says that at the end of history as we now experience it, Christ will return, not only to usher believers into a life of restored bodily existence in the presence of God, but also to restore the whole non-human creation. 'The creation itself will be set free from its bondage to decay and will obtain the freedom of the glory of the children of God' (Rom. 8:21, NRSV). In that restored earth, I expect to go sailing with my great-grandchildren on a replenished Aral Sea.

20 The last book of the Bible uses a beautiful metaphor about the tree of life growing beside an unpolluted river, pure as crystal, that purges human civilization of its brokenness and evil so that the glory and honour of the nations may enter into the holy city of the future (Rev. 21:22–22:2). Unlike Christian Platonists and Hindu Monists who see the material world as an evil or as an illusion to escape, biblical people believe that it matters so much that the Creator will eventually restore its broken beauty. Knowing God's grand design, Christians can work to initiate now what God will later complete.

21 Few things are more controversial today than the status of persons in relationship to the non-human world. Some, including some Christians, suppose that the only purpose of the non-human world is to serve humanity. Therefore, they conclude, we can ravage and destroy species and ecological systems at will. A liveable-in environment cannot survive another century of such thinking. At the other extreme are those who reject any distinction between monkeys, moles and people, denouncing any claim to superior status for people as speciesism. If that is correct, then human civilization itself becomes impossible. What right have we to use plants and animals for our food and shelter if we are of no more importance than they?

22 Biblical faith offers another perspective. The Bible teaches both that the non-human creation has worth and significance, quite apart from its usefulness to humanity, and also that persons alone are created in God's image and called to be stewards of God's good garden.

23 Anyone who thinks God created the non-human world merely for the benefit of persons has not read the Bible carefully. God feeds the birds and clothes the lilies (Matt. 6:26–30). God watches over the deer hind in the mountains, counting the months of her pregnancy and watching over her when she gives birth, though she never encounters a human being (Job 39:1–2). In the story of the flood, God makes a covenant not just with Noah and his family, but also with the non-human creation: 'I am establishing my covenant with you and your descendants after you, and with every living creature that is with you, the birds, the domestic animals and every animal of the earth' (Gen. 9:9–10, NRSV). Knowing that they all give joy to their Creator, Christians will treasure every species.

24   The independent worth of the non-human creation and humanity's interdependence with it do not, however, mean that we should forget another central biblical claim: human beings alone are created in the image of God, and we alone have been given a special dominion or stewardship of the Earth (Gen. 1:27–28). If one abandons that truth, the whole project of civilization crumbles.

25   Genesis 2:15 says God put people in the garden 'to work it and take care of it'. The word *'ābad'*, translated as 'work', means 'to serve'. The related noun actually means 'slave' or 'servant'. The word *šāmar*, translated as 'take care of', suggests watchful care and preservation of the earth. (Psalm 121 repeatedly uses this same verb to describe the way the Lord unceasingly watches over his people.) We are to serve and watch lovingly over God's good garden, not rape it.

26   The Mosaic law offers explicit commands designed to prevent exploitation of the Earth. Every seventh year, for instance, the Israelites' land was to lie fallow because 'the land is to have a sabbath of rest' (Lev. 25:4).

27   Created in the divine image, we alone have been placed in charge of the Earth. At the same time, our dominion must be the gentle care of a loving gardener, not the callous exploitation of a self centred lordling. So we should not wipe out species or waste the non-human creation. Only a careful, stewardly use of plants and animals by human beings is legitimate.

28   Biblical faith also provides a framework for dealing with the destructive rat race of unbridled consumption. The planet cannot sustain ten billion people living the kind of ever-expanding lifestyle that North Americans now demand. The Creator who made us, both body and soul, wants us to enjoy the gorgeous bounty of the material world. At the same time, we are created in such a way that human wholeness and fulfilment come not only from material things, but also from right relationships with neighbour and God. Both the call to care for our neighbour and the summons to sabbatical worship of God place limits on human acquisition and consumption. Material things are very good, but less important than spending time and enjoying right relationships with neighbour and God.

29   The eighteenth century abandoned the biblical worldview. The isolated, autonomous individual replaced God at the centre of reality.
The scientific method became the only avenue to truth and reality.

30   We can measure an ever-increasing GNP and an expanding stock
portfolio. We cannot easily measure the goodness of community in
the extended family, or the value of caring for the neighbour, not to
mention the value of a personal relationship with God. Frantically,
each individual seeks fulfilment in more and more material things,
even though our very nature makes it impossible for such things to
satisfy our deepest needs. The destructive, unbridled consumerism
of modern society is rooted in this narcissistic individualism and
materialistic naturalism that flow from the Enlightenment. Biblical
faith, on the other hand, provides a framework within which we can
both enjoy material abundance and understand its limits.

31   I believe biblical faith provides a solid foundation for caring for the
creation entrusted to us by the Creator. Perhaps if more Christians
engaged in environmental practices that were consistent with biblical
teaching, more environmentalists would be ready to explore again
the claim that a biblical framework would offer our best hope for a
comprehensive Earth-healing.

Community

This passage, known as the "Sermon on the Mount," contains many of Jesus's instructions for what it means to follow Jesus individually and in a community. In the Beatitudes (Matt. 5:3–10), Christ bestows blessings on people with traits not always valued by the world, such as purity of heart, meekness, or a desire for peace. He goes on to exhort his followers to set a good example, pray privately, follow the law as it is fulfilled by Him, and give generously to the needy. When these and the rest of Jesus's instructions in the Sermon on the Mount are followed, Christians can live in fellowship with one another as the disciples did and fulfill God's intent for community among his people.

Matthew 5–7 (NRSV)

The Beatitudes

5 When Jesus saw the crowds, he went up the mountain; and after he sat down, his disciples came to him. **2** Then he began to speak, and taught them, saying:

3 "Blessed are the poor in spirit, for theirs is the kingdom of heaven.

4 "Blessed are those who mourn, for they will be comforted.

5 "Blessed are the meek, for they will inherit the earth.

6 "Blessed are those who hunger and thirst for righteousness, for they will be filled.

7 "Blessed are the merciful, for they will receive mercy.

8 "Blessed are the pure in heart, for they will see God.

9 "Blessed are the peacemakers, for they will be called children of God.

10 "Blessed are those who are persecuted for righteousness' sake, for theirs is the kingdom of heaven.

11 "Blessed are you when people revile you and persecute you and utter all kinds of evil against you falsely on my account. **12** Rejoice and be glad, for your reward is great in heaven, for in the same way they persecuted the prophets who were before you.

Salt and Light

13 "You are the salt of the earth; but if salt has lost its taste, how can its saltiness be restored? It is no longer good for anything, but is thrown out and trampled under foot.

14 "You are the light of the world. A city built on a hill cannot be hid. **15** No one after lighting a lamp puts it under the bushel basket, but on the lampstand, and it gives light to all in the house. **16** In the same way, let your light shine before others, so that they may see your good works and give glory to your Father in heaven.

The Law and the Prophets

17 "Do not think that I have come to abolish the law or the prophets; I have come not to abolish but to fulfill. **18** For truly I tell you, until heaven and earth pass away, not one letter, not one stroke of a letter, will pass from the law until all is accomplished. **19** Therefore, whoever breaks one of the least of these commandments, and teaches others to do the same, will be called least in the kingdom of heaven; but whoever does them and teaches them will be called great in the kingdom of heaven. **20** For I tell you, unless your righteousness exceeds that of the scribes and Pharisees, you will never enter the kingdom of heaven.

Concerning Anger

21 "You have heard that it was said to those of ancient times, 'You shall not murder'; and 'whoever murders shall be liable to judgment.' **22** But I say to you that if you are angry with a brother or sister, you will be liable to judgment; and if you insult a brother or sister, you will be liable to the council; and if you say, 'You fool,' you will be liable to the hell of fire. **23** So when you are offering your gift at the altar, if you remember that your brother or sister has something against you, **24** leave your gift there before the altar and go; first be reconciled to your brother or sister, and then come and offer your gift. **25** Come to terms quickly with your accuser while you are on the way to court with him, or your accuser may hand you over to the judge, and the judge to the guard, and you will be thrown into prison. **26** Truly I tell you, you will never get out until you have paid the last penny.

Concerning Adultery

27 "You have heard that it was said, 'You shall not commit adultery.' **28** But I say to you that everyone who looks at a woman with lust has already committed adultery with her in his heart. **29** If your right eye causes you to sin, tear it out and throw it away; it is better for you to lose one of your members than for your whole body to be thrown into hell. **30** And if your right hand causes you to sin, cut it off and throw it away; it is better for you to lose one of your members than for your whole body to go into hell.

Concerning Divorce

31 "It was also said, 'Whoever divorces his wife, let him give her a certificate of divorce.' **32** But I say to you that anyone who divorces his wife, except on the ground of unchastity, causes her to commit adultery; and whoever marries a divorced woman commits adultery.

Concerning Oaths

33 "Again, you have heard that it was said to those of ancient times, 'You shall not swear falsely, but carry out the vows you have made to the Lord.' **34** But I say to you, Do not swear at all, either by heaven, for it is the throne of God, **35** or by the earth, for it is his footstool, or by Jerusalem, for it is the city of the great King. **36** And do not swear by your head, for you cannot make one hair white or black. **37** Let your word be 'Yes, Yes' or 'No, No'; anything more than this comes from the evil one.

Concerning Retaliation

38 "You have heard that it was said, 'An eye for an eye and a tooth for a tooth.' **39** But I say to you, Do not resist an evildoer. But if anyone strikes you on the right cheek, turn the other also; **40** and if anyone wants to sue you and take your coat, give your cloak as well; **41** and if anyone forces you to go one mile, go also the second mile. **42** Give to everyone who begs from you, and do not refuse anyone who wants to borrow from you.

Love for Enemies

43 "You have heard that it was said, 'You shall love your neighbor and hate your enemy.' **44** But I say to you, Love your enemies and pray for those who persecute you, **45** so that you may be children of your Father in heaven; for he makes his sun rise on the evil and on the good, and sends rain on the righteous and on the unrighteous. **46** For if you love those who love you, what reward do you have? Do not even the tax collectors do the same? **47** And if you greet only your brothers and sisters, what more are you doing than others? Do not even the Gentiles do the same? **48** Be perfect, therefore, as your heavenly Father is perfect.

Concerning Almsgiving

6 "Beware of practicing your piety before others in order to be seen by them; for then you have no reward from your Father in heaven. **2** "So whenever you give alms, do not sound a trumpet before you, as the hypocrites do in the synagogues and in the streets, so that they may be praised by others. Truly I tell you, they have received their reward. **3** But when you give alms, do not let your left hand know what your right hand is doing, **4** so that your alms may be done in secret; and your Father who sees in secret will reward you.

Concerning Prayer

5 "And whenever you pray, do not be like the hypocrites; for they love to stand and pray in the synagogues and at the street corners, so that they may be seen by others. Truly I tell you, they have received their reward. **6** But whenever you pray, go into your room and shut the door and pray to your Father who is in secret; and your Father who sees in secret will reward you.

7 "When you are praying, do not heap up empty phrases as the Gentiles do; for they think that they will be heard because of their many words. **8** Do not be like them, for your Father knows what you need before you ask him.

9   "Pray then in this way:
     Our Father in heaven,
       hallowed be your name.
10   Your kingdom come.
      Your will be done,
        on earth as it is in heaven.
11   Give us this day our daily bread.
12   And forgive us our debts,
       as we also have forgiven our debtors.
13   And do not bring us to the time of trial,
      but rescue us from the evil one.

14 For if you forgive others their trespasses, your heavenly Father will also forgive you; 15 but if you do not forgive others, neither will your Father forgive your trespasses.

Concerning Fasting

16 "And whenever you fast, do not look dismal, like the hypocrites, for they disfigure their faces so as to show others that they are fasting. Truly I tell you, they have received their reward. 17 But when you fast, put oil on your head and wash your face, 18 so that your fasting may be seen not by others but by your Father who is in secret; and your Father who sees in secret will reward you.

Concerning Treasures

19 "Do not store up for yourselves treasures on earth, where moth and rust consume and where thieves break in and steal; 20 but store up for yourselves treasures in heaven, where neither moth nor rust consumes and where thieves do not break in and steal. 21 For where your treasure is, there your heart will be also.

The Sound Eye

22 "The eye is the lamp of the body. So, if your eye is healthy, your whole body will be full of light; 23 but if your eye is unhealthy, your whole body will be full of darkness. If then the light in you is darkness, how great is the darkness!

Serving Two Masters

24 "No one can serve two masters; for a slave will either hate the one and love the other, or be devoted to the one and despise the other. You cannot serve God and wealth.

Do Not Worry

25 "Therefore I tell you, do not worry about your life, what you will eat or what you will drink, or about your body, what you will wear. Is not life more than food, and the body more than clothing? 26 Look at the birds of the air; they neither sow nor reap nor gather into barns, and yet your heavenly Father feeds them. Are you not of more value than they? 27 And can any of you by worrying add a single hour to your span of life? 28 And why do you worry about clothing? Consider the lilies of the field, how they grow; they neither toil nor spin, 29 yet I tell you, even Solomon in all

his glory was not clothed like one of these. **30** But if God so clothes the grass of the field, which is alive today and tomorrow is thrown into the oven, will he not much more clothe you—you of little faith? **31** Therefore do not worry, saying, 'What will we eat?' or 'What will we drink?' or 'What will we wear?' **32** For it is the Gentiles who strive for all these things; and indeed your heavenly Father knows that you need all these things. **33** But strive first for the kingdom of God and his righteousness, and all these things will be given to you as well.

34 "So do not worry about tomorrow, for tomorrow will bring worries of its own. Today's trouble is enough for today.

Judging Others

7 "Do not judge, so that you may not be judged. **2** For with the judgment you make you will be judged, and the measure you give will be the measure you get. **3** Why do you see the speck in your neighbor's eye, but do not notice the log in your own eye? **4** Or how can you say to your neighbor, 'Let me take the speck out of your eye,' while the log is in your own eye? **5** You hypocrite, first take the log out of your own eye, and then you will see clearly to take the speck out of your neighbor's eye.

Profaning the Holy

6 "Do not give what is holy to dogs; and do not throw your pearls before swine, or they will trample them under foot and turn and maul you.

Ask, Search, Knock

7 "Ask, and it will be given you; search, and you will find; knock, and the door will be opened for you. **8** For everyone who asks receives, and everyone who searches finds, and for everyone who knocks, the door will be opened. **9** Is there anyone among you who, if your child asks for bread, will give a stone? **10** Or if the child asks for a fish, will give a snake? **11** If you then, who are evil, know how to give good gifts to your children, how much more will your Father in heaven give good things to those who ask him!

The Golden Rule

12 "In everything do to others as you would have them do to you; for this is the law and the prophets.

The Narrow Gate

13 "Enter through the narrow gate; for the gate is wide and the road is easy that leads to destruction, and there are many who take it. **14** For the gate is narrow and the road is hard that leads to life, and there are few who find it.

A Tree and Its Fruit

15 "Beware of false prophets, who come to you in sheep's clothing but inwardly are ravenous wolves. **16** You will know them by their fruits. Are grapes gathered from thorns, or figs from thistles? **17** In the same way, every good tree bears good fruit, but the bad tree bears bad fruit. **18** A good tree cannot bear bad fruit, nor can a bad tree bear good fruit. **19** Every tree that does not bear good fruit is cut down and thrown into the fire. **20** Thus you will know them by their fruits.

Concerning Self-Deception

21 "Not everyone who says to me, 'Lord, Lord,' will enter the kingdom of heaven, but only the one who does the will of my Father in heaven. **22** On that day many will say to me, 'Lord, Lord, did we not prophesy in your name, and cast out demons in your name, and do many deeds of power in your name?' **23** Then I will declare to them, 'I never knew you; go away from me, you evildoers.'

Hearers and Doers

24 "Everyone then who hears these words of mine and acts on them will be like a wise man who built his house on rock. **25** The rain fell, the floods came, and the winds blew and beat on that house, but it did not fall, because it had been founded on rock. **26** And everyone who hears these words of mine and does not act on them will be like a foolish man who built his house on sand. **27** The rain fell, and the floods came, and the winds blew and beat against that house, and it fell—and great was its fall!"

28 Now when Jesus had finished saying these things, the crowds were astounded at his teaching, **29** for he taught them as one having authority, and not as their scribes.

everal locations in Acts describe the community ethos of the early Church. These passages make clear that Christ's disciples did not keep any possessions for themselves, but shared freely among the community so that every person had what he or she needed. Personal possessions, such as Joseph of Cyprus's field, were sold and the money was contributed to the community to provide for everyone. As Christians, we can look to these accounts for an example of how we should live in community with each other. Rather than keeping a firm grasp on our own blessings, both spiritual and material, we can maximize their full potential by sharing them with others.

Acts 2:37–47 and 4:32–37 (NRSV)

The First Converts

2 37 Now when they heard this, they were cut to the heart and said to Peter and to the other apostles, "Brothers, what should we do?" **38** Peter said to them, "Repent, and be baptized every one of you in the name of Jesus Christ so that your sins may be forgiven; and you will receive the gift of the Holy Spirit. **39** For the promise is for you, for your children, and for all who are far away, everyone whom the Lord our God calls to him." **40** And he testified with many other arguments and exhorted them, saying, "Save yourselves from this corrupt generation." **41** So those who welcomed his message were baptized, and that day about three thousand persons were added. **42** They devoted themselves to the apostles' teaching and fellowship, to the breaking of bread and the prayers.

Life among the Believers

43 Awe came upon everyone, because many wonders and signs were being done by the apostles. **44** All who believed were together and had all things in common; **45** they would sell their possessions and goods and distribute the proceeds to all, as any had need. **46** Day by day, as they spent much time together in the temple, they broke bread at home and ate their food with glad and generous hearts, **47** praising God and having the goodwill of all the people. And day by day the Lord added to their number those who were being saved.

The Believers Share Their Possessions

4 32 Now the whole group of those who believed were of one heart and soul, and no one claimed private ownership of any possessions, but everything they owned was held in common. **33** With great power the apostles gave their testimony to the resurrection of the Lord Jesus, and great grace was upon them all. **34** There was not a needy person among them, for as many as owned lands or houses sold them and brought the proceeds of what was sold. **35** They laid it at the apostles' feet, and it was distributed to each as any had need. **36** There was a Levite, a native of Cyprus, Joseph, to whom the apostles gave the name Barnabas (which means "son of encouragement"). **37** He sold a field that belonged to him, then brought the money, and laid it at the apostles' feet.

*H*arold S. Bender (1897–1962) was a well-known professor of theology, who wanted to help Anabaptists and Mennonites during World War II to retain their convictions. To do this, Bender pointed out the beginnings of the religious movement that produced Anabaptist and Mennonite communities. In this excerpt from The Anabaptist Vision, Bender analyzes the history of the movement to emphasize the main tenets of Anabaptism. His three important "points of emphasis" emphasize the importance of and form a model for Christian community.

from The Anabaptist Vision

Harold S. Bender

1   Having defined genuine Anabaptism in its Reformation setting, we are ready to examine its central teachings. The Anabaptist vision included three major points of emphasis; first, a new conception of the essence of Christianity as discipleship; second, a new conception of the church as a brotherhood; and third, a new ethic of love and nonresistance. We turn now to an exposition of these points.

2   First and fundamental in the Anabaptist vision was the conception of the essence of Christianity as discipleship. It was a concept which meant the transformation of the entire way of life of the individual believer and of society so that it should be fashioned after the teachings and example of Christ.[1] The Anabaptists could not understand a Christianity which made regeneration, holiness, and love primarily a matter of intellect, of doctrinal belief, or of subjective "experience," rather than one of the transformation of life. They demanded an outward expression of the inner experience. Repentance must be "evidenced" by newness of behavior. "In evidence" is the keynote which rings through the testimonies and challenges of the early Swiss Brethren when they are called to give an account of themselves. The whole life was to be brought literally under the lordship of Christ in a covenant of discipleship, a covenant which the Anabaptist writers delighted to emphasize.[2] The focus of the Christian life was to be not so much the inward experience of the grace of God, as it was for

Luther, but the outward application of that grace to all human conduct and the consequent Christianization of all human relationships.
The true test of the Christian, they held, is discipleship. The great
word of the Anabaptists was not "faith" as it was with the reformers,
but "following" (*Nachfolge Christi*). And baptism, the greatest of
Christian symbols, was accordingly to be for them the "covenant of a
good conscience toward God" (1 Peter 3:21),[3] the pledge of a complete commitment to obey Christ, and not primarily the symbol of a
past experience. The Anabaptists had faith, indeed, but they used it
to produce a life. Theology was for them a means, not an end.

3   That the Anabaptists not only proclaimed the ideal of full Christian
discipleship but achieved, in the eyes of their contemporaries and
even of their opponents, a measurably higher level of performance
than the average, is fully witnessed by the sources. The early Swiss
and South German reformers were keenly aware of this achievement
and its attractive power. Zwingli knew it best of all, but Bullinger,
Capito, Vadian, and many others confirm his judgment that the
Anabaptist Brethren were unusually sincere, devoted, and effective
Christians. However, since the Brethren refused to accept the state
church system which the reformers were building, and in addition
made "radical" demands which might have changed the entire social
order, the leaders of the Reformation were completely baffled in their
understanding of the movement, and professed to believe that the
Anabaptists were hypocrites of the darkest dye. Bullinger, for
instance, calls them "devilish enemies and destroyers of the Church
of God."[4] Nevertheless they had to admit the apparent superiority of
their life. In Zwingli's last book against the Swiss Brethren (1527), for
instance, the following is found:

> If you investigate their life and conduct, it seems at first contact irre-
> proachable, pious, unassuming, attractive, yea, above this world. Even
> those who are inclined to be critical will say that their lives are excellent.[5]

Bullinger, himself, who wrote bitter diatribes against them, was compelled to admit of the early Swiss Brethren that

> Those who unite with them will by their ministers be received into their
> church by rebaptism and repentance and newness of life. They hence-
> forth lead their lives under a semblance of a quite spiritual conduct.
> They denounce covetousness, pride, profanity, the lewd conversation
> and immorality of the world, drinking and gluttony. In short, their
> hypocrisy is great and manifold.[6]

Bullinger's lament (1531) that "the people are running after them as though they were the living saints" has been reported earlier. Vadian, the reformer of St. Gall, testified, that "none were more favorably inclined toward Anabaptism and more easily entangled with it than those who were of pious and honorable disposition."[7] Capito, the reformer of Strassburg, wrote in 1527 concerning the Swiss Brethren:

> I frankly confess that in most [Anabaptists] there is in evidence piety and consecration and indeed a zeal which is beyond any suspicion of insincerity. For what earthly advantage could they hope to win by enduring exile, torture, and unspeakable punishment of the flesh? I testify before God that I cannot say that on account of a lack of wisdom they are somewhat indifferent toward earthly things, but rather from divine motives.[8]

4   The preachers of the Canton of Berne admitted in a letter to the Council of Berne in 1532 that

> The Anabaptists have the semblance of outward piety to a far greater degree than we and all the churches which unitedly with us confess Christ, and they avoid offensive sins which are very common among us.[9]

Walter Klarer, the Reformed chronicler of Appenzell, Switzerland, wrote:

> Most of the Anabaptists are people who at first had been the best with us in promulgating the word of God.[10]

And the Roman Catholic theologian, Franz Agricola, in his book of 1582, *Against the Terrible Errors of the Anabaptists,* says:

> Among the existing heretical sects there is none which in appearance leads a more modest or pious life than the Anabaptist. As concerns their outward public life they are irreproachable. No lying, deception, swearing, strife, harsh language, no intemperate eating and drinking, no outward personal display, is found among them, but humility, patience, uprightness, neatness, honesty, temperance, straightforwardness in such measure that one would suppose that they had the Holy Spirit of God.[11]

A mandate against the Swiss Brethren published in 1585 by the Council of Berne states that offensive sins and vices were common among the preachers and the membership of the Reformed Church, adding, "And this is the greatest reason that many pious, God-fearing people who seek Christ from their heart are offended and forsake our church [to unite with the Brethren]."[12]

5 One of the finest contemporary characterizations of the Anabaptists is that given in 1531 by Sebastian Franck, an objective and sympathetic witness, though an opponent of the Anabaptists, who wrote as follows:

> The Anabaptists . . . soon gained a large following, . . . drawing many sincere souls who had a zeal for God, for they taught nothing but love, faith, and the cross. They showed themselves humble, patient under much suffering; they brake bread with one another as an evidence of unity and love. They helped each other faithfully, and called each other brothers. . . . They died as martyrs, patiently and humbly enduring all persecution.[13]

6 A further confirmation of the above evaluation of the achievement of the Anabaptists is found in the fact that in many places those who lived a consistent Christian life were in danger of falling under the suspicion of being guilty of Anabaptist heresy. Caspar Schwenckfeld, for instance, declared, "I am being maligned, by both preachers and others, with the charge of being Anabaptist, even as all others who lead a true, pious Christian life are now almost everywhere given this name."[14] Bullinger himself complained that

> . . . there are those who in reality are not Anabaptists but have a pronounced averseness to the sensuality and frivolity of the world and therefore reprove sin and vice and are consequently called or misnamed Anabaptists by petulant persons.[15]

7 The great collection of Anabaptist source materials, commonly called the *Täufer-Akten*, now in its third volume, contains a number of specific illustrations of this. In 1562 a certain Caspar Zacher of Wailblingen in Württemberg was accused of being an Anabaptist, but the court record reports that since he was an envious man who could not get along with others, and who often started quarrels, as well as being guilty of swearing and cursing and carrying a weapon, he was not considered to be an Anabaptist.[16] On the other hand in 1570 a certain Hans Jäger of Vöhringen in Württemberg was brought before the court on suspicion of being an Anabaptist primarily because he did not curse but lived an irreproachable life.[17]

8 As a second major element in the Anabaptist vision, a new concept of the church was created by the central principle of newness of life and applied Christianity. Voluntary church membership based upon true conversion and involving a commitment to holy living and discipleship was the absolutely essential heart of this concept. This vision

stands in sharp contrast to the church concept of the reformers who retained the medieval idea of a mass church with membership of the entire population from birth to the grave compulsory by law and force.

9　It is from the standpoint of this new conception of the church that the Anabaptist opposition to infant baptism must be interpreted. Infant baptism was not the cause of their disavowal of the state church; it was only a symbol of the cause. How could infants give a commitment based upon a knowledge of what true Christianity means? They might conceivably passively experience the grace of God (though Anabaptists would question this), but they could not respond in pledging their lives to Christ. Such infant baptism would not only be meaningless, but would in fact become a serious obstacle to a true understanding of the nature of Christianity and membership in the church. Only adult baptism could signify an intelligent life commitment.

10　An inevitable corollary of the concept of the church as a body of committed and practicing Christians pledged to the highest standard of New Testament living was the insistence on the separation of the church from the world, that is nonconformity of the Christian to the worldly way of life. The world would not tolerate the practice of true Christian principles in society, and the church could not tolerate the practice of worldly ways among its membership. Hence, the only way out was separation ("*Absonderung*"), the gathering of true Christians into their own Christian society where Christ's way could and would be practiced. On this principle of separation Menno Simons says:

> All the evangelical scriptures teach us that the church of Christ was and is, in doctrine, life, and worship, a people separated from the world [18]

In the great debate of 1532 at Zofingen, spokesmen of the Swiss Brethren said:

> The true church is separated from the world and is conformed to the nature of Christ. If a church is yet at one with the world we cannot recognize it is a true church.[19]

In a sense, this principle of nonconformity to the world is merely a negative expression of the positive requirement of discipleship, but it goes further in the sense that it represents a judgment on the contemporary social order, which the Anabaptists called "the world," as non-Christian, and sets up a line of demarcation between the Christian community and worldly society.

11   A logical outcome of the concept of nonconformity to the world was the concept of the suffering church. Conflict with the world was inevitable for those who endeavored to live an earnest Christian life. The Anabaptists expected opposition; they took literally the words of Jesus when He said, " In the world ye shall have tribulation," but they also took literally His words of encouragement, "But be of good cheer; I have overcome the world." Conrad Grebel said in 1524:

> True Christian believers are sheep among wolves, sheep for the slaughter; they must be baptized in anguish and affliction, tribulation, persecution, suffering, and death; they must be tried with fire and must reach the fatherland of eternal rest not by killing them bodily, but by mortifying their spiritual, enemies. [20]

Professor Ernest Staehelin of Basel, Switzerland, says:

> Anabaptism by its earnest determination to follow in life and practice the primitive Christian Church has kept alive the conviction that he who is in Christ is a new creature and that those who are identified with his cause will necessarily encounter the opposition of the world.[21]

12   Perhaps it was persecution that made the Anabaptists so acutely aware of the conflict between the church and the world, but this persecution was due to the fact that they refused to accept what they considered the sub-Christian way of life practiced in European Christendom. They could have avoided the persecution had they but conformed, or they could have suspended the practice of their faith to a more convenient time and sailed under false colors as did David Joris, but they chose with dauntless courage and simple honesty to live their faith, to defy the existing world order, and to suffer the consequences.

13   Basic to the Anabaptist vision of the church was the insistence on the practice of true brotherhood and love among the members of the church.[22] This principle was understood to mean not merely the expression of pious sentiments, but the actual practice of sharing possessions to meet the needs of others in the spirit of true mutual aid. Hans Leopold, a Swiss Brethren martyr of 1528, said of the Brethren:

> If they know of any one who is in need, whether or not he is a member of their church, they believe it their duty, out of love to God, to render help and aid.[23]

Heinrich Seiler, a Swiss Brethren martyr of 1535 said:

> I do not believe it wrong that a Christian has property of his own, but yet he is nothing more than a steward.[24]

An early Hutterian book states that one of the questions addressed by the Swiss Brethren to applicants for baptism was: "Whether they would consecrate themselves with all their temporal possessions to the service of God and His people."[25] A Protestant of Strassburg, visitor at a Swiss Brethren baptismal service in that city in 1557, reports that a question addressed to all applicants for baptism was: "Whether they, if necessity require it, would devote all their possessions to the service of the brotherhood, and would not fail any member that is in need, if they were able to render aid."[26] Heinrich Bullinger, the bitter enemy of the Brethren, states:

> They teach that every Christian is under duty before God from motives of love, to use, if need be, all his possessions to supply the necessities of life to any of the brethren who are in need.[27]

This principle of full brotherhood and stewardship was actually practiced, and not merely speculatively considered. In its absolute form of Christian communism, with the complete repudiation of private property, it became the way of life of the Hutterian Brotherhood in 1528 and has remained so to this day, for the Hutterites held that private property is the greatest enemy of Christian love. One of the inspiring stories of the sixteenth and seventeenth centuries is the successful practice of the full communal way of life by this group.[28]

14   The third great element in the Anabaptist vision was the ethic of love and nonresistance as applied to all human relationships. The Brethren understood this to mean complete abandonment of all warfare, strife, and violence, and of the taking of human life.[29] Conrad Grebel, the Swiss, said in 1524:

> True Christians use neither worldly sword nor engage in war, since among them taking human life has ceased entirely, for we are no longer under the Old Covenant. . . . The Gospel and those who accept it are not to be protected with the sword, neither should they thus protect themselves.[30]

Pilgram Marpeck, the South German leader, in 1544, speaking of Matthew 5, said:

> All bodily, worldly, carnal, earthly fightings, conflicts, and wars are annulled and abolished among them through such law . . . which law of love Christ . . . Himself observed and thereby gave His followers a pattern to follow after.[31]

Peter Riedemann, the Hutterian leader, wrote in 1545:

> Christ, the Prince of Peace, has established His Kingdom, that is, His Church, and has purchased it by His blood. In this kingdom all worldly warfare has ended. Therefore a Christian has no part in war nor does he wield the sword to execute vengeance.[32]

Menno Simons, of Holland, wrote in 1550:

> [The regenerated do not go to war, nor engage in strife.] . . . They are the children of peace who have beaten their swords into plowshares and their spears into pruning hooks, and know of no war. . . . Spears and swords of iron we leave to those who, alas, consider human blood and swine's blood of well-nigh equal value.[33]

In this principle of nonresistance, or biblical pacifism, which was thoroughly believed and resolutely practiced by all the original Anabaptist Brethren and their descendants throughout Europe from the beginning until the last century,[34] the Anabaptists were again creative leaders, far ahead of their times, in this ante-dating the Quakers by over a century and a quarter. It should also be remembered that they held this principle in a day when both Catholic and Protestant churches not only endorsed war as an instrument of state policy, but employed it in religious conflicts. It is true, of course, that occasional earlier prophets, like Peter Chelcicky, had advocated similar views, but they left no continuing practice of the principle behind them.

15 As we review the vision of the Anabaptists, it becomes clear that there are two foci in this vision. The first focus relates to the essential nature of Christianity. Is Christianity primarily a matter of the reception of divine grace through a sacramental-sacerdotal institution (Roman Catholicism), is it chiefly enjoyment of the inner experience of the grace of God through faith in Christ (Lutheranism), or is it most of all the transformation of life through discipleship (Anabaptism)? The Anabaptists were neither institutionalists, mystics, nor pietists, for they laid the weight of their emphasis upon following Christ in life. To them it was unthinkable for one truly to be a Christian without creating a new life on divine principles both for himself and for all men who commit themselves to the Christian way.

16 The second focus relates to the church. For the Anabaptist, the church was neither an institution (Catholicism), nor the instrument of God for the proclamation of the divine Word (Lutheranism), nor a resource group for individual piety (Pietism). It was a brotherhood of love in which the fullness of the Christian life ideal is to be expressed.

17   The Anabaptist vision may be further clarified by comparison of the social ethics of the four main Christian groups of the Reformation period, Catholic, Calvinist, Lutheran, and Anabaptist. Catholic and Calvinist alike were optimistic about the world, agreeing that the world can be redeemed; they held that the entire social order can be brought under the sovereignty of God and Christianized, although they used different means to attain this goal. Lutheran and Anabaptist were pessimistic about the world, denying the possibility of Christianizing the entire social order; but the consequent attitudes of these two groups toward the social order were diametrically opposed. Lutheranism said that since the Christian must live in a world order that remains sinful, he must make a compromise with it. As a citizen he cannot avoid participation in the evil of the world, for instance in making war, and for this his only recourse is to seek forgiveness by the grace of God; only within his personal private experience can the Christian truly Christianize his life. The Anabaptist rejected this view completely. Since for him no compromise dare be made with evil, the Christian may in no circumstance participate in any conduct in the existing social order which is contrary to the spirit and teaching of Christ and the apostolic practice. He must consequently withdraw from the worldly system and create a Christian social order within the fellowship of the church brotherhood. Extension of this Christian order by the conversion of individuals and their transfer out of the world into the church is the only way by which progress can be made in Christianizing the social order.

18   However, the Anabaptist was realistic. Down the long perspective of the future he saw little chance that the mass of humankind would enter such a brotherhood with its high ideals. Hence he anticipated a long and grievous conflict between the church and the world. Neither did he anticipate the time when the church would rule the world; the church would always be a suffering church. He agreed with the words of Jesus when He said that those who would be His disciples must deny themselves and take up their cross daily and follow Him, and that there would be few who would enter the strait gate and travel the narrow way of life. If this prospect should seem too discouraging, the Anabaptist would reply that the life within the Christian brotherhood is satisfyingly full of love and joy.

19   The Anabaptist vision was not a detailed blueprint for the recon-
     struction of human society, but the Brethren did believe that Jesus
     intended that the kingdom of God should be set up in the midst of
     earth, here and now, and this they proposed to do forthwith. We shall
     not believe, they said, that the Sermon on the Mount or any other
     vision that He had is only a heavenly vision meant but to keep His
     followers in tension until the last great day, but we shall practice
     what He taught, believing that where He walked we can by His grace
     follow in His steps.

Notes

[1]   Johannes Kuhn, *Toleranz und Offenbarung* (Leipzig, 1923), 224 says: "With the
      Anabaptists everything was based on a central idea. This central idea was con-
      cretely religious. It was Jesus' command to follow Him in a holy life of fellow-
      ship." Professor Alfred Hegler of Tübingen describes the Anabaptist ideal as
      "liberty of conscience, rejection of all state-made Christianity, the demand for
      personal holiness, and a vital personal acceptance of Christian truth." Professor
      Paul Wernle says, "Their vital characteristic was the earnestness with which
      they undertook the practical fulfillment of New Testament requirements both
      for the individual and for the church." These and other similar quotations are
      to be found in Horsch. "The Character of the Evangelical Anabaptists as
      Reported by Contemporary Reformation Writers." *Mennonite Quarterly Review*
      (July 1934), VIII, 135.

[2]   Pilgram Marpeck, the outstanding writer of the Swiss and South German
      Brethren, is an example. See J. C. Wenger, "The Theology of Pilgram Marpeck."
      Mennonite Quarterly Review (October 1938), XII, 247.

[3]   The German (Luther) translation of I Peter 3:21 calls baptism "Der Bund eines
      guten Gewissens mit Gott."

[4]   Bullinger, *Von dem unverschampten fräfel* (1531), fol. 75 r.

[5]   S. M. Jackson, *Selected Works of Huldreich Zwingli* (Philadelphia, 1901), 127.

[6]   Bullinger, *Der Widertäufferen Ursprung*, fol. 15 v.

[7]   Joachim von Watt, *Deutsche Historische Schriften*, ed. Ernst Götzinger (St. Gall,
      1879), II, 408.

[8]   C. A. Cornelius, *Geschichte des Münsterschen Aufruhrs* (Leipzig, 1860), II, 52.

[9]   W. J. McGlothlin, *Die Berner Täufer bis 1532* (Berlin, 1902), 36.

[10] J. J. Simler, *Sammlung alter und neuer Urkunden* (Zurich, 1757), I, 824.

[11] Karl Rembert, *Die Wiedertäufer im Herzogtum Jülich* (Berlin, 1899), 564.

[12] Ernst Müller, *Geschichte der Bernischen Taüfer* (Frauenfeld, 1895), 88. Müller
      speaks (p. 89) of the mandate of 1585 as conceiving of "das Tüuferwesen" as a
      just judgment of God on the church and the people of Berne.

[13] Sebastian Franck, *Chronica, Zeitbuch und Geschichtbibel* (Strassburg, 1531), folio 444v.

[14] Schwenckfeld's *Epistolar* (1564), I, 203.

[15] Bullinger, *Der Widertäufferen Ursprung* (1561), fol. 170r.

[16] *Quellen zur Geschichte der Wiederläufer, I. Band Herzogtum Württemberg*, ed. Gustav Bossert (Leipzig, 1930), 216 f.

[17] *Ibid.*, 259 ff.

[18] *Complete Works of Menno Simons* (Elkhart, Indiana, 1871), II, 37b.

[19] *Handlung oder Acta der Disputation gehalten zu Zofingen* (Zurich, 1532).

[20] Böhmer-Kirn, *op. cit.*, 97.

[21] Horsch, *op cit.*, 386.

[22] P. Tschackert, *Die Entstehung der Lutherischen und reformierten Kirchenlehre* (Göttingen, 1910), 133, says of the Anabaptists that they were "a voluntary Christian fellowship, striving to conform to the Christian spirit for the practice of brotherly love."

[23] Johannes Kühn, *op. cit.*, 231. fol. 22 v.

[24] Ernst Müller, *op. cit.*, 44. See Ernst Correll, *op. cit.*, 15 f. on the attitude of the various Anabaptist groups on community of goods.

[25] Horsch, *op. cit.*, 317.

[26] A. Hulshof *Geschiedenis van de Doopsgezinden te Straatsburg van 1525 tot 1557* (Amsterdam, 1905), 216.

[27] Bullinger, *Der Widertäufferen Ursprung*, fol. 129v.

[28] John Horsch, *The Hutterian Brethren 1528–1931* (Goshen, Indiana, 1931), gives the only adequate account in English of the Hutterian Brethren. It is of interest to note that Erasmus, Melanchthon, and Zwingli condemned private ownership of property as a sin. See Paul Wernle, *Renaissance und Reformation* (Tübingen, 1912), 54, 55, for the citations of Erasmus and Melanchthon, and Horsch, *Hutterian Brethren*, 132, footnote 126, for the citation of Zwingli. Wilhelm Pauck says that Bucer's ideal state was that of Christian communism, "Martin Bucer's Conception of a Christian State," in *Princeton Theological Review* (January 1928), XXVI, 88.

[29] Not all the Anabaptists were completely nonresistant: Balthasar Hubmaier for instance for a brief period (1526–28) led a group of Anabaptists at Nikolsburg in Moravia who agreed to carry the sword against the Turk and pay special war taxes for this purpose. This group, which became extinct in a short time, was known as the "Schwertler" in distinction from other Moravian Anabaptists called the "Stäbler," who later became the Hutterites and have continued to the present. It is obvious that Hubmaier and the "Schwertler" represent a transient aberration from original and authentic Anabaptism. Bullinger (*Von dem unverschampten fräfel* [1531] fol. 139v.) testifies that the Swiss Brethren considered war to be "das ergist uebel das man erdencken mag," and (*Der Widertäufferen*

Ursprung [1561] fol. 16 r.) says "they do not defend themselves, therefore they do not go to war and are not obedient to the government on this point." See also, extensive compilation of evidence by John Horsch in his booklet, *The Principle of Nonresistance as Held by the Mennonite Church, A Historical Survey* (Scottdale, Pa., 1927), 60 pages.

30 Letter of Grebel to Müntzer, Böhmer-Kirn, *op. cit.*, 97.

31 (Pilgrim Marpeck), *Testamenterleütterung* (n.d., n.p., ca. 1544), fol. 313r.

32 (Peter Riedemann), *Rechenschaft unserer Religion, Lehre und Glaubens, von den Bruedern die Man die Hutterischen nennt* (Berne, Indiana, 1902), 105.

33 *The Complete Works of Menno Simons* (Elkhart, Indiana, 1871), I, 170b and 81b. The quotations were revised by comparison with the Dutch editions of 1646 and 1681.

34 Mennonites of Holland, Germany, France, and Switzerland gradually abandoned nonresistance in the course of the nineteenth century. The emigrant Mennonites in Russia and North America have maintained it. The Mennonites of the United States furnish 40 percent of all conscientious objectors in Civilian Public Service in the present war, and the Mennonites of Canada a still higher percent of the conscientious objectors in that country.

*R*obert Frost (1874–1963) was an American poet renowned for his ability to infuse his poetry about rural New England life with incisive social commentary. In "Mending Wall," Frost examines the social boundaries that exist even between neighbors. While destructive forces constantly work to undermine these boundaries, people continue to build them back up despite the ostensible futility of this endeavor. The narrator of the poem clearly sees the folly of this tradition of wall-building, and yet is an active participant and initiates the repairs himself. The implications for Christians trying to live in community with one another can be significant, given the entrenchment of such boundaries in society.

Mending Wall

Robert Frost

Something there is that doesn't love a wall,
That sends the frozen-ground-swell under it,
And spills the upper boulders in the sun,
And makes gaps even two can pass abreast.
5   The work of hunters is another thing:
I have come after them and made repair
Where they have left not one stone on a stone,
But they would have the rabbit out of hiding,
To please the yelping dogs. The gaps I mean,
10   No one has seen them made or heard them made,
But at spring mending-time we find them there.
I let my neighbor know beyond the hill;
And on a day we meet to walk the line
And set the wall between us once again.
15   We keep the wall between us as we go.
To each the boulders that have fallen to each.
And some are loaves and some so nearly balls
We have to use a spell to make them balance:
"Stay where you are until our backs are turned!"
20   We wear our fingers rough with handling them.
Oh, just another kind of outdoor game,
One on a side. It comes to little more:

There where it is we do not need the wall:
He is all pine and I am apple orchard.
25   My apple trees will never get across
And eat the cones under his pines, I tell him.
He only says, "Good fences make good neighbors."
Spring is the mischief in me, and I wonder
If I could put a notion in his head:
30   "*Why* do they make good neighbors? Isn't it
Where there are cows? But here there are no cows.
Before I built a wall I'd ask to know
What I was walling in or walling out,
And to whom I was like to give offense.
31   Something there is that doesn't love a wall,
That wants it down." I could say "Elves" to him,
But it's not elves exactly, and I'd rather
He said it for himself. I see him there
Bringing a stone grasped firmly by the top
40   In each hand, like an old-stone savage armed.
He moves in darkness as it seems to me,
Not of woods only and the shade of trees.
He will not go behind his father's saying,
And he likes having thought of it so well
45   He says again, "Good fences make good neighbors."

Robert D. Putnam (1941–) is a political scientist and professor of public policy at the Harvard University John F. Kennedy School of Government. In "Bowling Alone," he uses the example of individual versus league bowling to illustrate the instance of declining involvement in social organizations in communities across the United States. While this essay generated a lot of controversy over Putnam's qualification of what serves as social capital, and how it is measured, the central point of Putnam's argument remains clear: membership in traditional social organizations has declined steadily since its apex in the 1960s. In "Bowling Alone," Putnam explores possible reasons for this, and how this may be a negative trend for America as a whole.

Bowling Alone:
America's Declining Social Capital

Robert D. Putnam

1   Many students of the new democracies that have emerged over the past decade and a half have emphasized the importance of a strong and active civil society to the consolidation of democracy. Especially with regard to the postcommunist countries, scholars and democratic activists alike have lamented the absence or obliteration of traditions of independent civic engagement and a widespread tendency toward passive reliance on the state. To those concerned with the weakness of civil societies in the developing or postcommunist world, the advanced Western democracies and above all the United States have typically been taken as models to be emulated. There is striking evidence, however, that the vibrancy of American civil society has notably declined over the past several decades.

2   Ever since the publication of Alexis de Tocqueville's *Democracy in America*, the United States has played a central role in systematic studies of the links between democracy and civil society. Although this is in part because trends in American life are often regarded as harbingers of social modernization, it is also because America has traditionally been considered unusually "civic" (a reputation that, as we shall later see, has not been entirely unjustified).

3   When Tocqueville visited the United States in the 1830s, it was the Americans' propensity for civic association that most impressed him as the key to their unprecedented ability to make democracy work. "Americans of all ages, all stations in life, and all types of disposition," he observed, "are forever forming associations. There are not only commercial and industrial associations in which all take part, but others of a thousand different types—religious, moral, serious, futile, very general and very limited, immensely large and very minute. . . . Nothing, in my view, deserves more attention than the intellectual and moral associations in America."[1]

4   Recently, American social scientists of a neo-Tocquevillean bent have unearthed a wide range of empirical evidence that the quality of public life and the performance of social institutions (and not only in America) are indeed powerfully influenced by norms and networks of civic engagement. Researchers in such fields as education, urban poverty, unemployment, the control of crime and drug abuse, and even health have discovered that successful outcomes are more likely in civically engaged communities. Similarly, research on the varying economic attainments of different ethnic groups in the United States has demonstrated the importance of social bonds within each group. These results are consistent with research in a wide range of settings that demonstrates the vital importance of social networks for job placement and many other economic outcomes.

5   Meanwhile, a seemingly unrelated body of research on the sociology of economic development has also focused attention on the role of social networks. Some of this work is situated in the developing countries, and some of it elucidates the peculiarly successful "network capitalism" of East Asia.[2] Even in less exotic Western economies, however, researchers have discovered highly efficient, highly flexible "industrial districts" based on networks of collaboration among workers and small entrepreneurs. Far from being paleoindustrial anachronisms, these dense interpersonal and interorganizational networks undergird ultramodern industries, from the high tech of Silicon Valley to the high fashion of Benetton.

6   The norms and networks of civic engagement also powerfully affect the performance of representative government. That, at least, was the central conclusion of my own 20-year, quasi-experimental study of subnational governments in different regions of Italy.[3] Although all

these regional governments seemed identical on paper, their levels of effectiveness varied dramatically. Systematic inquiry showed that the quality of governance was determined by long-standing traditions of civic engagement (or its absence). Voter turnout, newspaper readership, membership in choral societies and football clubs—these were the hallmarks of a successful region. In fact, historical analysis suggested that these networks of organized reciprocity and civic solidarity, far from being an epiphenomenon of socioeconomic modernization, were a precondition for it.

7   No doubt the mechanisms through which civic engagement and social connectedness produce such results—better schools, faster economic development, lower crime, and more effective government—are multiple and complex. While these briefly recounted findings require further confirmation and perhaps qualification, the parallels across hundreds of empirical studies in a dozen disparate disciplines and subfields are striking. Social scientists in several fields have recently suggested a common framework for understanding these phenomena, a framework that rests on the concept of *social capital*.[4] By analogy with notions of physical capital and human capital—tools and training that enhance individual productivity —"social capital" refers to features of social organization such as networks, norms, and social trust that facilitate coordination and cooperation for mutual benefit.

8   For a variety of reasons, life is easier in a community blessed with a substantial stock of social capital. In the first place, networks of civic engagement foster sturdy norms of generalized reciprocity and encourage the emergence of social trust. Such networks facilitate coordination and communication, amplify reputations, and thus allow dilemmas of collective action to be resolved. When economic and political negotiation is embedded in dense networks of social interaction, incentives for opportunism are reduced. At the same time, networks of civic engagement embody past success at collaboration, which can serve as a cultural template for future collaboration. Finally, dense networks of interaction probably broaden the participants' sense of self, developing the "I" into the "we," or (in the language of rational-choice theorists) enhancing the participants' "taste" for collective benefits.

9   I do not intend here to survey (much less contribute to) the development of the theory of social capital. Instead, I use the central premise

of that rapidly growing body of work—that social connections and civic engagement pervasively influence our public life, as well as our private prospects—as the starting point for an empirical survey of trends in social capital in contemporary America. I concentrate here entirely on the American case, although the developments I portray may in some measure characterize many contemporary societies.

Whatever Happened to Civic Engagement?

10   We begin with familiar evidence on changing patterns of political participation, not least because it is immediately relevant to issues of democracy in the narrow sense. Consider the well-known decline in turnout in national elections over the last three decades. From a relative high point in the early 1960s, voter turnout had by 1990 declined by nearly a quarter; tens of millions of Americans had forsaken their parents' habitual readiness to engage in the simplest act of citizenship. Broadly similar trends also characterize participation in state and local elections.

11   It is not just the voting booth that has been increasingly deserted by Americans. A series of identical questions posed by the Roper Organization to national samples ten times each year over the last two decades reveals that since 1973 the number of Americans who report that "in the past year" they have "attended a public meeting on town or school affairs" has fallen by more than a third (from 22 percent in 1973 to 13 percent in 1993). Similar (or even greater) relative declines are evident in responses to questions about attending a political rally or speech, serving on a committee of some local organization, and working for a political party. By almost every measure, Americans' direct engagement in politics and government has fallen steadily and sharply over the last generation, despite the fact that average levels of education—the best individual-level predictor of political participation—have risen sharply throughout this period. Every year over the last decade or two, millions more have withdrawn from the affairs of their communities.

12   Not coincidentally, Americans have also disengaged psychologically from politics and government over this era. The proportion of Americans who reply that they "trust the government in Washington" only "some of the time" or "almost never" has risen steadily from 30 percent in 1966 to 75 percent in 1992.

13 These trends are well known, of course, and taken by themselves would seem amenable to a strictly political explanation. Perhaps the long litany of political tragedies and scandals since the 1960s (assassinations, Vietnam, Watergate, Irangate, and so on) has triggered an understandable disgust for politics and government among Americans, and that in turn has motivated their withdrawal. I do not doubt that this common interpretation has some merit, but its limitations become plain when we examine trends in civic engagement of a wider sort.

14 Our survey of organizational membership among Americans can usefully begin with a glance at the aggregate results of the General Social Survey, a scientifically conducted, national-sample survey that has been repeated 14 times over the last two decades. Church-related groups constitute the most common type of organization joined by Americans; they are especially popular with women. Other types of organizations frequently joined by women include school-service groups (mostly parent-teacher associations), sports groups, professional societies, and literary societies. Among men, sports clubs, labor unions, professional societies, fraternal groups, veterans' groups, and service clubs are all relatively popular.

15 Religious affiliation is by far the most common associational membership among Americans. Indeed, by many measures America continues to be (even more than in Tocqueville's time) an astonishingly "churched" society. For example, the United States has more houses of worship per capita than any other nation on Earth. Yet religious sentiment in America seems to be becoming somewhat less tied to institutions and more self-defined.

16 How have these complex crosscurrents played out over the last three or four decades in terms of Americans' engagement with organized religion? The general pattern is clear: The 1960s witnessed a significant drop in reported weekly churchgoing—from roughly 48 percent in the late 1950s to roughly 41 percent in the early 1970s. Since then, it has stagnated or (according to some surveys) declined still further. Meanwhile, data from the General Social Survey show a modest decline in membership in all "church-related groups" over the last 20 years. It would seem, then, that net participation by Americans, both in religious services and in church-related groups, has declined modestly (by perhaps a sixth) since the 1960s.

17 For many years, labor unions provided one of the most common organizational affiliations among American workers. Yet union membership has been falling for nearly four decades, with the steepest decline occurring between 1975 and 1985. Since the mid-1950s, when union membership peaked, the unionized portion of the nonagricultural work force in America has dropped by more than half, falling from 32.5 percent in 1953 to 15.8 percent in 1992. By now, virtually all of the explosive growth in union membership that was associated with the New Deal has been erased. The solidarity of union halls is now mostly a fading memory of aging men.[5]

18 The parent-teacher association (PTA) has been an especially important form of civic engagement in twentieth-century America because parental involvement in the educational process represents a particularly productive form of social capital. It is, therefore, dismaying to discover that participation in parent-teacher organizations has dropped drastically over the last generation, from more than 12 million in 1964 to barely 5 million in 1982 before recovering to approximately 7 million now.

19 Next, we turn to evidence on membership in (and volunteering for) civic and fraternal organizations. These data show some striking patterns. First, membership in traditional women's groups has declined more or less steadily since the mid-1960s. For example, membership in the national Federation of Women's Clubs is down by more than half (59 percent) since 1964, while membership in the League of Women Voters (LWV) is off 42 percent since 1969.[6]

20 Similar reductions are apparent in the numbers of volunteers for mainline civic organizations, such as the Boy Scouts (off by 26 percent since 1970) and the Red Cross (off by 61 percent since 1970). But what about the possibility that volunteers have simply switched their loyalties to other organizations? Evidence on "regular" (as opposed to occasional or "drop-by") volunteering is available from the Labor Department's Current Population Surveys of 1974 and 1989. These estimates suggest that serious volunteering declined by roughly one-sixth over these 15 years, from 24 percent of adults in 1974 to 20 percent in 1989. The multitudes of Red Cross aides and Boy Scout troop leaders now missing in action have apparently not been offset by equal numbers of new recruits elsewhere.

21   Fraternal organizations have also witnessed a substantial drop in membership during the 1980s and 1990s. Membership is down significantly in such groups as the Lions (off 12 percent since 1983), the Elks (off 18 percent since 1979), the Shriners (off 27 percent since 1979), the Jaycees (off 44 percent since 1979), and the Masons (down 39 percent since 1959). In sum, after expanding steadily throughout most of this century, many major civic organizations have experienced a sudden, substantial, and nearly simultaneous decline in membership over the last decade or two.

22   The most whimsical yet discomfiting bit of evidence of social disengagement in contemporary America that I have discovered is this: more Americans are bowling today than ever before, but bowling in organized leagues has plummeted in the last decade or so. Between 1980 and 1993 the total number of bowlers in America increased by 10 percent, while league bowling decreased by 40 percent. (Lest this be thought a wholly trivial example, I should note that nearly 80 million Americans went bowling at least once during 1993, *nearly a third more than voted in the 1994 congressional elections* and roughly the same number as claim to attend church regularly. Even after the 1980s' plunge in league bowling, nearly 3 percent of American adults regularly bowl in leagues.) The rise of solo bowling threatens the livelihood of bowling-lane proprietors because those who bowl as members of leagues consume three times as much beer and pizza as solo bowlers, and the money in bowling is in the beer and pizza, not the balls and shoes. The broader social significance, however, lies in the social interaction and even occasionally civic conversations over beer and pizza that solo bowlers forgo. Whether or not bowling beats balloting in the eyes of most Americans, bowling teams illustrate yet another vanishing form of social capital.

Countertrends

23   At this point, however, we must confront a serious counterargument. Perhaps the traditional forms of civic organization whose decay we have been tracing have been replaced by vibrant new organizations. For example, national environmental organizations (like the Sierra Club) and feminist groups (like the National Organization for Women) grew rapidly during the 1970s and 1980s and now count

hundreds of thousands of dues-paying members. An even more dramatic example is the American Association of Retired Persons (AARP), which grew exponentially from 400,000 card-carrying members in 1960 to 33 million in 1993, becoming (after the Catholic Church) the largest private organization in the world. The national administrators of these organizations are among the most feared lobbyists in Washington, in large part because of their massive mailing lists of presumably loyal members.

24   These new mass-membership organizations are plainly of great political importance. From the point of view of social connectedness, however, they are sufficiently different from classic "secondary associations" that we need to invent a new label—perhaps "tertiary associations." For the vast majority of their members, the only act of membership consists in writing a check for dues or perhaps occasionally reading a newsletter. Few ever attend any meetings of such organizations, and most are unlikely ever (knowingly) to encounter any other member. The bond between any two members of the Sierra Club is less like the bond between any two members of a gardening club and more like the bond between any two Red Sox fans (or perhaps any two devoted Honda owners): they root for the same team and they share some of the same interests, but they are unaware of each other's existence. Their ties, in short, are to common symbols, common leaders, and perhaps common ideals, but not to one another. The theory of social capital argues that associational membership should, for example, increase social trust, but this prediction is much less straightforward with regard to membership in tertiary associations. From the point of view of social connectedness, the Environmental Defense Fund and a bowling league are just not in the same category.

25   If the growth of tertiary organizations represents one potential (but probably not real) counterexample to my thesis, a second countertrend is represented by the growing prominence of nonprofit organizations, especially nonprofit service agencies. This so-called third sector includes everything from Oxfam and the Metropolitan Museum of Art to the Ford Foundation and the Mayo Clinic. In other words, although most secondary associations are nonprofits, most nonprofit agencies are not secondary associations. To identify trends in the size of the nonprofit sector with trends in social connectedness would be another fundamental conceptual mistake.[7]

26   A third potential countertrend is much more relevant to an assessment of social capital and civic engagement. Some able researchers have argued that the last few decades have witnessed a rapid expansion in "support groups" of various sorts. Robert Wuthnow reports that fully 40 percent of all Americans claim to be "currently involved in [a] small group that meets regularly and provides support or caring for those who participate in it."8 Many of these groups are religiously affiliated, but many others are not. For example, nearly 5 percent of Wuthnow's national sample claim to participate regularly in a "self-help" group, such as Alcoholics Anonymous, and nearly as many say they belong to book-discussion groups and hobby clubs.

27   The groups described by Wuthnow's respondents unquestionably represent an important form of social capital, and they need to be accounted for in any serious reckoning of trends in social connectedness. On the other hand, they do not typically play the same role as traditional civic associations. As Wuthnow emphasizes,

> Small groups may not be fostering community as effectively as many of their proponents would like. Some small groups merely provide occasions for individuals to focus on themselves in the presence of others. The social contract binding members together asserts only the weakest of obligations. Come if you have time. Talk if you feel like it. Respect everyone's opinion. Never criticize. Leave quietly if you become dissatisfied. . . . We can imagine that [these small groups] really substitute for families, neighborhoods, and broader community attachments that may demand lifelong commitments, when, in fact, they do not.9

28   All three of these potential countertrends—tertiary organizations, nonprofit organizations, and support groups—need somehow to be weighed against the erosion of conventional civic organizations. One way of doing so is to consult the General Social Survey.

29   Within all educational categories, total associational membership declined significantly between 1967 and 1993. Among the college-educated, the average number of group memberships per person fell from 2.8 to 2.0 (a 26-percent decline); among high-school graduates, the number fell from 1.8 to 1.2 (32 percent),and among those with fewer than 12 years of education, the number fell from 1.4 to 1. 1 (25 percent). In other words, at *all* educational (and hence social) levels of American society, and counting *all* sorts of group memberships, *the average number of associational memberships has fallen by about a fourth over the last quarter-century.* Without controls for educational levels,

the trend is not nearly so clear, but the central point is this: *more Americans than ever before are in social circumstances that foster associational involvement (higher education, middle age, and so on), but nevertheless aggregate associational membership appears to be stagnant or declining.*

30   Broken down by type of group, the downward trend is most marked for church-related groups, for labor unions, for fraternal and veterans' organizations, and for school-service groups. Conversely, membership in professional associations has risen over these years, although less than might have been predicted, given sharply rising educational and occupational levels. Essentially the same trends are evident for both men and women in the sample. In short, the available survey evidence confirms our earlier conclusion: American social capital in the form of civic associations has significantly eroded over the last generation.

Good Neighborliness and Social Trust

31   I noted earlier that most readily available quantitative evidence on trends in social connectedness involves formal settings, such as the voting booth, the union hall, or the PTA. One glaring exception is so widely discussed as to require little comment here: the most fundamental form of social capital is the family, and the massive evidence of the loosening of bonds within the family (both extended and nuclear) is well known. This trend, of course, is quite consistent with—and may help to explain—our theme of social decapitalization.

32   A second aspect of informal social capital on which we happen to have reasonably reliable time-series data involves neighborliness. In each General Social Survey since 1974 respondents have been asked, "How often do you spend a social evening with a neighbor?" The proportion of Americans who socialize with their neighbors more than once a year has slowly but steadily declined over the last two decades, from 72 percent in 1974 to 61 percent in 1993. (On the other hand, socializing with "friends who do not live in your neighborhood" appears to be on the increase, a trend that may reflect the growth of workplace-based social connections.)

33   Americans are also less trusting. The proportion of Americans saying that most people can be trusted fell by more than a third between 1960, when 58 percent chose that alternative, and 1993, when only 37 percent did. The same trend is apparent in all educational groups; indeed, because social trust is also correlated with education and

because educational levels have risen sharply, the overall decrease in social trust is even more apparent if we control for education.

34 Our discussion of trends in social connectedness and civic engagement has tacitly assumed that all the forms of social capital that we have discussed are themselves coherently correlated across individuals. This is in fact true. Members of associations are much more likely than non-members to participate in politics, to spend time with neighbors, to express social trust, and so on.

35 The close correlation between social trust and associational membership is true not only across time and across individuals, but also across countries. Evidence from the 1991 World Values Survey demonstrates the following:[10]

1. Across the 35 countries in this survey, social trust and civic engagement are strongly correlated; the greater the density of associational membership in a society, the more trusting its citizens. Trust and engagement are two facets of the same underlying factor—social capital.

2. America still ranks relatively high by cross-national standards on both these dimensions of social capital. Even in the 1990s, after several decades' erosion, Americans are more trusting and more engaged than people in most other countries of the world.

3. The trends of the past quarter-century, however, have apparently moved the United States significantly lower in the international rankings of social capital. The recent deterioration in American social capital has been sufficiently great that (if no other country changed its position in the meantime) another quarter-century of change at the same rate would bring the United States, roughly speaking, to the midpoint among all these countries, roughly equivalent to South Korea, Belgium, or Estonia today. Two generations' decline at the same rate would leave the United States at the level of today's Chile, Portugal, and Slovenia.

Why Is U.S. Social Capital Eroding?

36 As we have seen, something has happened in America in the last two or three decades to diminish civic engagement and social connectedness. What could that "something" be? Here are several possible explanations, along with some initial evidence on each.

37   *The movement of women into the labor force.* Over these same two or three decades, many millions of American women have moved out of the home into paid employment. This is the primary, though not the sole, reason why the weekly working hours of the average American have increased significantly during these years. It seems highly plausible that this social revolution should have reduced the time and energy available for building social capital. For certain organizations, such as the PTA, the League of Women Voters, the Federation of Women's Clubs, and the Red Cross, this is almost certainly an important part of the story. The sharpest decline in women's civic participation seems to have come in the 1970s; membership in such "women's" organizations as these has been virtually halved since the late 1960s. By contrast, most of the decline in participation in men's organizations occurred about ten years later; the total decline to date has been approximately 25 percent for the typical organization. On the other hand, the survey data imply that the aggregate declines for men are virtually as great as those for women. It is logically possible, of course, that the male declines might represent the knock-on effect of women's liberation, as dishwashing crowded out the lodge, but time-budget studies suggest that most husbands of working wives have assumed only a minor part of the housework. In short, something besides the women's revolution seems to lie behind the erosion of social capital.

38   *Mobility: The "re-potting" hypothesis.* Numerous studies of organizational involvement have shown that residential stability and such related phenomena as homeownership are clearly associated with greater civic engagement. Mobility, like frequent re-potting of plants, tends to disrupt root systems, and it takes time for an uprooted individual to put down new roots. It seems plausible that the automobile, suburbanization, and the movement to the Sun Belt have reduced the social rootedness of the average American, but one fundamental difficulty with this hypothesis is apparent: the best evidence shows that residential stability and homeownership in America have risen modestly since 1965, and are surely higher now than during the 1950s, when civic engagement and social connectedness by our measures was definitely higher.

39   *Other demographic transformations.* A range of additional changes have transformed the American family since the 1960s—fewer marriages,

more divorces, fewer children, lower real wages, and so on. Each of these changes might account for some of the slackening of civic engagement, since married, middle-class parents are generally more socially involved than other people. Moreover, the changes in scale that have swept over the American economy in these years—illustrated by the replacement of the corner grocery by the supermarket and now perhaps of the supermarket by electronic shopping at home, or the replacement of community-based enterprises by outposts of distant multinational firms—may perhaps have undermined the material and even physical basis for civic engagement.

40 *The technological transformation of leisure.* There is reason to believe that deep-seated technological trends are radically "privatizing" or "individualizing" our use of leisure time and thus disrupting many opportunities for social-capital formation. The most obvious and probably the most powerful instrument of this revolution is television. Time-budget studies in the 1960s showed that the growth in time spent watching television dwarfed all other changes in the way Americans passed their days and nights. Television has made our communities (or, rather, what we experience as our communities) wider and shallower. In the language of economics, electronic technology enables individual tastes to be satisfied more fully, but at the cost of the positive social externalities associated with more primitive forms of entertainment. The same logic applies to the replacement of vaudeville by the movies and now of movies by the VCR. The new "virtual reality" helmets that we will soon don to be entertained in total isolation are merely the latest extension of this trend. Is technology thus driving a wedge between our individual interests and our collective interests? It is a question that seems worth exploring more systematically.

What Is to Be Done?

41 The last refuge of a social-scientific scoundrel is to call for more research. Nevertheless, I cannot forbear from suggesting some further lines of inquiry.

- We must sort out the dimensions of social capital, which clearly is not a unidimensional concept, despite language (even in this essay) that implies the contrary. What types of organizations and networks most effectively embody—or generate—social capital, in the sense of mutual reciprocity, the resolution of dilemmas of collective action, and the broadening of social identities? In this essay I have emphasized the density of associational life. In earlier work I stressed the structure of networks, arguing that "horizontal" ties represented more productive social capital than vertical ties.[11]

- Another set of important issues involves macrosociological cross-currents that might intersect with the trends described here. What will be the impact, for example, of electronic networks on social capital? My hunch is that meeting in an electronic forum is not the equivalent of meeting in a bowling alley—or even in a saloon—but hard empirical research is needed. What about the development of social capital in the workplace? Is it growing in counterpoint to the decline of civic engagement, reflecting some social analogue of the first law of thermodynamics—social capital is neither created nor destroyed, merely redistributed? Or do the trends described in this essay represent a deadweight loss?

- A rounded assessment of changes in American social capital over the last quarter-century needs to count the costs as well as the benefits of community engagement. We must not romanticize small-town, middle-class civic life in the America of the 1950s. In addition to the deleterious trends emphasized in this essay, recent decades have witnessed a substantial decline in intolerance and probably also in overt discrimination, and those beneficent trends may be related in complex ways to the erosion of traditional social capital. Moreover, a balanced accounting of the social-capital books would need to reconcile the insights of this approach with the undoubted insights offered by Mancur Olson and others who stress that closely knit social, economic, and political organizations are prone to inefficient cartelization and to what political economists term "rent seeking" and ordinary men and women call corruption.[12]

- Finally, and perhaps most urgently, we need to explore creatively how public policy impinges on (or might impinge on) social-capital formation. In some well-known instances, public policy has destroyed highly effective social networks and norms. American slum-clearance policy of the 1950s and 1960s, for example, renovated physical capital, but at a very high cost to existing social capital. The consolidation of country post offices and small school districts has promised administrative and financial efficiencies, but full-cost accounting for the effects of these policies on social capital might produce a more negative verdict. On the other hand, such past initiatives as the county agricultural-agent system, community colleges, and tax deductions for charitable contributions illustrate that government can encourage social-capital formation. Even a recent proposal in San Luis Obispo, California, to require that all new houses have front porches illustrates the power of government to influence where and how networks are formed.

42　The concept of "civil society" has played a central role in the recent global debate about the preconditions for democracy and democratization. In the newer democracies this phrase has properly focused attention on the need to foster a vibrant civic life in soils traditionally inhospitable to self-government. In the established democracies, ironically, growing numbers of citizens are questioning the effectiveness of their public institutions at the very moment when liberal democracy has swept the battlefield, both ideologically and geopolitically. In America, at least, there is reason to suspect that this democratic disarray may be linked to a broad and continuing erosion of civic engagement that began a quarter-century ago. High on our scholarly agenda should be the question of whether a comparable erosion of social capital may be under way in other advanced democracies, perhaps in different institutional and behavioral guises. High on America's agenda should be the question of how to reverse these adverse trends in social connectedness, thus restoring civic engagement and civic trust.

Notes

1　Alexis de Tocqueville, *Democracy in America*, ed. J.P. Maier, trans. George Lawrence (Garden City, N.Y.: Anchor Books, 1969), 513–17.

2　On social networks and economic growth in the developing world, see Milton J. Esman and Norman Uphoff, *Local Organizations: Intermediaries in Rural Development* (Ithaca: Cornell University Press, 1984), esp. 15–42 and 99–180; and Albert O. Hirschman, *Getting Ahead Collectively: Grassroots Experiences in Latin America* (Elmsford, N.Y. : Pergamon Press, 1984), esp. 42–77. On East Asia, see Gustav Papanek, "The New Asian Capitalism: An Economic Portrait," in Peter L. Berger and Hsin-Huang Michael Hsiao, eds., *In Search of an East Asian Development Model* (New Brunswick, N.J.: Transaction, 1987), 27–80; Peter B. Evans, "The

State as Problem and Solution: Predation, Embedded Autonomy and Structural Change," in Stephan Haggard and Robert R. Kaufman, eds., *The Politics of Economic Adjustment* (Princeton: Princeton University Press, 1992), 139–81; and Gary G. Hamilton, William Zeile, and Wan-Jin Kim, "Network Structure of East Asian Economies," in Stewart R. Clegg and S. Gordon Redding, eds., *Capitalism in Contrasting Cultures* (Hawthome, N.Y.: De Gruyter, 1990), 105–29. See also Gary G. Hamilton and Nicole Woolsey Biggart, "Market, Culture, and Authority: A Comparative Analysis of Management and Organization in the Far East," *American Journal of Sociology* (Supplement) 94 (1988): S52–S94; and Susan Greenhalgh, "Families and Networks in Taiwan's Economic Development," in Edwin Winckler and Susan Greenhalgh, eds., *Contending Approaches to the Political Economy of Taiwan* (Armonk, N.Y.: M.E. Sharpe, 1987), 224–45.

[3] Robert D. Putnam, *Making Democracy Work: Civic Traditions in Modern Italy* (Princeton: Princeton University Press, 1993).

[4] James S. Coleman deserves primary credit for developing the "social capital" theoretical framework. See his "Social Capital in the Creation of Human Capital," *American Journal of Sociology* (Supplement) 94 (1988): S95–S 120, as well as his *The Foundations of Social Theory* (Cambridge: Harvard University Press, 1990), 300–21. See also Mark Granovetter, "Economic Action and Social Structure: The Problem of Embeddedness," *American Journal of Sociology* 91 (1985): 481–510; Glenn C. Loury, "Why Should We Care About Group Inequality?" *Social Philosophy and Policy* 5 (1987): 249–71; and Robert D. Putnam, "The Prosperous Community: Social Capital and Public Life," *American Prospect* 13 (1993): 35–42. To my knowledge, the first scholar to use the term "social capital" in its current sense was Jane Jacobs, in *The Death and Life of Great American Cities* (New York: Random House, 1961), 138.

[5] Any simplistically political interpretation of the collapse of American unionism would need to confront the fact that the steepest decline began more than six years before the Reagan administration's attack on PATCO. Data from the General Social Survey show a roughly 40–percent decline in reported union membership between 1975 and 1991.

[6] Data for the LWV are available over a longer time span and show an interesting pattern: a sharp slump during the Depression, a strong and sustained rise after World War II that more than tripled membership between 1945 and 1969, and then the post-1969 decline, which has already erased virtually all the postwar gains and continues still. This same historical pattern applies to those men's fraternal organizations for which comparable data are available—steady increases for the first seven decades of the century, interrupted only by the Great Depression, followed by a collapse in the 1970s and 1980s that has already wiped out most of the postwar expansion and continues apace.

[7] Cf. Lester M. Salamon, "The Rise of the Nonprofit Sector," *Foreign Affairs* 73 (July–August 1994): 109–22. See also Salamon, "Partners in Public Service: The Scope and Theory of Government-Nonprofit Relations," in Walter W. Powell, ed., *The Nonprofit Sector: A Research Handbook* (New Haven: Yale University Press, 1987), 99–117. Salamon's empirical evidence does not sustain his broad

claims about a global "associational revolution" comparable in significance to the rise of the nation-state several centuries ago.

[8] Robert Wuthnow, *Sharing the Journey: Support Groups and America's New Quest for Community* (New York: The Free Press, 1994), 45.

[9] Ibid., 3–6.

[10] I am grateful to Ronald Inglehart, who directs this unique cross-national project, for sharing these highly useful data with me. See his "The Impact of Culture on Economic Development: Theory, Hypotheses, and Some Empirical Tests" (unpublished manuscript, University of Michigan, 1994).

[11] See my *Making Democracy Work*, esp. ch. 6.

[12] See Mancur Olson, *The Rise and Decline of Nations: Economic Growth, Stagflation, and Social Rigidities* (New Haven: Yale University Press, 1982), 2.

In "Still Bowling Alone? The Post-9/11 Split," Thomas H. Sander and Robert D. Putnam celebrate the increase in civic engagement in the wake of 9/11, which shows most significantly in the "9/11 generation." However, Sander and Putnam also express reservations about demographic aspects of this increase in social participation. Engagement has increased far more in the white upper-middle class than in any other demographic, and this split poses the risk of exacerbating the widening social gaps among American communities. The authors suggest that increased civic engagement is a good thing, but that it is necessary to examine the potential negative consequences of continued improvement only in the upper socioeconomic classes.

Still Bowling Alone?
The Post-9/11 Split

Thomas H. Sander and Robert D. Putnam

1 Exactly fifteen years ago, the *Journal of Democracy* published in its fifth anniversary issue an article by Robert D. Putnam entitled "Bowling Alone: America's Declining Social Capital."[1] The essay struck a chord with readers who had watched their voting precincts empty out, their favorite bowling alleys or Elks lodges close for lack of patrons and members, and their once-regular card games and dinner parties become sporadic. Marshaling evidence of such trends, the article galvanized widespread concern about the weakening of civic engagement in the United States. But it also roused deep interest in the broader concept of "social capital"—a term that social scientists use as shorthand for social networks and the norms of reciprocity and trust to which those networks give rise. No democracy, and indeed no society, can be healthy without at least a modicum of this resource.

2 Even though Putnam's article and subsequent book-length study *Bowling Alone: The Collapse and Revival of American Community*[2] focused on the United States, scholars and political leaders around the world were seized by the question of how to foster the growth

138

and improve the quality of social capital.[3] This interest was not altogether surprising, as research in a variety of fields was demonstrating that social capital makes citizens happier and healthier, reduces crime, makes government more responsive and honest, and improves economic productivity.[4]

3 The trend that "Bowling Alone" spotlighted was alarming: By many measures, since the 1960s or 1970s Americans had been withdrawing from their communities. Attendance at public meetings plunged by nearly half between 1973 and 1994. The family dinner seemed at risk of becoming an endangered species. Trust in strangers took a sharp drop: In the early 1960s, more than half of all Americans said that they trusted others; fewer than a third say the same thing today. In the 1990s, as Americans' social connections withered, they increasingly watched *Friends* rather than had friends. Sociologists who had once been skeptical of Putnam's findings found to their dismay that over the last two decades the incidence of close friendships had declined.[5] As of 2004, a quarter of those polled in the United States reported that they lacked a confidant with whom to discuss important personal matters (the 1983 figure had been less than half that), and nearly half of all respondents reported being only one confidant away from social isolation. Since social isolation (that is, the lack of any confidants) strongly predicts premature death, these are sobering statistics.

4 Both *Bowling Alone* and a 2001 Harvard report known as *Better Together*[6] argued that America could be civically restored in two ways: by encouraging adults to socialize more, join more groups, or volunteer more; and by teaching the young, whose habits are more malleable, to be increasingly socially connected.

5 Americans need only look back two generations to see just how committed to civic life a generation can be. The "Greatest Generation" celebrated by Tom Brokaw's book of that name grew up amid the sense of solidarity generated by the Second World War and before the rise of television and its civically noxious influence. In comparison with their grandchildren, Americans born before 1930 were twice as trusting, 75 percent more likely to vote, and more than twice as likely to take part in community projects.[7] But the Greatest Generation, who viewed helping others as downright American, never managed to pass their

civic traits on to their "Baby Boomer" children (born between 1946 and 1964) or their "Generation X" grandchildren (born during the late 1960s and the 1970s). As its older civic stalwarts have died off, America's population has become less engaged year by year.

6   Nevertheless, surveying the landscape of the late 1990s, *Bowling Alone* spotted one hopeful trend: an increase in youth volunteering that potentially heralded broader generational engagement. Putnam noted that the task of sparking this greater engagement "would be eased by a palpable national crisis, like war or depression or natural disaster, but for better and for worse, America at the dawn of the new century faces no such galvanizing crisis."[8]

Newly Engaged? The Rise of the Post-9/11 Generation

7   Just a year after those words were written, a massive national crisis struck. The terrorists who carried out the 9/11 attacks were aiming to ruin America's confidence and resolve, but the roughly three-thousand

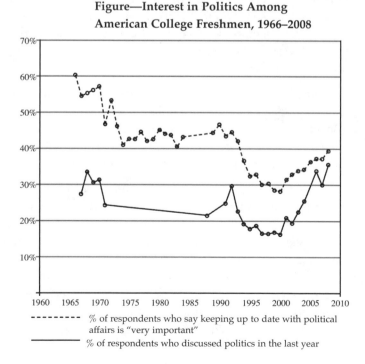

Figure—Interest in Politics Among American College Freshmen, 1966–2008

- - - - - - - -   % of respondents who say keeping up to date with political affairs is "very important"

————————   % of respondents who discussed politics in the last year

days that have passed since that fateful day seem instead to have strengthened the civic conscience of young people in the United States.

8 Whether they were in college, high school, or even grade school when the twin towers and the Pentagon were hit, the members of the 9/11 generation[9] were in their most impressionable years and as a result seem to grasp their civic and mutual responsibilities far more firmly than do their parents. While the upswing in volunteering that Putnam observed in the mid-1990s may have been largely an effect of school-graduation requirements or the desire to gain an edge while seeking admission to selective colleges,[10] the years since 9/11 have brought an unmistakable expansion of youth interest in politics and public affairs. For example, young collegians' interest in politics has rapidly increased in the last eight years, an increase all the more remarkable given its arrival on the heels of thirty years of steady decline. From 1967 to 2000, the share of college freshmen who said that they had "discussed politics" in the previous twelve months dropped from 27 to 16 percent; since 2001, it has more than doubled and is now at an all-time high of 36 percent.

9 First-year college students also evince a long-term decline and then post-2001 rise in interest in "keeping up to date with political affairs."[11] Surveys of high-school seniors show a similar and simultaneous decline and then rise in civic engagement.[12] Moreover, between 2000 and 2008, voting rates rose more than three times faster for Americans under age 29 than they did for Americans over 30.[13] The turning point in 2001 is unmistakable. On college campuses nationwide, this civic-engagement "youth movement" has evoked the spirit of the early John F. Kennedy years.

10 While the post-9/11 spike in community-mindedness among adults was short-lived, the shift appears more lasting among those who experienced the attacks during their impressionable adolescent years.[14] Why? As we wrote four years after 9/11:

> The attacks and their aftermath demonstrated that our fates are highly interdependent. We learned that we need to—and can—depend on the kindness of strangers who happen to be near us in a plane, office building or subway. Moreover, regardless of one's political leanings, it is easy to see that we needed effective governmental action: to coordinate volunteers, police national borders, design emergency response preparedness, engage in diplomacy, and train police and firefighters. Government and politics

mattered. If young people used to wonder why they should bother to vote, Sept[ember] 11 . . . gave them an answer. [15]

11   If this effect persists among young people who lived through 9/11, the inevitable turnover of generations will provide the cause of civic engagement with a powerful following wind. Amid such generational change, even if no present-day *adults* deepen their community engagement, the United States may witness a gradual yet inexorable reversal of the civic decline that *Bowling Alone* chronicled.

12   The final size of the "Post-9/11 Generation" remains unclear, however, since its lower age boundary is still a mystery. How likely is it that those who were grade-schoolers in 2001 will be counted as members of this generation? One less than encouraging hint may be gleaned from anecdotal evidence suggesting that those born in the early to mid-1990s increasingly say that they cannot remember 9/11.[16] How decisive can that day be for those who never had or no longer possess a vivid firsthand memory of it? Educators are experimenting with programs to freshen the memory of 9/11 among younger Americans, but a solitary lesson plan is likely to have far less impact than the raw immediacy of the suicide attacks and the pervasive discussions and reflection that followed. This suggests that while the 9/11 Generation is real, the attack's effects may be most concentrated among Americans born in the 1980s.

13   In his 2008 campaign for the U.S. presidency, Barack Obama ably surfed this wave of post-9/11 youthful civic engagement. Though the initial ripple had been visible years before he became a national figure, he and his campaign mightily amplified it. Some credit Internet-based social networking for bolstering youthful interest in politics and community life, but the advent of the well-known social-networking sites Facebook (2004) and Twitter (2006) occurred years after the initial upturn in civic engagement by young people. Nonetheless, the Obama campaign adroitly deployed classic organizing techniques to expand the impact of such new technologies. For example, the campaign created an iPhone application to enable Obama supporters to rank-order the campaign phone calls that they should make to friends, based on whether their friends lived in swing states; it also compiled millions of mobile-phone numbers and e-mail addresses to mobilize citizens for old-style, face-to-face politicking during the

campaign and after. Campaign workers exploited cutting-edge tech-nology to find volunteers, decide which wards to visit, and record people's political leanings, but relied on old-school door-knocking as the chief means of actually connecting with voters.

14 The Obama campaign, with its heavy use of young volunteers and workers, not only counted on an upwelling of youth civic engage-ment, but contributed to it as well. In the United States, the share of those aged 18 to 29 who avowed complete agreement with the claim that "it's my duty as a citizen to always vote" rose by almost 50 per-cent between 1999 and 2009. During the same years, the comparable rate among those older than 30 stayed flat. A closer look at trends among the 18-to-29 group, moreover, reveals a spike in agreement during the years surrounding the Obama campaign.[17]

15 The long-term civic effects of the Obama campaign on the 9/11 Gen-eration remain uncertain. If Obama's campaign promises on issues such as health care, financial reform, and equality of opportunity go unrealized, young voters could become politically dispirited. Or per-haps such failure would only strengthen their political resolve. As Yogi Berra observed, prediction is hard, especially about the future.

Are Only the Young "Haves" Engaged?

16 The emergence of the 9/11 Generation since 2001 is undoubtedly to be cheered. But it is only part of an ominous larger and longer-term picture whose main feature is a growing civic and social gap in the United States between upper-middle-class young white people and their less affluent counterparts. (A similar gap has not appeared within the ranks of black youth, though an overall black-white gap in engagement remains wide and troubling.)

17 Over the last thirty years, and with growing intensity over the latter half of that period, white high-school seniors from upper middle-class families have steadily *deepened* the degree to which they are engaged in their communities, while white high-school seniors from working- or lower-class backgrounds have shown a propensity to withdraw from (or never undertake) such engagement.[18] Advantaged kids increasingly flocked to church, while working-class kids deserted the pews. Middle-class kids connected more meaningfully with parents,

while working-class kids were increasingly left alone, in large part because single parenting has proliferated among lower- and working-class whites, while becoming rarer among upper-middle-class families. Among "have-not" high-school seniors, trust in other people plummeted, while seniors from the "right side of the tracks" showed no decline at all in social trust. On indicator after indicator—general and academic self-esteem, academic ambition, social friendships, and volunteering—the kids who could be described as the "haves" grew in confidence and engagement while their not-so-well-off contemporaries slipped farther into disengagement with every year.[19] Among other things, this means that the overall rise in youth political engagement and volunteering since 9/11 masks a pair of subtrends that are headed in different directions, with lower-class youth growing less involved while better-off youngsters become more involved. Since public discussion in the United States often tends to conflate class and race, it is important to emphasize that *this* growing gap among different groups of young people is about the former and not just the latter.

18   If the United States is to avoid becoming two nations, it must find ways to expand the post-9/11 resurgence of civic and social engagement beyond the ranks of affluent young white people. The widening gaps that we are seeing in social capital, academic ambition, and self-esteem augur poorly for the life chances of working-class youngsters. If these gaps remain unaddressed, the United States could become less a land of opportunity than a caste society replete with the tightly limited social mobility and simmering resentments that such societies invariably feature.

19   The basic, if unstated, social contract in America is this: We generally do not worry about how high the socioeconomic ladder extends upward (even to the heights scaled by Bill Gates and Warren Buffett), as long as everyone has a chance to get on the ladder at roughly the same rung. Of course, the image of exact equality of opportunity has never been entirely realistic, but as a statement of our national aspiration, it has been important, and as the discrepancy between aspiration and reality grows, a fundamental promise of American life is endangered. The growing class gap among high-school seniors erodes this promise.

20   Having noted above that greater engagement on the part of adults is another path toward civic restoration, we may ask how adult Americans are behaving on this score. Are they becoming more civically engaged? While there is no convincing evidence of such an encouraging trend over the last decade, adult Americans are engaging *differently*. Graduates reconnect with lost classmates on Facebook. Stay-at-home moms befriend each other through Meetup. Americans can locate proximate friends through BeaconBuddy. Brief posts on Twitter (known as "tweets") convey people's meal or sock choices, instant movie reactions, rush-hour rants, and occasionally even their profound reflections. Measured against the arc of history, such technological civic invention is in its infancy. In a world where Facebook "friendship" can encompass people who have never actually met, we remain agnostic about whether Internet social entrepreneurs have found the right mix of virtual and real strands to replace traditional social ties. But technological innovators may yet master the elusive social alchemy that will enable online behavior to produce real and enduring civic effects. If such effects do come about, they will benefit young and adult Americans alike—and fortify the civic impact of our new 9/11 Generation.

Notes

[1] Robert D. Putnam, "Bowling Alone: America's Declining Social Capital," *Journal of Democracy* 6 (January 1995): 65–78.

[2] Robert D. Putnam, *Bowling Alone: The Collapse and Revival of American Community* (New York: Simon and Schuster, 2000).

[3] The year 1994 saw the publication of a dozen scholarly articles on social capital. For 2008, that figure was nearly fifty times greater, with a comparable rise in press mentions of the concept.

[4] See Putnam, *Bowling Alone*, section 4. While much of the work on social capital is correlational, some work done since 2000 consists of panel data suggesting that social capital *causes* these beneficial outcomes.

[5] Miller McPherson, Lynn Smith-Lovin, and Matthew E. Brashears, "Social Isolation in America: Changes in Core Discussion Networks over Two Decades," *American Sociological Review* 71 (June 2006): 353–75. For a subsequent methodological debate about this study, see Claude Fischer, "The 2004 GSS Finding of Shrunken Social Networks: An Artifact?" *American Sociological Review* 74 (August 2009): 657–69, plus the original authors' rejoinder, "Models and Marginals: Using Survey Evidence to Study Social Networks," *American Sociological Review* 74 (August 2009): 670–81.

[6]   Available at *www.bettertogether.org/thereport.htm.*

[7]   Putnam, *Bowling Alone*, 253.

[8]   Putnam, *Bowling Alone*, 402.

[9]   It is worth noting that at any *single* instant, one cannot differentiate *life-cycle patterns* (how frequently people do something at one age or another) from *generational patterns* (the variation in how frequently people born in different periods do something). In our discussion of age differences, we rely on evidence gathered over many years and emphasize differences between one generation and another rather than lifecycle-related differences.

[10] Such motivations may matter little, however: Those who are introduced to volunteerism while they are young typically volunteer more often throughout their lives.

[11] From 2000 to 2008, the share of first-year U.S. college students who responded to a survey taken by the U.S. Higher Education Research Institute by saying that they considered keeping up with political affairs to be "essential" or "very important" rose from 28.1 to 39.5 percent. That was still below the all-time high, which came in 1966, when 60 percent of college first years said that they considered keeping up with politics to be "essential" or "very important." See *www.gseis.ucla.edu/ heri/pr-display.php?prQry=28.*

[12] The data are from "Monitoring the Future," an annual survey of more than fifty-thousand U.S. high-school seniors that has been taken under the auspices of the U.S. National Institutes of Health since 1976. The survey's main focus is drug use, but there are also many questions on social attitudes, social capital, self-esteem, ambition, materialism, and so on. For more information, see *www.monitoringthefuture.org.* This class gap was discovered by Rebekah Crooks Horowitz in her 2005 Harvard College senior thesis, "Minding the Gap: An Examination of the Growing Class Gap in Youth Volunteering and Political Participation."

[13] According to U.S. Current Population Survey data compiled by the U.S. Census Bureau and Labor Department, 60 percent of U.S. registered voters aged 30 or older actually cast ballots in 1996 and 2000, while only 36 percent of those aged 18 to 29 did so. In 2008, turnout among the over-30s rose modestly to 68 percent even as it shot up to 51 percent for those aged 18 to 29. Since 2000, campaign volunteering has risen at an average rate of about 5.5 percent per presidential election among Americans over 30, and by almost 20 percent among those from 18 to 29 years old.

[14] During the first six weeks after 9/11, Americans in general reported rising trust in government, rising trust in the police, greater interest in politics, more frequent attendance at political meetings, and more work on community projects. Among adults surveyed, all these increases had vanished by March 2002. See Robert D. Putnam, "Bowling Together," *American Prospect*, 11 February 2002.

15 Thomas H. Sander and Robert D. Putnam, "Sept. 11 as Civics Lesson," *Washington Post*, 10 September 2005.

16 Sarah Schweitzer, "When Students Don't Know 9/11," *Boston Globe*, 11 September 2009.

17 See the report by the Pew Research Center for the People and the Press, "Trends in Political Values and Core Attitudes: 1987–2009: Independents Take Center Stage in Obama Era," 21 May 2009, 75. Available at *http://people-press.org/reports/pdf/517.pdf*. Statistics also from crosstabs conducted by Leah Christian at the Pew Research Center for the People and the Press, 25 September 2009.

18 Social class in this analysis is measured by parental educational levels, so by "upper middle class" we mean kids with at least [one]parent who has a postgraduate education, whereas by "working [or lower] class" we mean kids whose parents have not gone beyond high school, if that.

19 These results come from our unpublished analyses of "Monitoring the Future" data.

Several white clergymen in Birmingham, Alabama published "A Call for Unity" in the local newspaper after civil rights protesting caused what they viewed as excessive upheaval and turmoil. They asserted that they supported equal rights for all, but focused their criticism on the methods of civil disobedience employed by many protestors. This, they claimed, forced the community to pay too high a price. Rather, they advocated that any civil rights activity should work through the legal system and not produce tension within the community.

A Call for Unity

Clergymen of Alabama

April 12, 1963

1   We the undersigned clergymen are among those who, in January, issued "An Appeal for Law and Order and Common Sense," in dealing with racial problems in Alabama. We expressed understanding that honest convictions in racial matters could properly be pursued in the courts, but urged that decisions of those courts should in the meantime be peacefully obeyed.

2   Since that time there had been some evidence of increased forebearance and a willingness to face facts. Responsible citizens have undertaken to work on various problems which cause racial friction and unrest. In Birmingham, recent public events have given indication that we all have opportunity for a new constructive and realistic approach to racial problems.

3   However, we are now confronted by a series of demonstrations by some of our Negro citizens, directed and led in part by outsiders. We recognize the natural impatience of people who feel that their hopes are slow in being realized. But we are convinced that these demonstrations are unwise and untimely.

4   We agree rather with certain local Negro leadership which has called for honest and open negotiation of racial issues in our area. And we believe this kind of facing of issues can best be accomplished by citizens of our own metropolitan area, white and Negro, meeting with their

knowledge and experience of the local situation. All of us need to face that responsibility and find proper channels for its accomplishment.

5 Just as we formerly pointed out that "hatred and violence have no sanction in our religious and political traditions," we also point out that such actions as incite to hatred and violence, however technically peaceful those actions may be, have not contributed to the resolution of our local problems. We do not believe that these days of new hope are days when extreme measures are justified in Birmingham.

6 We commend the community as a whole, and the local news media and law enforcement officials in particular, on the calm manner in which these demonstrations have been handled. We urge the public to continue to show restraint should the demonstrations continue, and the law enforcement officials to remain calm and continue to protect our city from violence.

7 We further strongly urge our own Negro community to withdraw support from these demonstrations, and to unite locally in working peacefully for a better Birmingham. When rights are consistently denied, a cause should be pressed in the courts and in negotiations among local leaders, and not in the streets. We appeal to both our white and Negro citizenry to observe the principles of law and order and common sense.

8 C.C.J. Carpenter, D.D., L.L.D., Bishop of Alabama; Joseph A. Durick, D.D., Auxiliary Bishop, Diocese of Mobile-Birming-ham; Rabbi Milton L. Grafman, Temple Emanu-El, Birming-ham, Alabama; Bishop Paul Hardin, Bishop of the Alabama-West Florida Conference of the Methodist Church; Bishop Nolan B. Harmon, Bishop of the North Alabama Conference of the Methodist Church; George M. Murray, D.D., L.L.D., Bishop Coadjutor, Episcopal Diocese of Alabama; Edward V. Ramage, Moderator, Synod of the Alabama Presbyterian Church in the United States; Earl Stallings, Pastor, First Baptist Church, Birmingham, Alabama.

*M*artin Luther King Jr. (1929–1968) was a renowned leader in the American civil rights movement, and "Letter from Birmingham Jail" is one of
his most well-known and compelling essays. King's letter is written in response
to the Alabama clergymen's publication of "A Call for Unity." In this letter, King
enumerates and defends his reasons for promoting the method of civil disobedience to bring the issue of civil rights into the national spotlight. He articulates
the role of community membership in his presence as well as the interdependence
of communities.

Letter from Birmingham Jail

Martin Luther King Jr.

April 16, 1963

My Dear Fellow Clergymen:

1   While confined here in the Birmingham city jail, I came across your
recent statement calling my present activities "unwise and untimely."
Seldom do I pause to answer criticism of my work and ideas. If I
sought to answer all the criticisms that cross my desk, my secretaries
would have little time for anything other than such correspondence
in the course of the day, and I would have no time for constructive
work. But since I feel that you are men of genuine good will and that
your criticisms are sincerely set forth, I want to try to answer your
statement in what I hope will be patient and reasonable terms.

2   I think I should indicate why I am here in Birmingham, since you
have been influenced by the view which argues against "outsiders
coming in." I have the honor of serving as president of the Southern
Christian Leadership Conference, an organization operating in every
southern state, with headquarters in Atlanta, Georgia. We have some
eighty-five affiliated organizations across the South, and one of them
is the Alabama Christian Movement for Human Rights. Frequently
we share staff, educational and financial resources with our affiliates.
Several months ago the affiliate here in Birmingham asked us to be
on call to engage in a nonviolent direct-action program if such were

deemed necessary. We readily consented, and when the hour came we lived up to our promise. So I, along with several members of my staff, am here because I was invited here. I am here because I have organizational ties here.

3   But more basically, I am in Birmingham because injustice is here. Just as the prophets of the eighth century B.C. left their villages and carried their "thus saith the Lord" far beyond the boundaries of their home towns, and just as the Apostle Paul left his village of Tarsus and carried the gospel of Jesus Christ to the far corners of the Greco-Roman world, so am I compelled to carry the gospel of freedom beyond my own home town. Like Paul, I must constantly respond to the Macedonian call for aid.

4   Moreover, I am cognizant of the interrelatedness of all communities and states. I cannot sit idly by in Atlanta and not be concerned about what happens in Birmingham. Injustice anywhere is a threat to justice everywhere. We are caught in an inescapable network of mutuality, tied in a single garment of destiny. Whatever affects one directly, affects all indirectly. Never again can we afford to live with the narrow, provincial "outside agitator" idea. Anyone who lives inside the United States can never be considered an outsider anywhere within its bounds.

5   You deplore the demonstrations taking place in Birmingham. But your statement, I am sorry to say, fails to express a similar concern for the conditions that brought about the demonstrations. I am sure that none of you would want to rest content with the superficial kind of social analysis that deals merely with effects and does not grapple with underlying causes. It is unfortunate that demonstrations are taking place in Birmingham, but it is even more unfortunate that the city's white power structure left the Negro community with no alternative.

6   In any nonviolent campaign there are four basic steps: collection of the facts to determine whether injustices exist; negotiation; self-purification; and direct action. We have gone through all these steps in Birmingham. There can be no gainsaying the fact that racial injustice engulfs this community. Birmingham is probably the most thoroughly segregated city in the United States. Its ugly record of brutality is widely known. Negroes have experienced grossly unjust treatment in the courts. There have been more unsolved bombings of Negro homes

and churches in Birmingham than in any other city in the nation. These are the hard, brutal facts of the case. On the basis of these conditions, Negro leaders sought to negotiate with the city fathers. But the latter consistently refused to engage in good-faith negotiation.

7   Then, last September, came the opportunity to talk with leaders of Birmingham's economic community. In the course of the negotiations, certain promises were made by the merchants—for example, to remove the stores' humiliating racial signs. On the basis of these promises, the Reverend Fred Shuttlesworth and the leaders of the Alabama Christian Movement for Human Rights agreed to a moratorium on all demonstrations. As the weeks and months went by, we realized that we were the victims of a broken promise. A few signs, briefly removed, returned; the others remained.

8   As in so many past experiences, our hopes had been blasted, and the shadow of deep disappointment settled upon us. We had no alternative except to prepare for direct action, whereby we would present our very bodies as a means of laying our case before the conscience of the local and the national community. Mindful of the difficulties involved, we decided to undertake a process of self-purification. We began a series of workshops on nonviolence, and we repeatedly asked ourselves: "Are you able to accept blows without retaliating?" "Are you able to endure the ordeal of jail?" We decided to schedule our direct-action program for the Easter season, realizing that except for Christmas, this is the main shopping period of the year. Knowing that a strong economic-withdrawal program would be the by-product of direct action, we felt that this would be the best time to bring pressure to bear on the merchants for the needed change.

9   Then it occurred to us that Birmingham's mayoral election was coming up in March, and we speedily decided to postpone action until after election day. When we discovered that the Commissioner of Public Safety, Eugene "Bull" Connor, had piled up enough votes to be in the run-off, we decided again to postpone action until the day after the run-off so that the demonstrations could not be used to cloud the issues. Like many others, we waited to see Mr. Connor defeated, and to this end we endured postponement after postponement. Having aided in this community need, we felt that our direct-action program could be delayed no longer.

10   You may well ask: "Why direct action? Why sit-ins, marches and so forth? Isn't negotiation a better path?" You are quite right in calling for negotiation. Indeed, this is the very purpose of direct action. Nonviolent direct action seeks to create such a crisis and foster such a tension that a community which has constantly refused to negotiate is forced to confront the issue. It seeks so to dramatize the issue that it can no longer be ignored. My citing the creation of tension as part of the work of the nonviolent-resister may sound rather shocking. But I must confess that I am not afraid of the word "tension." I have earnestly opposed violent tension, but there is a type of constructive, nonviolent tension which is necessary for growth. Just as Socrates felt that it was necessary to create a tension in the mind so that individuals could rise from the bondage of myths and half-truths to the unfettered realm of creative analysis and objective appraisal, so must we see the need for nonviolent gadflies to create the kind of tension in society that will help men rise from the dark depths of prejudice and racism to the majestic heights of understanding and brotherhood.

11   The purpose of our direct-action program is to create a situation so crisis-packed that it will inevitably open the door to negotiation. I therefore concur with you in your call for negotiation. Too long has our beloved Southland been bogged down in a tragic effort to live in monologue rather than dialogue.

12   One of the basic points in your statement is that the action that I and my associates have taken in Birmingham is untimely. Some have asked: "Why didn't you give the new city administration time to act?" The only answer that I can give to this query is that the new Birmingham administration must be prodded about as much as the outgoing one, before it will act. We are sadly mistaken if we feel that the election of Albert Boutwell as mayor will bring the millennium to Birmingham. While Mr. Boutwell is a much more gentle person than Mr. Connor, they are both segregationists, dedicated to maintenance of the status quo. I have hope that Mr. Boutwell will be reasonable enough to see the futility of massive resistance to desegregation. But he will not see this without pressure from devotees of civil rights. My friends, I must say to you that we have not made a single gain in civil rights without determined legal and nonviolent pressure. Lamentably, it is an historical fact that privileged groups seldom give up their

privileges voluntarily. Individuals may see the moral light and voluntarily give up their unjust posture; but, as Reinhold Niebuhr has reminded us, groups tend to be more immoral than individuals.

13   We know through painful experience that freedom is never voluntarily given by the oppressor; it must be demanded by the oppressed. Frankly, I have yet to engage in a direct-action campaign that was "well timed" in the view of those who have not suffered unduly from the disease of segregation. For years now I have heard the word "Wait!" It rings in the ear of every Negro with piercing familiarity. This "Wait" has almost always meant "Never." We must come to see, with one of our distinguished jurists, that "justice too long delayed is justice denied."

14   We have waited for more than 340 years for our constitutional and God-given rights. The nations of Asia and Africa are moving with jet-like speed toward gaining political independence, but we still creep at horse-and-buggy pace toward gaining a cup of coffee at a lunch counter. Perhaps it is easy for those who have never felt the stinging darts of segregation to say, "Wait." But when you have seen vicious mobs lynch your mothers and fathers at will and drown your sisters and brothers at whim; when you have seen hate-filled policemen curse, kick and even kill your black brothers and sisters; when you see the vast majority of your twenty million Negro brothers smothering in an airtight cage of poverty in the midst of an affluent society; when you suddenly find your tongue twisted and your speech stammering as you seek to explain to your six-year-old daughter why she can't go to the public amusement park that has just been advertised on television, and see tears welling up in her eyes when she is told that Funtown is closed to colored children, and see ominous clouds of inferiority beginning to form in her little mental sky, and see her beginning to distort her personality by developing an unconscious bitterness toward white people; when you have to concoct an answer for a five-year-old son who is asking: "Daddy, why do white people treat colored people so mean?"; when you take a cross-country drive and find it necessary to sleep night after night in the uncomfortable corners of your automobile because no motel will accept you; when you are humiliated day in and day out by nagging signs reading "white" and "colored"; when your first name becomes "nigger," your middle name becomes "boy" (however old you are) and your last

name becomes "John," and your wife and mother are never given the respected title "Mrs."; when you are harried by day and haunted by night by the fact that you are a Negro, living constantly at tiptoe stance, never quite knowing what to expect next, and are plagued with inner fears and outer resentments; when you are forever fighting a degenerating sense of "nobodiness"—then you will understand why we find it difficult to wait. There comes a time when the cup of endurance runs over, and men are no longer willing to be plunged into the abyss of despair. I hope, sirs, you can understand our legitimate and unavoidable impatience.

15   You express a great deal of anxiety over our willingness to break laws. This is certainly a legitimate concern. Since we so diligently urge people to obey the Supreme Court's decision of 1954 outlawing segregation in the public schools, at first glance it may seem rather paradoxical for us consciously to break laws. One may well ask: "How can you advocate breaking some laws and obeying others?" The answer lies in the fact that there are two types of laws: just and unjust. I would be the first to advocate obeying just laws. One has not only a legal but a moral responsibility to obey just laws. Conversely, one has a moral responsibility to disobey unjust laws. I would agree with St. Augustine that "an unjust law is no law at all."

16   Now, what is the difference between the two? How does one determine whether a law is just or unjust? A just law is a man-made code that squares with the moral law or the law of God. An unjust law is a code that is out of harmony with the moral law. To put it in the terms of St. Thomas Aquinas: An unjust law is a human law that is not rooted in eternal law and natural law. Any law that uplifts human personality is just. Any law that degrades human personality is unjust. All segregation statutes are unjust because segregation distorts the soul and damages the personality. It gives the segregator a false sense of superiority and the segregated a false sense of inferiority. Segregation, to use the terminology of the Jewish philosopher Martin Buber, substitutes an "I-it" relationship for an "I-thou" relationship and ends up relegating persons to the status of things. Hence segregation is not only politically, economically and sociologically unsound, it is morally wrong and sinful. Paul Tillich has said that sin is separation. Is not segregation an existential expression of

man's tragic separation, his awful estrangement, his terrible sinfulness? Thus it is that I can urge men to obey the 1954 decision of the Supreme Court, for it is morally right; and I can urge them to disobey segregation ordinances, for they are morally wrong.

17 Let us consider a more concrete example of just and unjust laws. An unjust law is a code that a numerical or power majority group compels a minority group to obey but does not make binding on itself. This is *difference* made legal. By the same token, a just law is a code that a majority compels a minority to follow and that it is willing to follow itself. This is *sameness* made legal.

18 Let me give another explanation. A law is unjust if it is inflicted on a minority that, as a result of being denied the right to vote, had no part in enacting or devising the law. Who can say that the legislature of Alabama which set up that state's segregation laws was democratically elected? Throughout Alabama all sorts of devious methods are used to prevent Negroes from becoming registered voters, and there are some counties in which, even though Negroes constitute a majority of the population, not a single Negro is registered. Can any law enacted under such circumstances be considered democratically structured?

19 Sometimes a law is just on its face and unjust in its application. For instance, I have been arrested on a charge of parading without a permit. Now, there is nothing wrong in having an ordinance which requires a permit for a parade. But such an ordinance becomes unjust when it is used to maintain segregation and to deny citizens the First-Amendment privilege of peaceful assembly and protest.

20 I hope you are able to see the distinction I am trying to point out. In no sense do I advocate evading or defying the law, as would the rabid segregationist. That would lead to anarchy. One who breaks an unjust law must do so openly, lovingly, and with a willingness to accept the penalty. I submit that an individual who breaks a law that conscience tells him is unjust, and who willingly accepts the penalty of imprisonment in order to arouse the conscience of the community over its injustice, is in reality expressing the highest respect for law.

21 Of course, there is nothing new about this kind of civil disobedience. It was evidenced sublimely in the refusal of Shadrach, Meshach and Abednego to obey the laws of Nebuchadnezzar, on the ground that a

higher moral law was at stake. It was practiced superbly by the early Christians, who were willing to face hungry lions and the excruciating pain of chopping blocks rather than submit to certain unjust laws of the Roman Empire. To a degree, academic freedom is a reality today because Socrates practiced civil disobedience. In our own nation, the Boston Tea Party represented a massive act of civil disobedience.

22   We should never forget that everything Adolf Hitler did in Germany was "legal" and everything the Hungarian freedom fighters did in Hungary was "illegal." It was "illegal" to aid and comfort a Jew in Hitler's Germany. Even so, I am sure that, had I lived in Germany at the time, I would have aided and comforted my Jewish brothers. If today I lived in a Communist country where certain principles dear to the Christian faith are suppressed, I would openly advocate disobeying that country's antireligious laws.

23   I must make two honest confessions to you, my Christian and Jewish brothers. First, I must confess that over the past few years I have been gravely disappointed with the white moderate. I have almost reached the regrettable conclusion that the Negro's great stumbling block in his stride toward freedom is not the White Citizen's Counciler or the Ku Klux Klanner, but the white moderate, who is more devoted to "order" than to justice; who prefers a negative peace which is the absence of tension to a positive peace which is the presence of justice; who constantly says: "I agree with you in the goal you seek, but I cannot agree with your methods of direct action"; who paternalistically believes he can set the timetable for another man's freedom; who lives by a mythical concept of time and who constantly advises the Negro to wait for a "more convenient season." Shallow understanding from people of good will is more frustrating than absolute misunderstanding from people of ill will. Lukewarm acceptance is much more bewildering than outright rejection.

24   I had hoped that the white moderate would understand that law and order exist for the purpose of establishing justice and that when they fail in this purpose they become the dangerously structured dams that block the flow of social progress. I had hoped that the white moderate would understand that the present tension in the South is a necessary phase of the transition from an obnoxious negative peace, in which the Negro passively accepted his unjust plight, to a substantive and positive peace, in which all men will respect the dignity and worth of

human personality. Actually, we who engage in nonviolent direct action are not the creators of tension. We merely bring to the surface the hidden tension that is already alive. We bring it out in the open, where it can be seen and dealt with. Like a boil that can never be cured so long as it is covered up but must be opened with all its ugliness to the natural medicines of air and light, injustice must be exposed, with all the tension its exposure creates, to the light of human conscience and the air of national opinion before it can be cured.

25   In your statement you assert that our actions, even though peaceful, must be condemned because they precipitate violence. But is this a logical assertion? Isn't this like condemning a robbed man because his possession of money precipitated the evil act of robbery? Isn't this like condemning Socrates because his unswerving commitment to truth and his philosophical inquiries precipitated the act by the misguided populace in which they made him drink hemlock? Isn't this like condemning Jesus because his unique God-consciousness and never-ceasing devotion to God's will precipitated the evil act of crucifixion? We must come to see that, as the federal courts have consistently affirmed, it is wrong to urge an individual to cease his efforts to gain his basic constitutional rights because the quest may precipitate violence. Society must protect the robbed and punish the robber.

26   I had also hoped that the white moderate would reject the myth concerning time in relation to the struggle for freedom. I have just received a letter from a white brother in Texas. He writes: "All Christians know that the colored people will receive equal rights eventually, but it is possible that you are in too great a religious hurry. It has taken Christianity almost two thousand years to accomplish what it has. The teachings of Christ take time to come to earth." Such an attitude stems from a tragic misconception of time, from the strangely irrational notion that there is something in the very flow of time that will inevitably cure all ills. Actually, time itself is neutral; it can be used either destructively or constructively. More and more I feel that the people of ill will have used time much more effectively than have the people of good will. We will have to repent in this generation not merely for the hateful words and actions of the bad people but for the appalling silence of the good people. Human progress never rolls in on wheels of inevitability; it comes through the tireless efforts of men willing to be co-workers with God, and without this hard work, time

itself becomes an ally of the forces of social stagnation. We must use time creatively, in the knowledge that the time is always ripe to do right. Now is the time to make real the promise of democracy and transform our pending national elegy into a creative psalm of brotherhood. Now is the time to lift our national policy from the quicksand of racial injustice to the solid rock of human dignity.

27 You speak of our activity in Birmingham as extreme. At first I was rather disappointed that fellow clergymen would see my nonviolent efforts as those of an extremist. I began thinking about the fact that I stand in the middle of two opposing forces in the Negro community. One is a force of complacency, made up in part of Negroes who, as a result of long years of oppression, are so drained of self-respect and a sense of "somebodiness" that they have adjusted to segregation; and in part of a few middle-class Negroes who, because of a degree of academic and economic security and because in some ways they profit by segregation, have become insensitive to the problems of the masses. The other force is one of bitterness and hatred, and it comes perilously close to advocating violence. It is expressed in the various black nationalist groups that are springing up across the nation, the largest and best-known being Elijah Muhammad's Muslim movement. Nourished by the Negro's frustration over the continued existence of racial discrimination, this movement is made up of people who have lost faith in America, who have absolutely repudiated Christianity, and who have concluded that the white man is an incorrigible "devil."

28 I have tried to stand between these two forces, saying that we need emulate neither the "do-nothingism" of the complacent nor the hatred and despair of the black nationalist. For there is the more excellent way of love and nonviolent protest. I am grateful to God that, through the influence of the Negro church, the way of nonviolence became an integral part of our struggle.

29 If this philosophy had not emerged, by now many streets of the South would, I am convinced, be flowing with blood. And I am further convinced that if our white brothers dismiss as "rabble-rousers" and "outside agitators" those of us who employ nonviolent direct action, and if they refuse to support our nonviolent efforts, millions of Negroes will, out of frustration and despair, seek solace and security

in black-nationalist ideologies—a development that would inevitably lead to a frightening racial nightmare.

30   Oppressed people cannot remain oppressed forever. The yearning for freedom eventually manifests itself, and that is what has happened to the American Negro. Something within has reminded him of his birthright of freedom, and something without has reminded him that it can be gained. Consciously or unconsciously, he has been caught up by the *Zeitgeist*, and with his black brothers of Africa and his brown and yellow brothers of Asia, South America and the Caribbean, the United States Negro is moving with a sense of great urgency toward the promised land of racial justice. If one recognizes this vital urge that has engulfed the Negro community, one should readily understand why public demonstrations are taking place. The Negro has many pent-up resentments and latent frustrations, and he must release them. So let him march; let him make prayer pilgrimages to the city hall; let him go on freedom rides—and try to understand why he must do so. If his repressed emotions are not released in nonviolent ways, they will seek expression through violence; this is not a threat but a fact of history. So I have not said to my people: "Get rid of your discontent." Rather, I have tried to say that this normal and healthy discontent can be channeled into the creative outlet of nonviolent direct action. And now this approach is being termed extremist.

31   But though I was initially disappointed at being categorized as an extremist, as I continued to think about the matter I gradually gained a measure of satisfaction from the label. Was not Jesus an extremist for love: "Love your enemies, bless them that curse you, do good to them that hate you, and pray for them which despitefully use you, and persecute you." Was not Amos an extremist for justice: "Let justice roll down like waters and righteousness like an ever-flowing stream." Was not Paul an extremist for the Christian gospel: "I bear in my body the marks of the Lord Jesus." Was not Martin Luther an extremist: "Here I stand; I cannot do otherwise, so help me God." And John Bunyan: "I will stay in jail to the end of my days before I make a butchery of my conscience." And Abraham Lincoln: "This nation cannot survive half slave and half free." And Thomas Jefferson: "We hold these truths to be self-evident, that all men are created equal . . ." So the question is not whether we will be extremists, but

what kind of extremists we will be. Will we be extremists for hate or for love? Will we be extremists for the preservation of injustice or for the extension of justice? In that dramatic scene on Calvary's hill three men were crucified. We must never forget that all three were crucified for the same crime—the crime of extremism. Two were extremists for immorality, and thus fell below their environment. The other, Jesus Christ, was an extremist for love, truth and goodness, and thereby rose above his environment. Perhaps the South, the nation and the world are in dire need of creative extremists.

32   I had hoped that the white moderate would see this need. Perhaps I was too optimistic; perhaps I expected too much. I suppose I should have realized that few members of the oppressor race can understand the deep groans and passionate yearnings of the oppressed race, and still fewer have the vision to see that injustice must be rooted out by strong, persistent and determined action. I am thankful, however, that some of our white brothers in the South have grasped the meaning of this social revolution and committed themselves to it. They are still all too few in quantity, but they are big in quality. Some—such as Ralph McGill, Lillian Smith, Harry Golden, James McBride Dabbs, Ann Braden and Sarah Patton Boyle—have written about our struggle in eloquent and prophetic terms. Others have marched with us down nameless streets of the South. They have languished in filthy, roach-infested jails, suffering the abuse and brutality of policemen who view them as "dirty nigger-lovers." Unlike so many of their moderate brothers and sisters, they have recognized the urgency of the moment and sensed the need for powerful "action" antidotes to combat the disease of segregation.

33   Let me take note of my other major disappointment. I have been so greatly disappointed with the white church and its leadership. Of course, there are some notable exceptions. I am not unmindful of the fact that each of you has taken some significant stands on this issue. I commend you, Reverend Stallings, for your Christian stand on this past Sunday, in welcoming Negroes to your worship service on a nonsegregated basis. I commend the Catholic leaders of this state for integrating Spring Hill College several years ago.

34   But despite these notable exceptions, I must honestly reiterate that I have been disappointed with the church. I do not say this as one of

those negative critics who can always find something wrong with the church. I say this as a minister of the gospel, who loves the church; who was nurtured in its bosom; who has been sustained by its spiritual blessings and who will remain true to it as long as the cord of life shall lengthen.

35   When I was suddenly catapulted into the leadership of the bus protest in Montgomery, Alabama, a few years ago, I felt we would be supported by the white church. I felt that the white ministers, priests and rabbis of the South would be among our strongest allies. Instead, some have been outright opponents, refusing to understand the freedom movement and misrepresenting its leaders; all too many others have been more cautious than courageous and have remained silent behind the anesthetizing security of stained-glass windows.

36   In spite of my shattered dreams, I came to Birmingham with the hope that the white religious leadership of this community would see the justice of our cause and, with deep moral concern, would serve as the channel through which our just grievances could reach the power structure. I had hoped that each of you would understand. But again I have been disappointed.

37   I have heard numerous southern religious leaders admonish their worshipers to comply with a desegregation decision because it is the law, but I have longed to hear white ministers declare: "Follow this decree because integration is morally right and because the Negro is your brother." In the midst of blatant injustices inflicted upon the Negro, I have watched white churchmen stand on the sideline and mouth pious irrelevancies and sanctimonious trivialities. In the midst of a mighty struggle to rid our nation of racial and economic injustice, I have heard many ministers say: "Those are social issues, with which the gospel has no real concern." And I have watched many churches commit themselves to a completely otherworldly religion which makes a strange, un-Biblical distinction between body and soul, between the sacred and the secular.

38   I have traveled the length and breadth of Alabama, Mississippi and all the other southern states. On sweltering summer days and crisp autumn mornings I have looked at the South's beautiful churches with their lofty spires pointing heavenward. I have beheld the impressive outlines of her massive religious-education buildings.

Over and over I have found myself asking: "What kind of people worship here? Who is their God? Where were their voices when the lips of Governor Barnett dripped with words of interposition and nullification? Where were they when Governor Wallace gave a clarion call for defiance and hatred? Where were their voices of support when bruised and weary Negro men and women decided to rise from the dark dungeons of complacency to the bright hills of creative protest?"

39 Yes, these questions are still in my mind. In deep disappointment I have wept over the laxity of the church. But be assured that my tears have been tears of love. There can be no deep disappointment where there is not deep love. Yes, I love the church. How could I do otherwise? I am in the rather unique position of being the son, the grandson and the great-grandson of preachers. Yes, I see the church as the body of Christ. But, oh! How we have blemished and scarred that body through social neglect and through fear of being nonconformists.

40 There was a time when the church was very powerful—in the time when the early Christians rejoiced at being deemed worthy to suffer for what they believed. In those days the church was not merely a thermometer that recorded the ideas and principles of popular opinion; it was a thermostat that transformed the mores of society. Whenever the early Christians entered a town, the people in power became disturbed and immediately sought to convict the Christians for being "disturbers of the peace" and "outside agitators." But the Christians pressed on, in the conviction that they were "a colony of heaven," called to obey God rather than man. Small in number, they were big in commitment. They were too God-intoxicated to be "astronomically intimidated." By their effort and example they brought an end to such ancient evils as infanticide and gladiatorial contests.

41 Things are different now. So often the contemporary church is a weak, ineffectual voice with an uncertain sound. So often it is an archdefender of the status quo. Far from being disturbed by the presence of the church, the power structure of the average community is consoled by the church's silent—and often even vocal—sanction of things as they are.

42 But the judgment of God is upon the church as never before. If today's church does not recapture the sacrificial spirit of the early

church, it will lose its authenticity, forfeit the loyalty of millions, and be dismissed as an irrelevant social club with no meaning for the twentieth century. Every day I meet young people whose disappointment with the church has turned into outright disgust.

43 Perhaps I have once again been too optimistic. Is organized religion too inextricably bound to the status quo to save our nation and the world? Perhaps I must turn my faith to the inner spiritual church, the church within the church, as the true *ekklesia* and the hope of the world. But again I am thankful to God that some noble souls from the ranks of organized religion have broken loose from the paralyzing chains of conformity and joined us as active partners in the struggle for freedom. They have left their secure congregations and walked the streets of Albany, Georgia, with us. They have gone down the highways of the South on tortuous rides for freedom. Yes, they have gone to jail with us. Some have been dismissed from their churches, have lost the support of their bishops and fellow ministers. But they have acted in the faith that right defeated is stronger than evil triumphant. Their witness has been the spiritual salt that has preserved the true meaning of the gospel in these troubled times. They have carved a tunnel of hope through the dark mountain of disappointment.

44 I hope the church as a whole will meet the challenge of this decisive hour. But even if the church does not come to the aid of justice, I have no despair about the future. I have no fear about the outcome of our struggle in Birmingham, even if our motives are at present misunderstood. We will reach the goal of freedom in Birmingham and all over the nation, because the goal of America is freedom. Abused and scorned though we may be, our destiny is tied up with America's destiny. Before the pilgrims landed at Plymouth, we were here. Before the pen of Jefferson etched the majestic words of the Declaration of Independence across the pages of history, we were here. For more than two centuries our forebears labored in this country without wages; they made cotton king; they built the homes of their masters while suffering gross injustice and shameful humiliation—and yet out of a bottomless vitality they continued to thrive and develop. If the inexpressible cruelties of slavery could not stop us, the opposition we now face will surely fail. We will win our freedom because the sacred heritage of our nation and the eternal will of God are embodied in our echoing demands.

45　Before closing I feel impelled to mention one other point in your statement that has troubled me profoundly. You warmly commended the Birmingham police force for keeping "order" and "preventing violence." I doubt that you would have so warmly commended the police force if you had seen its dogs sinking their teeth into unarmed, nonviolent Negroes. I doubt that you would so quickly commend the policemen if you were to observe their ugly and inhumane treatment of Negroes here in the city jail; if you were to watch them push and curse old Negro women and young Negro girls; if you were to see them slap and kick old Negro men and young boys; if you were to observe them, as they did on two occasions, refuse to give us food because we wanted to sing our grace together. I cannot join you in your praise of the Birmingham police department.

46　It is true that the police have exercised a degree of discipline in handling the demonstrators. In this sense they have conducted themselves rather "nonviolently" in public. But for what purpose? To preserve the evil system of segregation. Over the past few years I have consistently preached that nonviolence demands that the means we use must be as pure as the ends we seek. I have tried to make clear that it is wrong to use immoral means to attain moral ends. But now I must affirm that it is just as wrong, or perhaps even more so, to use moral means to preserve immoral ends. Perhaps Mr. Connor and his policemen have been rather nonviolent in public, as was Chief Pritchett in Albany, Georgia, but they have used the moral means of nonviolence to maintain the immoral end of racial injustice. As T. S. Eliot has said: "The last temptation is the greatest treason: To do the right deed for the wrong reason."

47　I wish you had commended the Negro sit-inners and demonstrators of Birmingham for their sublime courage, their willingness to suffer and their amazing discipline in the midst of great provocation. One day the South will recognize its real heroes. They will be the James Merediths, with the noble sense of purpose that enables them to face jeering and hostile mobs, and with the agonizing loneliness that characterizes the life of the pioneer. They will be old, oppressed, battered Negro women, symbolized in a seventy-two-year-old woman in Montgomery, Alabama, who rose up with a sense of dignity and with her people decided not to ride segregated buses, and who responded with ungrammatical profundity to one who inquired about her weariness: "My feets is tired, but my soul is at rest." They will be the young high school and college students, the young ministers of the gospel and a host of their elders, courageously and nonviolently sitting in at lunch counters and willingly going to jail for conscience' sake. One day the South will know that when these disinherited children of God sat down at lunch counters, they were in reality standing up for what is best in the American dream and for the most sacred values in our Judaeo-Christian heritage, thereby bringing our nation back to those great wells of democracy which were dug deep by the founding fathers in their formulation of the Constitution and the Declaration of Independence.

48 Never before have I written so long a letter. I'm afraid it is much too long to take your precious time. I can assure you that it would have been much shorter if I had been writing from a comfortable desk, but what else can one do when he is alone in a narrow jail cell, other than write long letters, think long thoughts and pray long prayers?

49 If I have said anything in this letter that overstates the truth and indicates an unreasonable impatience, I beg you to forgive me. If I have said anything that understates the truth and indicates my having a patience that allows me to settle for anything less than brotherhood, I beg God to forgive me.

50 I hope this letter finds you strong in the faith. I also hope that circumstances will soon make it possible for me to meet each of you, not as an integrationist or a civil-rights leader but as a fellow clergyman and a Christian brother. Let us all hope that the dark clouds of racial prejudice will soon pass away and the deep fog of misunderstanding will be lifted from our fear-drenched communities, and in some not too distant tomorrow the radiant stars of love and brotherhood will shine over our great nation with all their scintillating beauty.

Yours for the cause of Peace and Brotherhood,

Martin Luther King, Jr.

Wang Anyi's (1954–) fiction is shaped by her experience in China's Cultural Revolution (1966–1971). As a child in Shanghai, her family was accused of political crimes during the Cultural Revolution, and Wang had to interrupt her education. "The Destination" reflects the trials faced by people living during this period, including displacement and regimented conditions. Within this larger context, this short story deals with the intricacies and dynamics of Chinese family life, and explores the factors that make us call a place "home." These factors are what give us a sense of community, and what motivate Wang's character, Chen Xin, to sacrifice so much to return to his home of Shanghai.

The Destination

Wang Anyi

1 Over the loudspeaker came the announcement, "The train is arriving at Shanghai terminal. . . ."

2 Dozing passengers opened their eyes. "We're arriving in Shanghai."

3 "We're nearing the terminal."

4 The impatient ones removed their shoes and climbed onto their seats to reach for their luggage.

5 A group of middle-aged men from Xinjiang began making plans. "We'll take a bath as soon as we check into a hotel. Then we'll call the heavy-machinery plant and go out to a Western-style restaurant."

6 "Right. We'll have Western food." Their spirits rose. They had gone to work in Xinjiang after their university years in Beijing, Fuzhou and Jiangsu. Though they retained their accents, their appearance and temperament were "Xinjiangized," weatherbeaten and blunt. When Chen Xin asked casually about Xinjiang after he got on the train at Nanjing, they gave him a detailed and enthusiastic account of the region: the humor and wit of Xinjiang's different ethnic minorities, the beautiful songs they sang, the graceful dances and lively girls. They also described their own life there, how they fished and hunted. Expressive and eloquent, they painted an appealing picture.

167

7   "How long will you be in Shanghai?" one of the group, a man from Beijing, asked, patting Chen Xin on the shoulder.

8   With a smile, he turned around from gazing out the window. "I've come back for good."

9   "Got a transfer?"

10 "Right."

11 "Bringing your wife and children?"

12 "I haven't any," he blushed. "I couldn't have come back if I'd been married."

13 "My, you must be determined." Chen Xin's shoulder received a heartier slap. "You Shanghainese can't survive away from Shanghai."

14 "It's my home," Chen Xin said, justifying himself.

15 Chen Xin smiled.

16 "One should be able to find interesting things anywhere. You skate in Harbin, swim in Guangzhou, eat big chunks of mutton with your hands in Xinjiang and Western food in Shanghai. . . . Wherever fate lands you, you look for something interesting and enjoy it as best you can. Maybe that's what makes life interesting."

17 Chen Xin only smiled. Absentmindedly, he kept his eyes on the fields flitting past his window, fields carefully divided into small plots and planted like squares of embroidery—there were patches of yellow, dark and light green and, beside the river, purple triangles. To eyes used to the vast, fertile soil of the north, the highly utilized and carefully partitioned land struck him as narrow and jammed. But he had to admit that everything was as fresh and clean as if washed by water. This was the south, the outskirts of Shanghai. Oh, Shanghai!

18 The train hurtled past the fields and low walls and entered the suburbs. Chen Xin saw factories, buildings, streets, buses and pedestrians. . . . Shanghai became closer and tangible. His eyes moistened and his heart thumped. Ten years ago, when classes were suspended during the Cultural Revolution, he and other sent-down youth left for the countryside. At that time, as Shanghai faded into the distance, he had not expected to return. No. He probably had thought about it. In the countryside, he plowed, planted, harvested wheat, dredged rivers,

and tried to get a job or admittance to a university. . . . He finally enrolled in a teachers' college. After graduation he was assigned to teach in a middle school in a small town. Able to earn his own living at last, his struggles should have ended; he could start a new life. But he felt he had not arrived at his destination. Not yet. He was still unsettled and expectant, waiting for something. He only realized what he had been waiting for, what his destination really was, when large numbers of school-leavers returned to Shanghai after the fall of the Gang of Four.

19 In the past decade, he had been to Shanghai on holiday and on business. But with every visit he only felt the distance between him and Shanghai grow. He had become a stranger, an outsider, whom the Shanghainese looked down upon. And he found their superiority and conceit intolerable. The pity and sympathy of his friends and acquaintances were as unbearable. For at the back of that lay pride. Still he was forced to admire Shanghai's progress and superiority. The department stores were full of all kinds of goods and people dressed in the latest fashions. Clean, elegant restaurants. New films at the cinemas. Shanghai represented what was new in China. But above all there was his home, his mother, brothers, and dead father's ashes. . . . He smiled, his eyes brimming with tears. He would make any sacrifice to return. He had acted as soon as he learned that his mother was retiring and that one of her children could take her job. He had gone here and there to get his papers stamped, a troublesome and complicated business. He had fought a tense and energetic battle, but he had won.

20 The train pulled into the station. As Chen Xin opened the window, a cool breeze—a Shanghai breeze—rushed in. He saw his younger brother, now grown tall and handsome. Seeing him, the youth ran beside the train calling happily, "Second brother!" Chen Xin's heart shrank with regret. He calmed down, remembering how, ten years earlier, his elder brother had run beside the train too at his departure.

21 The train came to a halt. His younger brother caught up, panting. Chen Xin was too busy talking to him and handing him his luggage to notice that the cheerful group of middle-aged men were bidding him farewell.

22   "Elder brother, his wife, and Nannan are here too. They're outside. We only got one platform ticket with your telegram, saying you were coming. Have you got a lot of luggage?"

23   "I can manage. How's Mom?"

24   "She's OK. She's getting dinner ready. She got up at three this morning to buy food for you."

25   A lump rose in his throat; he lowered his head in silence. His brother fell silent too.

26   They moved quietly out of the long station. At the exit his elder brother, his wife, and son, Nannan, took his suitcases from him. They struggled under the weight for a few steps and then gave them back to him. Everybody laughed. His elder brother clasped him around his shoulders while his younger brother took his arm. His sister-in-law followed, carrying Nannan.

27   "Have you got all the necessary papers?" his elder brother inquired. "Tomorrow I'll ask for leave and take you to the labor bureau."

28   "I can take him. I haven't got anything to do," offered his younger brother.

29   Chen Xin's heart trembled again. He turned to him with a smile. "OK. No. 3 can take me."

30   It took three buses to reach home. His mother greeted him, lowering her head to wipe away tears. The three sons were at a loss for words, not knowing how and also too shy to express their feelings. All they could say was, "What's there to cry about?" It was his sister-in-law who knew how to stop her. She said, "This calls for a celebration, Mum. You should be rejoicing."

31   The tension lifted. "Let's eat," they said to one another. The table was moved from his mother's six-square-meter room to the big room his elder brother and his wife occupied. Chen Xin looked around. The room where he and his two brothers had once lived had a different appearance. The light green wallpaper was decorated with an oil painting and a wall light. Smart new furniture had been made to fit the room. The color was special too.

32   "What do you call this color?" asked Chen Xin.

33 "Reddish brown. It's the fashion," answered his younger brother with the air of an expert.

34 Nannan moved a stool over to a chest of drawers, climbed on it, and turned on the cassette player. The strong rhythm of the music raised everybody's spirits.

35 "You live well!" The excitement in Chen Xin's voice was obvious.

36 His elder brother smiled apologetically. After a long pause he said, "I'm glad you're finally back."

37 His sister-in-law carried in some food, "Now that you're back, you should find a sweetheart and get married."

38 "I'm old and ugly. Who'd want me?"

39 That made everyone laugh.

40 More than ten different dishes were placed on the table: diced pork and peanuts, braised spareribs, crucian carp soup. . . . Everybody piled food onto Chen Xin's plate. Even Nannan copied them. They went on serving him even when his plate was like a hill, as if to compensate for the ten hard years he had spent away from home. His elder brother almost emptied the stir-fried eel, Chen Xin's favorite dish, onto his plate. Though younger by three years, Chen Xin had always been his brother Chen Fang's protector. Chen Fang, tall and slender, had been nicknamed String Bean. His school marks were high, but outside of school he was poor at sports and had slow reflexes. His legs always got caught in the rope when it was his turn to jump. When playing cops and robbers, the side he was on was sure to lose. Chen Xin always fought for him when no one wanted him. "If you don't want my brother, I won't play either. And if I don't play, I'll make sure there'll be no game." And he meant what he said, so the boys compromised, fearing the terrible havoc he'd wreak on the one hand and hating to lose a popular, funny playmate on the other. Later, when Chen Fang had to wear glasses, he looked so scholarly that his nickname became Bookworm. For some reason Chen Xin considered this even more insulting than the previous one. He brought an end to it by bashing anyone who dared to utter it. When classes were suspended during the Cultural Revolution, he had finished junior middle and his brother senior middle school. The government's policy

was clear; only one son could work in Shanghai, the other must go to the countryside. His heartbroken mother had mumbled tearfully, "The palm and the back of my hand. . . . They are both my flesh and blood." Feeling sorry for her, Chen Xin volunteered, "I'll go to the countryside. Brother's a softy; he'll get bullied. Let him stay in Shanghai. I'll go. . . ." when he set out, Chen Fang had seen him off at the station, standing woodenly behind a group of friends, not daring to meet his eyes. As the train pulled out, Chen Fang moved forward to grasp Chen Xin's hand and run beside the train even after the speeding locomotive pulled them apart.

41   Chen Xin had finally returned. Overcome by all sorts of emotions, no one was particularly good at expressing them, so they transformed them into action. After supper his elder brother served tea while his wife made up a bed in the hut they had constructed in the courtyard. His younger brother stood in a queue for Chen Xin to go to the public bathhouse. When Chen Xin had eaten his fill and bathed, he lay on the double bed he was to share with his younger brother, feeling as relaxed as if he were drunk. The clean, warm bedding had a pleasant smell. The lamp on the desk beside the bed gave the simple hut a soft glow. Someone had placed a stack of magazines beside his pillow; the family knew and had remembered that he always read himself to sleep. Oh, home. This was home! He had returned home after ten years. Feeling a peace that he had never felt before, he closed his eyes and dozed off without reading. At dusk he woke up. Someone had come in and turned off the light. He opened his eyes in the darkened room and peacefully drifted back to slumber.

42   Early in the morning Chen Xin and his younger brother went to the labor bureau to start the formalities. The triangular lot beside the bus stop was filled with tailors' stalls and sewing machines. A young man with a measuring tape hanging round his neck accosted them. "Do you want something made?" They shook their heads and walked away. Curious, Chen Xin turned to look back at the young man who was dressed up like a model, soliciting customers.

43   His brother tugged at him. "The bus's coming. They're all school-leavers waiting for jobs. Shanghai's full of them." Chen Xin was astonished. His brother, shoving his way onto a bus, stopped at the door and called out to him, "Come on, Second Brother."

44 "Let's wait for the next one." The bus filled to bursting and the crowd at the bus stop made Chen Xin hesitate.

45 "More people will come. Get on quick." His brother's voice seemed to come from afar.

46 Chen Xin was strong. He could push. He shoved and squeezed until he caught the door handle and placed his feet on the steps. Then he mustered his strength and, amid cries and curses, pushed deeper into the bus to stand beside a window where he could hang on to the back of the seat. But he was crammed in and uncomfortable, bumping against people's heads or backs, having a hard time fitting in. All round him the passengers grumbled.

47 "Look at the way you're standing!"

48 "Just like a door plank."

49 "Outsiders are always so awkward on buses."

50 "Who're you calling an outsider?" An indignant No. 3 squeezed his way over, ready to pick a quarrel. Chen Xin tugged him. "Don't mind them. It's so crowded. Don't fight."

51 Softly, No. 3 gave him a tap. "Turn this way. Right. Hold the seat with your left hand. That's better. See?"

52 It was true. Chen Xin heaved a long sigh. He finally fitted in with his chest pressed against a back and his back against someone else's chest. At least his feet touched the floor. He turned his head to look and noticed a silent understanding among the passengers. Facing in the same direction, they all stood in a straight line, one behind the other. This way, the bus could fill to capacity. He thought of the remote town he had lived in where passengers squeezed in any old way, no scientific method at all. The bus held fewer people while the crowding and discomfort were the same. Shanghainese could adapt themselves to smaller spaces better.

53 The female conductor's voice came through a loudspeaker in Beijing and Shanghai dialects: "The next top is Xizang Zhong Road. Those who're getting off please get ready." With royal airs, these women looked proud and disdainful, like strict disciplinarians. But these announcements helped passengers. He recalled again the buses and women conductors in that little town: battered, dusty buses shooting

off before their doors were closed; unenthusiastic conductors never announcing stops, closing doors on passengers and catching their clothes in them. They had no rules at all. Things were shipshape in Shanghai. In that sort of environment, you had to do things properly.

54   When they got off the bus, No. 3 took Chen Xin down a street to one of the city's free markets. There were vegetables, fish, poultry, woollen sweaters, sandals, purses and hair clips, and stalls with fried food and meat dumplings. Below a placard announcing folk toys were paper lanterns and clay dolls. Seeing a market like that, Chen Xin had to laugh. What a strong contrast with Shanghai's wealthy, modern Nanjing Road.

55   "There are a lot of markets like this in Shanghai," explained No. 3. "The government encourages school-leavers to be self-employed."

56   The mention of the unemployed youth made Chen Xin frown. After pausing, he asked, "What was the matter with you, No. 3? Why did you fail the university entrance exam again?"

57   No. 3 lowered his head. "I don't know. I guess I'm stupid."

58   "Will you take it again next year?"

59   After a long silence, No. 3 said haltingly, "I might fail a third time."

60   That made Chen Xin angry. "You've no confidence in yourself."

61   No. 3 smiled honestly. "I'm not cut out to study. I forget what I learn."

62   "Your elder brother and I didn't have the chance to continue our studies. You're the only one in the family who can attend a university. But you've no ambition."

63   No. 3 fell silent.

64   "What are your plans then?"

65   No. 3 gave a laugh but said nothing. Just then someone called out behind them, "Chen Xin!"

66   They turned to face a woman leading a handsome little boy. She was in her thirties, with long permed hair and stylish clothes. Chen Xin couldn't place her.

67   "Have I grown so old that you don't recognize me?"

68 "Why, it's you, Yuan Xiaoxin! You don't look older, just prettier," Chen Xin laughed.

69 Yuan laughed with him. "Come on. We were in the same group in the countryside for two years, and yet you couldn't place me. What a poor memory!"

70 "No. It was just that I didn't expect to see you. Weren't you among the first batch to get a job? Are you still at Huaibei Colliery?"

71 "No. I came back to Shanghai last year."

72 "How come?"

73 "It's a long story. How about you?"

74 "I returned yesterday."

75 "Oh." She didn't show surprise. "Zhang Xinhu and Fang Fang are back too."

76 "Good," Chen Xin said excitedly. "So half the group has returned. We must get together sometime. Our hard times are finally over."

77 She gave a faint smile, revealing fine wrinkles at the corners of her eyes.

78 "Uncle," chirped the little boy. "You've got white hair like my grand-pa."

79 Chen Xin laughed, bending down to take the boy's hand, "This is your son?" he addressed Yuan.

80 "He's my sister's son," she explained blushing. "I'm not married. If I were I couldn't have come back."

81 "Oh." Chen Xin was surprised. Having graduated the same year as Chen Fang, Yuan must be thirty-three or thirty-four. "But why didn't you marry after your return?"

82 "Well, how shall I put it? One has to wait for an opportunity."

83 Chen Xin said nothing.

84 Caressing the little boy's fluffy hair she said softly, "Sometimes I felt that the sacrifices I made to return to Shanghai weren't worth it."

85 Chen Xin tried to console her, "Don't say that. It's good to be back."

86 "We'll be late for the film, Aunty," cried the boy.

87 "Right, we ought to be going." She looked up and smiled at Chen Xin. "Sorry if I dampened your spirits. But you're different. You're a man, and you're young. You'll find happiness."

88 Chen Xin's heart grew heavy as he watched her disappear into the crowd.

89 No. 3 commented, "She's a dead crab."

90 "What do you mean?"

91 "She's over thirty and hasn't got a boyfriend. She's like a dead crab. No hope."

92 "It isn't that she can't find one. She said she was waiting for someone to come along. Don't you see?"

93 Whether he understood or not, he answered disapprovingly, "Whatever you say, she's got a big problem. Men in their thirties are married, or else handicapped or ineligible. Eligible ones are hard to please and like young, beautiful girls. There are handfuls of twenty-year-old girls up for grabs."

94 Chen Xin meant to say that some people were waiting for love. But then he had second thoughts. That was beyond No. 3. Youngsters like him were so different from his generation. Throwing a sidelong glance at his brother, he said instead, "You really know a lot."

95 No. 3 looked very proud. The sarcasm was lost on him. Feeling apologetic, Chen Xin added in a kinder tone, "What do you do every day?"

96 "Nothing much except watch television, listen to the radio and sleep."

97 "What are your plans?"

98 He said nothing. When they were walking up the steps of the labor bureau, No. 3 confided, "I'd like to get a job."

99 Chen Xin halted. No. 3 turned to urge him, "Come on." His eyes were frank and sincere. Still Chen Xin avoided them.

100 He started work at his mother's factory, which was a long way away. It took him an hour and twenty minutes and three buses to get there. Assigned to work at a lathe, he had to learn from scratch; mockingly, he called himself a thirty-year-old apprentice. What he found hard was not the lathe but the adjustment to the new life and the fast pace. He had to run from the first bus to catch the second and then the third. . . . He mustn't miss any of the connections, which meant no smoking or daydreaming. He also found it hard to adjust to three rotating shifts. After a week on night shift it took more than two weeks to catch up on his sleep; as a result he was always tired. Within two months his face grew thinner. People said he looked better that way for the weight he had gained before he came home was not healthy. It was the result of the flour and stodge he had eaten in the North, whereas in Shanghai people ate rice.

101 Still he was glad he had returned to Shanghai even though his contentment was marred by a feeling of emptiness. Something was missing. The longing of the past ten years, an ache that had affected his sleep and appetite, had come to an end. But it had given him a goal to fight for. Now he was at a loss and felt empty. Maybe he was too happy being back? He must start a new life even though he had not given much serious thought to what it should be like. Things were only just beginning.

102 Ending the early shift, he dragged his legs, numb after eight hours' standing, to the bathroom, had a bath, changed, and left the factory. At the bus stop passengers spilled from the pavement onto the middle of the street. At least three buses were late. He waited for ten minutes but there was no sign of a bus. The passengers complained, assuming there must have been an accident. Losing patience, Chen Xin started to walk the few stops to catch the second bus. Li, a worker a year younger than he, had once shown him a shortcut. Relying on his memory, he went along a lane to a narrow cobbled street where people on both sides were washing honey buckets, cooking, knitting, reading, doing homework, playing chess or Ping-Pong, or sleeping on door planks, making the little street even narrower. The houses lining it resembled pigeon coops or the squares of a harmonica. Through the small, low windows he saw only beds, large and

small, two bunks and camp beds. So, recreation, work, other activities, all had to take place outdoors. What would they do when all those at work came home, or on rainy and snowy days? Suppose a grown-up son found a wife? If . . . behind the colorful shop windows, dazzling billboards, glamorous clothes and the latest film posters, there existed streets that narrow, rooms that crowded, lives that miserable. Shanghai was not as wonderful as one imagined.

103 It took him half an hour to reach the second bus stop. He shoved in and fitted his six-foot-high body into the smallest space as he had now learned to do, so that he wouldn't be taken for an outsider. It was already six when he got home, hungry and tired, expecting to find steaming hot food waiting for him, but supper was not ready. His mother had been shopping on Huaihai Avenue and had got home late, as it was impossible to rush through the teeming crowds on the streets, in stores, on buses. His sister-in-law had started to cook when she returned home from work. His mother helped wash and chop the vegetables.

104 "No. 3 does nothing but sleep and listen to his transistor radio," his mother said, showing her annoyance. "You could have sliced the meat for me, you layabout."

105 Frustrated, Chen Xin went over to his dark hut. A transistor radio was buzzing jarringly, half-talking and half-singing between two stations. He jumped in fright when, groping over toward his bed, he almost fell over a leg. His brother sat up and said, "You're back, Second Brother?"

106 Chen Xin turned on the desk lamp. "You're too lazy, No. 3. Why don't you give Mother a hand when you've nothing to do?" he stormed.

107 "I bought the rice and mopped the floor this afternoon," No. 3 said, defending himself.

108 "So what? When I was your age I was ploughing and harvesting in the countryside."

109 No. 3 fell silent.

110 "You're twenty this year. You should use your brains and do something useful. Get up. How can you while away your time doing nothing? Pull yourself together and act like a man."

111 No. 3 walked out silently. Chen Fang, just back from work, joined in. "You're an adult, No. 3. You should behave like one. We all need some rest when we come home from work. You should've helped."

112 Chen Xin added from the hut, "If you were studying for the university entrance exam, we wouldn't blame you, but would let you have as much time as you needed. . . ."

113 No. 3 remained silent. His mother interrupted to make peace. "It's all my fault. I didn't tell him what to do before I left. Supper'll soon be ready. Eat some biscuits first. Go and buy some vinegar for me, No. 3." When No. 3 had left, she told her two elder sons, "I'd rather he stayed at home and didn't roam around and get into trouble. Of all these unemployed youngsters, he's one of the nicest."

114 Supper was at last ready at half past seven. They ate in his mother's small room. No one felt like talking after the episode with No. 3, and with no chatting, no one enjoyed the meal. In an attempt to liven up the atmosphere, the sister-in-law broke the silence by saying, "My bureau has set up a club to help young bachelors who want to get married. Shall I get a form for you to fill in, Chen Xin?"

115 Chen Xin forced a smile. "Certainly not. I don't want to get married."

116 "Nonsense," his mother piped up. "Everyone gets married. With your looks, I'm sure you'll find a wife."

117 "Tall men like you are very popular nowadays with young girls," said a smiling No. 3, who had forgotten all about the reproaches he had received. He was still young.

118 "Getting married's no joke," his sister-in-law added. "You need to have at least a thousand yuan."

119 "We'll help even if we go bankrupt. Right, Chen Fang?" his mother asked.

120 "Hmm," his elder brother mumbled stupidly.

121 "But even if you've money, but no room, it's still hopeless," his sister-in-law went on.

122 "If we can't find a room I'll move out and sleep in the lane if he's getting married. Right, Chen Fang?" his mother asked again.

123 "Sure," his elder brother agreed.

124 "You mean what you say, Mum?" asked his sister-in-law, smiling.

125 His mother laughed. "Haven't I always meant what I said?"

126 "What sort of a joke is that?" Chen Xin put down his bowl. Although the three of them smiled, he sensed they were serious and full of hints. It was highly unpleasant.

127 He watched television in his brother's room. Before long he felt drowsy and could hardly keep his eyes open. He had to get up very early to go to work so he rose and retired to his hut where No. 3 was already in bed listening to the transistor radio, laughing at a comedy show, looking happy and comfortable.

128 "Bed so early?" Chen Xin asked.

129 "The television program was awful," No. 3 answered, but only when the program ended in applause. He reluctantly turned off the radio.

130 As usual, Chen Xin read for a few minutes and then switched out the light. In the darkness he heard his brother say, "I wish Dad was still alive. Then you could take his place while I took Mum's. Dad had a better job, working in an office."

131 Chen Yin's nose tingled. He wanted to hold his brother in his arms but he only turned and said hoarsely, "You should have tried to go to university."

132 After a while No. 3 began to snore. But Chen Xin's urge to sleep had vanished.

133 No. 3 could have had his mother's job but for him. . . .

134 He had called long distance saying, "No. 3 is living in Shanghai. He'll have a way out somehow. This is my only chance. . . ." His mother was silent at the other end. He had repeated, "I left home at eighteen, Mum, and I've been alone for ten years. Eighteen, and I've been all alone for ten years. Ten whole years, Mum." Still silence. He knew that his mother must be weeping and repeating to herself, "The palm and the back of my hand . . . Oh, the palm and the back of my hand . . ." In the end, No. 3 gave him the chance, which was only natural. Ten years ago, he had done the same for his elder brother. Like him, his younger brother had not complained or grumbled but was

nice to him. Turning in his sleep, No. 3 stretched one leg across him again. He did not push it away.

135 His brother was too lazy. Wouldn't everything be fine and everyone happy if he could enter the university? But not everyone could do that or go to a technical college. No. 3, ashamed at not having passed the exam, was amiable to everyone and never defended himself when he was criticized.

136 Chen Xin sighed. Life in Shanghai was not easy.

137 One evening, Aunt Shen, who worked in the same factory as Chen Xin's mother, was to bring a girl over to meet Chen Xin. As this had been arranged by his mother, he couldn't give a flat refusal although he found the situation awkward and silly. "You must start building a new life," said his elder brother. The statement had stunned him. When his new life became so concrete, he was not prepared for it and found it hard to accept. But, on second thought, he couldn't imagine a more significant and important new life. Maybe it just means marrying and having a child? Shaking his head, he smiled wryly, while an emptiness filled him. The ten years of longing for Shanghai, though gnawing, had been mixed with sweetness. It was like a dream, a yearning suffused with imagination. Anticipation was perhaps the best state. He remembered that when he was a child Saturday had always been better than Sunday.

138 But everyone in the family was full of enthusiasm. Preparations started after lunch. His sister-in-law swept and dusted her room, while his elder brother bought cakes and fruit. They planned to put Nannan to bed early in case he made a faux pas. It had happened once before when his grandmother was matchmaking and the young couple met at their place. Having always been present when grown-ups talked and not really understanding what it all was about, he suddenly pointed at the young man and girl and asked his mother, "Are they getting married, Mum?" It had been very embarrassing.

139 No. 3 was the busiest of all. He suggested that his mother cook lentil soup and offered Chen Xin his best clothes to wear. Chen Xin was annoyed by his excitement, which was just because he had nothing better to do.

140 His enthusiasm dampened, No. 3 still helped cook a large pot of lentil soup and made Chen Xin put on his bell-bottom trousers.

141 The girl arrived at seven-thirty; hiding shyly behind Aunt Shen and moving quickly over to an armchair in a corner, where she picked up a book to read. With her head lowered in the darkness, no one could see her features clearly.

142 "Chen Xin is a promising young man. The workers at the factory are very pleased with him. The ten years he spent in the small town in the countryside gave him a lot of experience. He's not irresponsible like new school-leavers," began Aunt Shen.

143 "Yes, it was hard for him, having to stay far away so long," said his mother, her eyes glancing over to the girl in the corner.

144 "How do you like working at a lathe, Chen Xin?" Aunt Shen turned to him. "Standing on your feet for eight hours is quite thing."

145 "It's OK. I don't mind it. I did all kinds of work in the countryside," replied Chen Xin, his attention fixed on the corner. He could see nothing except her profile, short hair and wide shoulders.

146 "Where's your son, Chen Fang? He must be a lively boy."

147 "He's sleeping. He's a nice boy," Chen Fang answered absentmindedly.

148 "He isn't so nice," countered his wife. "He's a little scamp. I don't want him."

149 "Don't talk like that. No one can take him away from you. Naughty boys are clever boys."

150 "That's true. . . ." Chen Xin's sister-in-law moved over to the corner. "Come and have some lentil soup."

151 Someone quicker had got to the corner first and switched on the standard lamp, saying, "You need some light to read." It was No. 3 who had slipped in unnoticed. Chen Xin was ready to throw him out, but he was grateful for his clever intervention.

152 The girl was bathed in light. All stopped talking and turned to her. Then all turned back to look at one another with disappointed expressions. After a while, his sister-in-law collected herself and said, "Don't read now. Come and have some lentil soup."

153 Very embarrassed, the girl finished her bowl of soup, wiped her mouth with a handkerchief and announced that she was leaving. No one made any attempt to stop her. After some polite remarks— "Please come again," "Take care of yourself"—they all rose to see her to the door, while Aunt Shen saw her out of the lane alone. This was the custom and all scrupulously obeyed it. Chen Xin, recently back, didn't know the rules. But No. 3 stood beside him, showing him what to do.

154 His mother asked, "How did you like her, Chen Xin?"

155 He laughed in reply.

156 "She's no good. Her cheekbones are too high. It's a sign that her husband'll die early," said No. 3.

157 "Don't be silly. No one's asking you."

158 "She's a bit short on looks," commented his elder brother.

159 "She's not pretty. I wonder what sort of person she is," said his mother.

160 The comments stopped when Aunt Shen returned. She addressed Chen Xin with a smile, "She seemed to like you. It all depends on what you think now."

161 Chen Xin remained silent smiling.

162 Realizing something was wrong, she added, "She's a nice girl, honest and simple. She's twenty-eight. Her parents are well-to-do. They don't mind whether the young man is well off or not, provided that he's nice. If he has no room, he can live with them. They have a spare room. . . . You'd better talk it over and give me a reply as soon as possible. . . . You must trust me, Chen Xin. I won't let you down. I've known you since you were a kid."

163 The whole family saw her to the entrance of the lane.

164 When they returned, his elder brother asked, "What's your impression of her?"

165 Chen Xin gave a frank reply. "Not good."

166 "Looks aren't important. You can date her for a while," suggested his sister-in-law.

167 "Looks are very important. Otherwise, my elder brother wouldn't have married you," Chen Xin teased her, causing general laughter.

168 His sister-in-law punched him on the shoulder, half laughing and half angry.

169 "I too think you could date her, Chen Xin. You mustn't go by looks alone," said his elder brother.

170 "Looks are very important when two people are introduced to each other. What would I fall in love with if not with her looks?" Chen Xin had his reasons.

171 "She doesn't have to be a beauty, but at least presentable." No. 3 had to voice his opinion.

172 "I think she's OK, Mum," his sister-in-law said, turning to his mother. "Besides, she has a room. That's very important in Shanghai."

173 Chen Xin retorted, "I'm marrying a girl, not a room."

174 "But it's an important factor. She's not ugly except that her face is a bit wide. Her eyes and eyebrows are all right."

175 "Forget the eyes and brows. For one thing, she doesn't attract me at all."

176 No. 3 laughed. This was something new to him.

177 "It's all for your own good. You can't live on attraction," said his sister-in-law.

178 "I agree," his elder brother added.

179 His mother broke in, "Let him decide for himself."

180 "Yes, yes," his elder brother seconded.

181 "Well, let's leave it at that," cried Chen Xin. It was all so pointless. "Don't bother about it anymore, Mum. I'll find my own wife. If I can't find a good wife, I'll remain a bachelor all my life." He retired to his hut.

182 In his dreams, a pair of eyes smiled at him, a pair of jade black eyes, in the shape of a new moon, eyes that smiled sweetly and gently. He woke up. From his window, only one-foot square, he saw a new moon.

183 Ah, eyes like a new moon. Where was she? Who was she? In the school where he had taught, every morning on his way to breakfast

in the canteen he saw a girl on an old-fashioned bicycle taking a shortcut from the back gate to the front. Elegant and petite, she always turned to look at him with those eyes. . . . He was confident that if he had asked, where are you going? she would have replied. He had never asked, and he would never know where she came from and where she was bound. Many people took a shortcut through his school. The front gate led to a hospital, cultural center, cultural troupe, and a machinery plant. At the back gate were a department store, playground, and cotton mill. She had passed by him hundreds, thousands of times and he had let her go even though he liked her and the sight of her made him happy. But his mind was set on Shanghai, his sole destination. He had finally returned to Shanghai, while she had become something in his past, something that would never return, leaving only a beautiful memory. He had few regrets as Shanghai carried more weight than a girl. Still he was a little sorry.

184 He remembered his school with its big garden, bigger than any school in Shanghai. The campus had a boulevard and a grove. In summer he iced melons in the well in front of his room. Several students used to bring food to him. But he had left these loyal students without saying good bye, afraid of complicating matters. He missed that school. That part of his life had touched his heart.

185 One morning his elder brother surprised them by telling his mother that his family wanted a separate residence card. He stammered, "Then . . . we can have . . . two rations of eggs. . . . Two rations of everything."

186 He avoided his mother's eyes when she looked up silently. Chen Xin wondered why he stuttered, as if it were something very embarrassing. After all it was a bright idea to get extra rations, which were given according to residence cards. He laughed. "What a brainstorm. How did you ever think of it?"

187 But his joke had made his brother flee in shame. His mother fixed her eyes on him, saying nothing.

188 Chen Xin left for work. Following behind him, No. 3 whispered as if it were a secret, "You know why elder brother wanted to have another residence card?"

189 "He wanted more eggs. . . ."

190 "Of course not," No. 3 cut him short. "He's after the room."

191 "The room?" Chen Xin halted, puzzled.

192 "Right," No. 3 affirmed. "The twenty-two-meter room belongs to him once he has his own residence card. It must be our sister-in-law's idea."

193 "Let him have it," Chen Xin moved on. "You don't put your brains to good use, yet you're very quick in such matters."

194 That day, Chen Xin was preoccupied, his brother's suggestion recurring in his mind. He had a feeling it implied something more. Then his younger brother's words rang in his ears: "He's after the room." He also recalled how his sister-in-law had harped about his marrying a girl with a room. Did it really mean that? Instinctively he waved his hand to deny it. "It can't be," he said almost aloud, scaring himself. Then he had to laugh.

195 When he returned home after work, he heard his mother saying to his elder brother, "You can't separate from us. Chen Xin has a right to that room too. He has been away working in the countryside for ten years. If he marries, you must divide it. Isn't that right?" His mother asked again when he didn't answer, "Isn't that right?" Only then did he echo, "Right." Bringing in a dish, his wife banged it loudly on the table. By coincidence?

196 A heavy cloud hung over the dinner table. His elder brother and wife sulked while his mother apologetically piled food in their bowls. No. 3 kept throwing meaningful glances at Chen Xin. "See?" he seemed to say. Disgusted, Chen Xin turned away, looking at no one. Luckily Nannan brightened the atmosphere by standing up and sitting down on the chair asking for this and that. He had thrown away his spoon and was grabbing with his fingers. His grandmother caught his hand and spanked him lightly on the palm. No. 3 made a face and cried "Hurrah!" while Nannan declared proudly, "It didn't hurt at all."

197 Everybody laughed. But Nannan's mother dragged him down from his chair and scolded, "You rude boy. You don't appreciate favors. You should thank your lucky stars that you're not kicked out." The laughter froze as everyone wondered whether to continue laughing or look solemn. "Oh, boy!" No. 3 said softly to ease the embarrassment.

198 Chen Xin's mother's face fell. "What do you mean?"

199 "Nothing," his sister-in-law countered.

200 "I know what you were driving at." His mother brought it into the open. "It's the room."

201 "No. I don't care about the room. But when my son grows up, I won't let him marry a girl if he doesn't have a room."

202 "Don't rub it in. I may be poor but I love all my sons and treat them all equally. The palm and the back of my hand, they're all my flesh. Chen Xin had to leave home because of Chen Fang. You shouldn't be so ungrateful." The old lady wept.

203 "Ungrateful? When other girls marry, they all get a suite of furniture including chairs and a standard lamp. When I married Chen Fang what did he have? Have I ever complained? And we never failed to send Chen Xin parcels and money every festival. What complaints can you have about such a daughter-in-law?" She wept too.

204 Chen Fang was stunned, not knowing whom to console.

205 No. 3 fled. He was useless, disappearing whenever a real crisis occurred.

206 "Don't cry." Chen Xin stood up. He was disturbed and agitated. "I don't want the room, Mother. I'm not marrying. I'm quite happy just back in Shanghai."

207 His mother was even sadder. Stealing a glance at him, his sister-in-law wept more softly.

208 At night, when everybody had retired to bed, his elder brother entered the hut smoking a cigarette. "Don't mind your sister-in-law," he said. "She's not mean, though she likes to grumble. I had no savings when we married. We had nothing except a bed and she's never complained. These last years, by scrimping and scraping, we bought some furniture and decorated the room. She was content with the improvement and wants to keep it. She's not bad and knows we should divide the room into two for you but just finds it hard to accept. I'll talk her round gradually."

209   "Forget it, Brother," Chen Xin stopped him. "I meant what I said. I
      swear I don't want the room. Please reassure her. Just don't separate
      from us. The old lady likes to have her whole family together."

210   His brother broke down, putting his arms around Chen Xin's shoul-
      ders. Though Chen Xin wanted to take him into his arms, he pushed
      him away and pulled the quilt over his head. Ten years had tough-
      ened him.

211   It was not easy to live in Shanghai.

212   Chen Xin, used to a carefree life, was very disturbed. The following
      morning, his day off, he got up at daybreak and went out, telling no
      one. He wanted to take a walk. Accustomed to the vast spaces in the
      north, he found Shanghai oppressive. High-rise buildings blocked
      out the breeze and the crowds made the air stale. Where could he go?
      He would go to the Bund.

213   He got off the bus and moved ahead. He could see the ships anchored
      in the Huangpu River on the other side of the road. On the bank there
      were green trees and red flowers, and old people doing taijiquan
      exercises, children playing and young people strolling and taking
      photos. He felt lighter. He crossed over to the river, the symbol of
      Shanghai. It was not blue, as he recalled, but muddy and stinking.
      Everything should be viewed from a distance, perhaps. A closer look
      only brought disappointment.

214   He came to the Bund Park, bought a ticket and went in. A fountain
      cascaded down a rock into a pool, rippling the water. He recalled that
      long, long ago, the water didn't fall directly into the pool but onto a
      statue of an umbrella under which a smiling mother and two chil-
      dren were sheltered. He had liked the sculpture so much when he
      first saw it as a child that he had stared at it refusing to be led away.
      It was like a symbol of his life. His father had died early and his
      mother had brought up her three sons, overcoming many difficulties.
      By sticking together, they had given one another warmth in hard
      times. When a typhoon hit Shanghai, the four of them had huddled
      together on the bed. The lightning, thunder, and howling wind had
      frightened and excited them. His younger brother had made exag-
      gerated shrieks, his mother playfully blamed the sky, and Chen Xin,
      acting as a protector, sat beside the light switch, which his elder

brother, having just learned something about electricity, was scared of. The storm was frightening and exhilarating. And there was a warmth. It was this that had attracted and drawn him home.

215 Water, falling on the pond, caused monotonous, empty ripples. A drop fell on his hand. He suddenly realized that it was from his eyes. What was the matter with him? When he had left home and his mother had sobbed her heart out, he hadn't shed a tear. Today . . . he experienced a tremendous disappointment, as if a most precious thing had suddenly been shattered. He turned and left the park.

216 The stores were opening and salespeople were removing the shutters outside the shop windows, which displayed a dazzling array of goods. The pedestrians on the street, so well dressed they looked like models, made his head spin. Unconsciously he stopped outside a shop window: Plump dolls with enormous heads were shooting down a slide, two others were swinging in each other's arms. In the background several Young Pioneers were flying model planes, which circled in a blue sky.

217 He couldn't move. It all reminded him of his childhood, his youth and the golden memory he had when he left Shanghai. He had mistaken this memory for Shanghai, to which he had struggled to return. Back home, he found he could never recapture the past.

218 The pedestrians increased, edging from the pavement onto the street. They seemed to be walking in file, and it was hard to move quickly. Life in such a compressed world was difficult. He remembered the struggles on buses. In restaurants, he had to stand beside tables for seats, and then others waited for him to leave while he ate. In the parks three couples sat on one bench and in the Yu-yuan Park lined up to have a picture taken on a rock mountain. Humans created not only wonders, but also problems. Why must he squeeze in? Why?

219 People rubbed shoulders, toes touched heels. Though they lived so closely, they were all strangers. Not knowing or understanding one another, they were proud and snobbish. He remembered a song his brother had recorded a few days ago: "People on earth are thronged like stars in the sky. Stars in the sky are as distant as people on earth."

220 A town was different. It was calm, maybe a little too deserted. One could run and stroll at ease on the streets and breathe freely. And in

a small town, the same people meeting constantly knew one another by sight, nodding to and greeting all acquaintances, creating a warm, friendly feeling. So a big city had its drawbacks, while a small town its advantages.

221 He moved with the stream of people, not caring where he was heading. He was dazed. The bittersweet yearning in the past decade disappeared, and with it the fullness he had felt in the past ten years. He had arrived at his destination. What was his next step? One must have a destination. Should he follow the new trend and equip himself with Western-style clothing, leather shoes, bellbottom trousers, and a cassette recorder . . . then find a sweet-heart and get married? . . . Yes. He could start doing that though it required effort and hard work. But would he find happiness if fashionable clothes concealed a heavy and miserable heart? If he married for the sake of getting married and the wife he chose was not understanding, wouldn't he be adding a burden to his life? Again he missed the new-moon eyes and the chances he had lost. A man's destination must be happiness, not misery. He suddenly felt that the destination he sought ought to be something bigger. Yes, bigger.

222 His spirits lifting, the dark clouds parted slightly to let through a dim light. Dim and hazy, it was still a light.

223 "Chen Xin."

224 He halted. Someone had called him.

225 "Chen Xin." He turned and saw a bus plowing slowly through the crowds on the street. His elder brother was leaning halfway out the window, reaching out to him. Behind him was his sister-in-law. They seemed agitated.

226 Shocked, he chased the bus. His elder brother grabbed his hands and gazed at him speechless and wooden, as he had done ten years ago when he ran after the train. Chen Xin was touched. His sister-in-law grabbed him too. "Chen Xin, you mustn't do anything drastic." She broke down.

227 "What nonsense!" Chen Xin laughed, tears rolling down his face.

228 "Come home," said his brother.

229 "Yes. I'll come home." Home was, after all, home. Quarrels were caused by poverty. I made you suffer, my loved ones. He was suddenly ashamed of having used the ten years as a trump card. His mother, two brothers and sister-in-law had also endured those difficult years. And besides, life meant joy, fun, pleasure. For instance, the boulevard, tree groves, the well, innocent pupils, and eyes like a new moon. . . . He had overlooked them all. But ahead of him there would be another ten, twenty and thirty years, a long, long time. He must give his future some serious thought.

230 Another train was leaving the station. Where was it bound? He knew that his destination would be farther, greater, and he would have to wander more than a decade, maybe two or three decades, a lifetime. He might never settle down. But he believed that once he arrived at his true destination, he would have no doubts, troubles, or sense of rootlessness.

*S*t. Augustine (354–430 CE) was a fourth-century philosopher and theologian whose ideas regarding divine grace, original sin, the Trinity, justice in war, and salvation have influenced the Christian church community. In this excerpt from his famous autobiography The Confessions, St. Augustine describes the crushing loss of a close friend, and his realization that friendship can only be truly fulfilling when it is based on mutual love for God. The relational dynamics of friendship and loss are examined both personally and in community.

from The Confessions

St. Augustine

4

1 In those years I started teaching grammar in the city of my birth, Thagaste. There I became attached to another close friend who, like myself, had arrived at the flower of young manhood; and with whom I shared both studies and outside interests. Actually we had grown up together as boys, had gone to school and played together. In childhood, however, he was not such an intimate friend as he later became, though even our later relationship could hardly be described in the truest sense as friendship. That, my God, is because true friendship exists only when you solder it together, and when human hearts stick to you in the love that has been poured into our hearts through the Holy Spirit which has been given to us.

2 Still it was a very dear friendship to us, ripened by the warmth of our common interests. I managed to deflect him from the Christian faith, which he had not really accepted internally; and so got him tangled in the superstitions and destructive fables that had kept my mother in tears over me. His mind wandered into error together with mine, until my soul could not get along without him. But all the while you were close behind your fugitives, for you are a God of vengeance and a Fountain of mercy. You convert us to yourself in wonderful ways. Thus when our friendship had scarcely completed its first year you

took him away, out of this life, and cut off what I valued as sweet above everything else in existence.

3   Who is there that can, through his own personal experiences, really "show forth all your praise"? What did you do at that time, my God? "How unsearchable are your judgments, and your ways past finding out." For my friend was stricken with a fever and for a long time lay unconscious in a lethal sweat. Then one day when his life was despaired of, without his being aware of it, he was baptized. I paid no attention to the incident, for I assumed that he would naturally retain what he had imbibed from me, and would hardly be affected by something performed on his body while he lay senseless. But things turned out differently. He began to recover his health and immediately, as soon as I was able to speak with him (which I could do because I never left him; in fact we hung onto each other too much for our own good), I tried to joke with him. I thought he would be ready to laugh with me at the baptism which (as he had learned) he had received while lying there incapable of thought or feeling. But he drew away from me horrified as if I were an enemy. In a sudden show of independence that startled me, he warned me that if I wished to remain his friend, I should never speak to him that way again. I was astonished and shaken up by his outburst, but concealed my feelings until he should convalesce to a state of health sufficient for me to deal with him and "set him straight." But he was snatched away from my rantings and placed in your keeping for my future consolation. Within a few days the fever returned, and at a moment when I was absent from his bedside, he died.

4   My heart was now darkened by grief, and everywhere I looked I saw death. My native haunts became a scene of torture to me, and my own home a misery. Without him everything we had done together turned into an excruciating ordeal. My eyes kept looking for him without finding him. I hated all the places where we used to meet, because they could no longer say to me, "Look, here he comes," as they once did. I became a problem to myself and kept asking, "Why are you cast down, O my soul, and why are you disquieted within me?" But my soul didn't know what to answer. If I added the words, "Hope thou in God," then my soul quite properly refused to comply. Why should it hope in God? The man my soul had loved and lost was

far more real and valuable than any fantasy such as I proposed to trust. Only tears were sweet to me, and only tears were able to take the place my friend had filled in my heart's delight.

5

5   But now, Lord, all these things lie in the past, and time has healed my wound. Let me listen to you who are the Truth. Let the ears of my heart move closer to your mouth, so you can tell me why tears are so sweet to those in misery. Have you, who are present everywhere, placed our troubles out of your reach? You reside within yourself, but we ricochet from one rugged experience to another; and if we weren't able to pour our troubles into your ears, what hope would be left us? How can there be such a sweet flavor in the bitter fruit we pluck from life—with all its groans, tears, sighs, and wailings? Does the sweetness come from the hope that you will hear us? In the case of prayer I would say Yes, for prayer is built on a longing to get through to you. But is it also the case when one is overwhelmed by grief and anguish over something lost, as I was? (I had no hope of my friend's coming back to life; in all my weeping I never once looked for it. I just grieved and let the tears fall, for my joy had disappeared and I was heartbroken.) Or is it that weeping is a bitter thing that gives us pleasure only because it relieves the tension created by sorrow?

6

6   Why speak of it now? This is not the time to ask questions but, rather, to confess to you. I was a dismal mess, along with every other soul who is chained to the things of this life. When we lose these things we're all torn to pieces; then we realize we were miserable even while we had them. That's the way it was with me. I wept bitterly and found release in bitterness. Wretched as I was, I could still put my own life ahead of my friend's on whose account I felt so wretched. For while I would gladly have changed my life, I was not about to lose it even for him. Whether or not it's true, they say that Orestes and Pylades were ready to die for each other, together, because each of them held life to be worse than death without each other. I felt exactly the opposite. It was a weird kind of sensation; I was fed up with living and very much afraid of dying. I suppose it was because of my great love for him that I hated and feared death as the cruel enemy that had stolen him away from me. I imagined that death

would suddenly destroy all men as it had destroyed him. I still remember thinking that way.

7   Look into my heart, my God, look deeply into it. Notice the things that I remember. You are my hope; you cleanse me of impure motives such as these. "My eyes are ever toward the Lord, for he will pluck my feet out of the net." I marveled that other mortals kept on living when he was dead, for I had loved him as though he would never die. I marveled even more that I could go on living with him dead. Someone has correctly described a friend as being "the soul's other half." I felt that my soul and my friend's soul were one, but we happened to be living in two bodies; and my life became a horrible thing to me because I didn't want to live as half soul.

7

8   What do you think of a madness that doesn't know enough to love men for what they are—men? What do you think of a simple-minded man who can't take what every man has to put up with? I raved, I sighed, I wept, and it became so distracting that I was unable to rest or even think. I could find no place to lay down the burden of my cut-up and bleeding soul. Neither in pleasant woods and fields, nor in laughter and music, nor in the fragrance of a garden, nor in the pomp and conviviality of banqueting, nor in the voluptuous delights of the bed and couch, nor even in books and poetry could I find rest. I hated everything, even the light itself; and when my soul finally stopped its crying, a heavy burden of misery kept it depressed.

9   To you, Lord, my soul should have been lifted, for I know you could have taken care of it. But I had neither the strength nor the will-power to do it. What made my situation even more trying was that I couldn't conceive of you as something firm and solid. I had some kind of empty fantasy that wasn't you at all, and so my error became my god. If I tried to unload my burden and rest it on that, it simply fell through and landed on me again. I couldn't stand my life, yet I couldn't escape it. Where could my heart go to hide from itself? Where could I go to leave myself behind? Where would I not follow myself? But I did finally leave the place of my birth. I found my eyes weren't always unconsciously searching for my missing friend if I went to places where they weren't used to seeing him. So I left the town of Thagaste and came to Carthage.

8

10 Time never takes time off. As it rolls on its deliberate way it affects our senses and does strange things to our minds. The days came and went, one after another, and they introduced me to other hopes and fresh memories. Little by little my soul was patched up as I resumed the kind of pleasures I had once enjoyed. The heartache began to ease and the place of sadness was occupied not by other sorrows, but by the cause of future sorrows. Why had that first great grief so easily pierced me to the quick, if it weren't that I had poured out my soul on the sand by loving a mortal as though he were immortal? What renewed and refreshed me was the consolation of other friends, with whom I went on loving the things I had formerly loved instead of you. I mean in particular the enormous myth, the bald-faced lie which our minds listened to with itching ears, and which corrupted us with its adulterous message. But as far as I was concerned that religious fable would not die the way some of my friends did.

11 In Carthage I was charmed by the company of new friends. I loved the talk, the laughter, the courteous little gestures toward one another, the sharing of the study of books of eloquence, the companionship that was sometimes serious and sometimes hilariously nonsensical, the differences of opinion that left no more bad feeling than if a man were disagreeing with his own self, the rare disputes that simply seasoned the normal consensus of agreement. We took turns listening to each other and teaching each other. We became restless if one of us was absent, and happily welcomed him back with open arms. These are the signs of genuine affection between friends who love and are loved in return. They can be recognized through the facial expression, the tongue, the eyes, and a thousand different motions and gestures. And by those signs our souls were kindled into a blaze and melted and fused together as one.

9

12 This is what we like to see in our friends. We like it so much that we have a guilty conscience if we don't respond to those who love us by loving them, without asking anything else in return. That is why we feel so distressed over a friend's death, and become gloomy and sad. Such an occasion turns joy into bitterness so that the heart is steeped in tears, and life becomes a total loss—a living death because of the

death of the living. Oh, happy is the man who loves you, my God, and his friend in you, and his enemy because of you. Such a man is the only person who never loses those who are dear to him, for they are all beloved in you, our God, and you are the God who is never lost. You made heaven and earth and fill them with your presence—for it was by filling them that you made them. The only way a man can lose you is to leave you; and if he leaves you, where does he go? He can run only from your pleasure to your wrath. Where does he end up without finding your law fulfilled in his punishment? Your law is the truth and you are truth.

*P*aul J. Wadell is a professor of religious studies at St. Norbert College in Wisconsin. He has written extensively on the subject of friendship, including his book Becoming Friends, *which explores the connections between friendship, worship, justice, and the life we are called to live. In this personal essay, Wadell makes the point that friendship is not always easy, but requires grace and a decision to care for another person despite the difficulties presented by the relationship. This is even more true for Christians, who must struggle to imitate the unconditional love of a God of infinite generosity and grace. Wadell's essay suggests that friendship plays an important role in Christian community.*

Shared Lives: The Challenges of Friendship

Paul J. Wadell

1   Friendships are possible only if we are willing to make space for another person in our lives. But this is risky and sometimes gets messy, because the very people we are initially delighted to make room for in our lives can hurt and disappoint us as the friendships unfold. Then our inclination is not to create space but to close it off and protect ourselves by writing our friends out of our story.

2   That's how it was with my friendship with Jim. Jim was one of my dearest lifelong friends, but it's surprising that our friendship ever began—much less continued—because Jim and I were startlingly different from one another. Aristotle said that too touch dissimilarity between persons makes friendship impossible. Jim and I proved him wrong—though not right away. I met Jim on August 28, 1965, our first day at a high school seminary in rural Missouri. I remember it vividly because I immediately knew that no one could ever confuse one of us for the other. Jim was an outgoing, charismatic, energetic Italian-American from the south side of St. Louis who loved adventure, was never afraid to take chances and was pretty good at getting into trouble. Growing up in the suburbs of Louisville, I was much more reserved than Jim (well, everybody was), liked routines more than adventures and thought "playing it safe" was not a bad way to live.

198

Still, I had a hunch that if I made room for Jim in my life, it would be good for me.

3   But little did I know how much this friendship would challenge me. Of course, no one enters a friendship thinking of ways it might go wrong; friendships are based in attraction and carry a sense of possibility. We are drawn to some persons more than others because of something we see in them. It can be their personality and temperament, their outlook on life, their goodness, their sense of humor or, as with Jim, it can be because they clearly are not who we are. But we also open our lives to them because we believe there is something promising in the friendship. We don't know what the friends will ask of us—or where the friendship will take us—but we risk investing in it because we believe that sharing life with these persons will bless us.

4   And it usually does, but not always in the ways we anticipate. Friendships are morally important because they draw us out of ourselves and teach us how to care for others for their own sake. Friendships create obligations and responsibilities because a friendship is a promise to attend to another's well-being over time. At first this is easy. There is nothing we want more than to be with our friends because we are enlivened by the goodness we see in them and by the love we receive from them. But friendships are living things—they are graced by unpredictable adventures—and this means that friendships don't always soar; sometimes they plod along, sometimes they stall, sometimes they stop for a while and sometimes they die. What does it mean to seek the good of a friend then?

5   It is easy to sentimentalize friendship, to think that friendships should always be uplifting, comforting and relatively easy relationships. But this is a silly and shallow view of friendship because it fails to recognize that our friends are just as flawed and fractured as we are. Jesus commands us to love our neighbors, and sometimes friends can be the hardest neighbors to love precisely because we know them so well. In friendships we see the other person's goodness—we see the image of God alive in that person—but we also become intimately aware of his or her shortcomings and weaknesses, of imperfections that may never disappear and struggles that may never end.

6   This was certainly true for Jim and me. As we moved from high school to college to graduate school, Jim changed in ways that were hard for me to understand. Though we were members of the same religious community, his life moved in directions that excluded me. He developed new friendships that left me questioning the status of our own and made me feel marginal to his life. As our interests increasingly diverged, it was harder to find what connected us. I began to wonder if the friend who was once a stranger might have become a stranger again.

7   But it worked both ways. I changed in a way that was extremely hard for Jim to accept when I left the religious community the two of us had belonged to for over 30 years. Jim was baffled, hurt and angered by my decision, particularly because he heard about it before I was able to tell him myself. He felt I had abandoned him at a time when he wasn't certain about his own future. But then Jim did something wonderful. Instead of counting his losses and moving on without me, he reached out to me. He would not let a decision he found hard to understand destroy a friendship that, despite all its turbulence, had always been a blessing and a gift. In his inimitable way, he continued to love me whether through a surprise phone call on a Saturday afternoon, a memorable meal at a Mongolian restaurant in Louisville or by showing up at my wedding on a sultry July morning in Green Bay.

8   I tried to do the same for Jim by giving him the time and space he needed to discover who he was, by being patient with him and by being with him when he was seriously ill. I wanted him to know that I loved him.

9   Friendships are narratives of hope, but they can be sustained only by a generosity of heart and spirit that enables the friends to work through the struggles and setbacks that mark any real relationship, in order to recover its original grace. Generosity of heart and spirit means that friends will not allow each other's very real failures and shortcomings to obscure the good they see in one another. Without this generosity, our vision of the other grows twisted and distorted and our recollection of them grievously selective. We forget the good that attracted us to them in the first place and are unwilling to acknowledge that along with whatever misdeeds we can trace to them, there is also a narrative of love, kindness and undeserved goodness and support.

10   Rooted in humility, a generosity of heart and spirit nurtures compassion, mercy and forgiveness, as well as a healthy sense of humor. It frees us to be patient with the foibles of our friends because we are honest enough to acknowledge our own. Lacking this virtue, we are much more likely to judge our friends harshly and ungraciously instead of charitably, because we think better of ourselves than we should and not nearly as well of them as they deserve. It is an essential virtue for friendship, because through it friends give one another the time each needs to struggle, to grow, to repent and be forgiven and to experience from one another the love of a God who never gives up on any of us.

11   Isn't that the heart of the matter? Christians think differently about friendship because their understanding of friendship is rooted not in rosy accounts of human perfectibility but in a God who remains ever faithful to us and who never, no matter how egregious our failings, writes us out of the story of divine love. Imitating such a scandalously uncalculating love is daunting; it demands not only that we stand by our friends when they are struggling or discouraged or suffering, but also that we do so when others have abandoned them and given up hope in them.

12   What does it mean to seek the good of a friend when a wrong he has done has removed him from the community? What does love require of us when a friend is in prison? Or when everyone else has turned against her? What is required of spouses when the bond of love in marriage has been irreparably broken, and the partner who was thought to be a lifelong companion has become more an enemy whom it is easy to hate than a friend whom we are given to love? These are not easy questions to answer. But Christians must wrestle with them as they navigate the challenges of friendship because they have been befriended by a God of limitless love and are disciples of one whose life, death and resurrection should make it hard for them to close their hearts to anyone.

13   My friend Jim died in January 2006. In the life of our friendship we celebrated one another's gifts, rejoiced in the life we shared with one another and hopefully made one another better. Yes, Jim sometimes turned my world upside down—but he also left it immeasurably

graced. I learned from him that what Augustine said was true: friends are God's gift to us and God loves us through them. But Augustine also said that friendships are "schools of love" and sanctifying ways of life, because by faithfully seeking the good of one who, like ourselves, can be both companion and stranger, heartfelt friend as well as occasional enemy, we help one another along on our way to God by growing together in the love of God

14   Jim was always full of surprises. Perhaps his most blessed surprise was teaching me that sometimes salvation comes to us from the person we are most tempted to write out of our story.

John Henry Newman (1801–1890) played a significant role in England's reli-gious history both as an Anglican priest as a young man and then after his conversion to Roman Catholicism. Following this, he became a leader in the Oxford Movement which tried to return England to a more Catholic religious tradition. In "What Is a University?," Newman defines a university both by popular definition and what he believes to be ultimately true. He focuses on importance of the community in the university, including close teacher-student relationships and the intimate connection between the university and its stu-dents. He also stresses that there is much more to be gained from a university education than what we can glean from books.

What Is a University?

John Henry Newman

1   If I were asked to describe as briefly and popularly as I could, what a University was, I should draw my answer from its ancient designa-tion of a *Studium Generale*, or "School of Universal Learning." This description implies the assemblage of strangers from all parts in one spot;—*from all parts*; else, how will you find professors and students for every department of knowledge? and *in one spot*; else, how can there be any school at all? Accordingly, in its simple and rudimental form, it is a school of knowledge of every kind, consisting of teacher and learners from every quarter. Many things are requisite to com-plete and satisfy the idea embodied in this description; but such as this a University seems to be in its essence, a place for the communi-cation and circulation of thought, by means of personal intercourse, through a wide extent of country.

2   There is nothing far-fetched or unreasonable in the idea thus presented to us; and if this be a University, then a University does but contemplate a necessity of our nature, and is but one specimen in a particular medi-um, out of many which might be adduced in others, of a provision for that necessity. Mutual education, in a large sense of the word, is one of the great and incessant occupations of human society, carried on partly with set purpose, and partly not. One generation forms another; and

the existing generation is ever acting and reacting upon itself in the persons of its individual members. Now, in this process, books, I need scarcely say, that is, the *litera scripta*, are one special instrument. It is true; and emphatically so in this age. Considering the prodigious powers of the press, and how they are developed at this time in the never-intermitting issue of periodicals, tracts, pamphlets, works in series, and light literature, we must allow there never was a time which promised fairer for dispensing with every other means of information and instruction. What can we want more, you will say, for the intellectual education of the whole man, and for every man, than so exuberant and diversified and persistent a promulgation of all kinds of knowledge? Why, you will ask, need we go up to knowledge, when knowledge comes down to us? The Sibyl wrote her prophecies upon the leaves of the forest, and wasted them; but here such careless profusion might be prudently indulged, for it can be afforded without loss, in consequence of the almost fabulous fecundity of the instrument which these latter ages have invented. We have sermons in stones, and books in the running brooks; works larger and more comprehensive than those which have gained for ancients an immortality, issue forth every morning, and are projected onwards to the ends of the earth at the rate of hundreds of miles a day. Our seats are strewed, our pavements are powdered, with swarms of little tracts; and the very bricks of our city walls preach wisdom, by informing us by their placards where we can at once cheaply purchase it.

3   I allow all this, and much more; such certainly is our popular education, and its effects are remarkable. Nevertheless, after all, even in this age, whenever men are really serious about getting what, in the language of trade, is called "a good article," when they aim at something precise, something refined, something really luminous, something really large, something choice, they go to another market; they avail themselves, in some shape or other, of the rival method, the ancient method, of oral instruction, of present communication between man and man, of teachers instead of learning, of the personal influence of a master, and the humble initiation of a disciple, and, in consequence, of great centres of pilgrimage and throng, which such a method of education necessarily involves. This, I think, will be found to hold good in all those departments or aspects of society, which possess an

interest sufficient to bind men together, or to constitute what is called "a world." It holds in the political world, and in the high world, and in the religious world; and it holds also in the literary and scientific world.

4   If the actions of men may be taken as any test of their convictions, then we have reason for saying this, viz.:—that the province and the inestimable benefit of the *litera scripta* is that of being a record of truth, and an authority of appeal, and an instrument of teaching in the hands of a teacher; but that, if we wish to become exact and fully furnished in any branch of knowledge which is diversified and complicated, we must consult the living man and listen to his living voice. I am not bound to investigate the cause of this, and anything I may say will, I am conscious, be short of its full analysis;—perhaps we may suggest, that no books can get through the number of minute questions which it is possible to ask on any extended subject, or can hit upon the very difficulties which are severally felt by each reader in succession. Or again, that no book can convey the special spirit and delicate peculiarities of its subject with that rapidity and certainty which attend on the sympathy of mind with mind, through the eyes, the look, the accent, and the manner, in casual expressions thrown off at the moment, and the unstudied turns of familiar conversation. But I am already dwelling too long on what is but an incidental portion of my main subject. Whatever be the cause, the fact is undeniable. The general principles of any study you may learn by books at home; but the detail, the colour, the tone, the air, the life which makes it live in us, you must catch all these from those in whom it lives already. You must imitate the student in French or German, who is not content with his grammar, but goes to Paris or Dresden: you must take example from the young artist, who aspires to visit the great Masters in Florence and in Rome. Till we have discovered some intellectual daguerreotype, which takes off the course of thought, and the form, lineaments, and features of truth, as completely and minutely, as the optical instrument reproduces the sensible object, we must come to the teachers of wisdom to learn wisdom, we must repair to the fountain, and drink there. Portions of it may go from thence to the ends of the earth by means of books; but the fulness is in one place alone. It is in such assemblages and congregations of intellect that books themselves, the masterpieces of human genius, are written, or at least originated.

5   The principle on which I have been insisting is so obvious, and
    instances in point are so ready, that I should think it tiresome to pro-
    ceed with the subject, except that one or two illustrations may serve
    to explain my own language about it, which may not have done jus-
    tice to the doctrine which it has been intended to enforce.

6   For instance, the polished manners and high-bred bearing which are so
    difficult of attainment, and so strictly personal when attained,—which
    are so much admired in society, from society are acquired. All that goes
    to constitute a gentleman,—the carriage, gait, address, gestures, voice;
    the ease, the self-possession, the courtesy, the power of conversing, the
    talent of not offending; the lofty principle, the delicacy of thought, the
    happiness of expression, the taste and propriety, the generosity and
    forbearance, the candour and consideration, the openness of hand;—
    these qualities, some of them come by nature, some of them may be
    found in any rank, some of them are a direct precept of Christianity;
    but the full assemblage of them, bound up in the unity of an individ-
    ual character, do we expect they can be learned from books? are they
    not necessarily acquired, where they are to be found, in high society?
    The very nature of the case leads us to say so; you cannot fence with-
    out an antagonist, nor challenge all comers in disputation before you
    have supported a thesis; and in like manner, it stands to reason, you
    cannot learn to converse till you have the world to converse with;
    you cannot unlearn your natural bashfulness, or awkwardness, or
    stiffness, or other besetting deformity, till you serve your time in
    some school of manners. Well, and is it not so in matter of fact? The
    metropolis, the court, the great houses of the land, are the centres to
    which at stated times the country comes up, as to shrines of refine-
    ment and good taste; and then in due time the country goes back
    again home, enriched with a portion of the social accomplishments,
    which those very visits serve to call out and heighten in the gracious
    dispensers of them. We are unable to conceive how the "gentleman-
    like" can otherwise be maintained; and maintained in this way it is.

7   And now a second instance: and here too I am going to speak with-
    out personal experience of the subject I am introducing. I admit I
    have not been in Parliament, any more than I have figured in the *beau
    monde*; yet I cannot but think that statesmanship, as well as high
    breeding, is learned, not by books, but in certain centres of education.
    If it be not presumption to say so, Parliament puts a clever man *au*

courant with politics and affairs of state in a way surprising to himself. A member of the Legislature, if tolerably observant, begins to see things with new eyes, even though his views undergo no change. Words have a meaning now, and ideas a reality, such as they had not before. He hears a vast deal in public speeches and private conversation, which is never put into print. The bearings of measures and events, the action of parties, and the persons of friends and enemies, are brought out to the man who is in the midst of them with a distinctness, which the most diligent perusal of newspapers will fail to impart to them. It is access to the fountain-heads of political wisdom and experience, it is daily intercourse, of one kind or another, with the multitude who go up to them, it is familiarity with business, it is access to the contributions of feet and opinion thrown together by many witnesses from many quarters, which does this for him. However, I need not account for a fact, to which it is sufficient to appeal; that the Houses of Parliament and the atmosphere around them are a sort of University of politics.

8   As regards the world of science, we find a remarkable instance of the principle which I am illustrating, in the periodical meetings for its advance, which have arisen in the course of the last twenty years, such as the British Association. Such gatherings would to many persons appear at first sight simply preposterous. Above all subjects of study, Science is conveyed, is propagated, by books, or by private teaching; experiments and investigations are conducted in silence; discoveries are made in solitude. What have philosophers to do with festive celebrities, and panegyrical solemnities with mathematical and physical truth? Yet on a closer attention to the subject, it is found that not even scientific thought can dispense with the suggestions, the instruction, the stimulus, the sympathy, the intercourse with mankind on a large scale, which such meetings secure. A fine time of year is chosen, when days are long, skies are bright, the earth smiles, and all nature rejoices; a city or town is taken by turns, of ancient name or modern opulence, where buildings are spacious and hospitality hearty. The novelty of place and circumstance, the excitement of strange, or the refreshment of well-known faces, the majesty of rank or of genius, the amiable charities of men pleased both with themselves and with each other; the elevated spirits, the circulation of thought, the curiosity; the morning sections, the outdoor exercise,

the well-furnished, well-earned board, the not ungraceful hilarity, the evening circle; the brilliant lecture, the discussions or collisions or guesses of great men one with another, the narratives of scientific processes, of hopes, disappointments, conflicts, and successes, the splendid eulogistic orations; these and the like constituents of the annual celebration, are considered to do something real and substantial for the advance of knowledge which can be done in no other way. Of course they can but be occasional; they answer to the annual Act, or Commemoration of a University, not to its ordinary condition; but they are of a University nature; and I can well believe in their utility. They issue in the promotion of a certain living and, as it were, bodily communication of knowledge from one to another, of a general interchange of ideas, and a comparison and adjustment of science with science, of an enlargement of mind, intellectual and social, of an ardent love of the particular study, which may be chosen by each individual, and a noble devotion to its interests.

9   Such meetings, I repeat, are but periodical, and only partially represent the idea of a University. The bustle and whirl which are their usual concomitants, are in ill keeping with the order and gravity of earnest intellectual education. We desiderate means of instruction which involve no interruption of our ordinary habits; nor need we seek it long, for the natural course of things brings it about, while we debate over it. In every great country, the metropolis itself becomes a sort of necessary University, whether we will or no. As the chief city is the seat of the court, of high society, of politics, and of law, so as a matter of course is it the seat of letters also; and at this time, for a long term of years, London and Paris are in fact and in operation Universities, though in Paris its famous University is no more, and in London a University scarcely exists except as a board of administration. The newspapers, magazines, reviews, journals, and periodicals of all kinds, the publishing trade, the libraries, museums, and academies there found, the learned and scientific societies, necessarily invest it with the functions of a University; and that atmosphere of intellect, which in a former age hung over Oxford or Bologna or Salamanca, has, with the change of times, moved away to the centre of civil government. Thither come up youths from all parts of the country, the students of law, medicine, and the fine arts, and the *employés* and *attachés* of literature. There they live, as chance determines; and they are satisfied with their temporary home, for they find in it all that we

promised to them there. They have not come in vain, as far as their own object in coming is concerned. They have not learned any particular religion, but they have learned their own particular profession well. They have, moreover, become acquainted with the habits, manner, and opinions of their place of sojourn, and done their part in maintaining the tradition of them. We cannot then be without virtual Universities; a metropolis is such: the simple question is, whether the education sought and given should be based on principle, formed upon rule, directed to the highest ends, or left to the random succession of masters and schools, one after another, with a melancholy waste of thought and an extreme hazard of truth.

10 Religious teaching itself affords us an illustration of our subject to a certain point. It does not indeed seat itself merely in centres of the world; this is impossible from the nature of the case. It is intended for the many not the few; its subject matter is truth necessary for us, not truth recondite and rare; but it concurs in the principle of a University so far as this, that its great instrument, or rather organ, has ever been that which nature prescribes in all education, the personal presence of a teacher, or, in theological language, Oral Tradition. It is the living voice, the breathing form, the expressive countenance, which preaches, which catechises. Truth, a subtle, invisible, manifold spirit, is poured into the mind of the scholar by his eyes and ears, through his affections, imagination, and reason; it is poured into his mind and is sealed up there in perpetuity, by propounding and repeating it, by questioning and requestioning, by correcting and explaining, by progressing and then recurring to first principles, by all those ways which are implied in the word "catechising." In the first ages, it was a work of a long time; months, sometimes years, were devoted to the arduous task of disabusing the mind of the incipient Christian of its pagan errors, and of moulding it upon the Christian faith. The Scriptures indeed were at hand for the study of those who could avail themselves of them; but St. Irenaeus does not hesitate to speak of whole races, who had been converted to Christianity, without being able to read them. To be unable to read or write was in those times no evidence of want of learning: the hermits of the deserts were, in this sense of the word, illiterate; yet the great St. Anthony, though he knew not letter, was a match in disputation for the learned philosophers who came to try him. Didymus again, the great Alexandrian theologian, was blind. The ancient discipline, called the *Disciplina*

Arcani, involved the same principle. The more sacred doctrines of Revelation were not committed to books but passed on by successive tradition. The teaching on the Blessed Trinity and the Eucharist appears to have been so handed down for some hundred years; and when at length reduced to writing, it has filled many folios, yet has not been exhausted.

11   But I have said more than enough in illustration; I end as I began;—a University is a place of concourse, whither students come from every quarter for every kind of knowledge. You cannot have the best of every kind everywhere; you must go to some great city or emporium for it. There you have all the choicest productions of nature and art all together, which you find each in its own separate place elsewhere. All the riches of the land, and of the earth, are carried up thither; there are the best markets, and there the best workmen. It is the centre of trade, the supreme court of fashion, the umpire of rival talents, and the standard of things rare and precious. It is the place for seeing: galleries of first-rate pictures, and for hearing wonderful voices and performers of transcendent skill. It is the place for great preachers, great orators, great nobles, great statesmen. In the nature of things, greatness and unity go together; excellence implies a centre. And such, for the third or fourth time, is a University; I hope I do not weary out the reader by repeating it. It is the place to which a thousand schools make contributions; in which the intellect may safely range and speculate, sure to find its equal in some antagonist activity, and its judge in the tribunal of truth. It is a place where inquiry is pushed forward, and discoveries verified and perfected, and rashness rendered innocuous, and error exposed, by the collision of mind with mind, and knowledge with knowledge. It is the place where the professor becomes eloquent, and is a missionary and a preacher, displaying his science in its most complete and most winning form, pouring it forth with the zeal of enthusiasm, and lighting up his own love of it in the breasts of his hearers. It is the place where the catechist makes good his ground as he goes, treading in the truth day by day into the ready memory, and wedging and tightening it into the expanding reason. It is a place which wins the admiration of the young by its celebrity, kindles the affections of the middle-aged by its beauty, and rivets the fidelity of the old by its associations. It is a seat of wisdom, a light of

the world, a minister of the faith, an Alma Mater of the rising generation. It is this and a great deal more, and demands a somewhat better head and hand than mine to describe it well.

12 Such is a University in its idea and in its purpose; such in good measure has it before now been in fact. Shall it ever be again? We are going forward in the strength of the Cross, under the patronage of the Blessed Virgin, in the name of St Patrick, to attempt it.

*E*rnest L. Boyer Sr. (1928–1995) was arguably the most influential educator in the last quarter of the twentieth century. Highlights of his forty-year career include service as chancellor of the State University of New York; a member of national education commissions under Presidents Nixon, Ford, and Carter, and then U.S. Commissioner of Education. As president of The Carnegie Foundation for the Advancement of Teaching, he influenced educational policy and practice from early childhood through graduate education. Despite his place in the national spotlight, Ernie Boyer retained a special affection for Messiah College, having graduated from Messiah Academy in 1948. In this essay, revised from a Convocation address given on the occasion of the College's seventy-fifth birthday, Boyer argues that amidst the College's history, four particular values remain prominent.

Retaining the Legacy of Messiah College

Ernest L. Boyer Sr.

1   Since its founding in 1909 Messiah Bible School, now Messiah College, has been a very special place. It was a special place that first fall semester when twelve students enrolled, no tuition was charged, the room rate was 50 cents a week, and the weekly charge for meals was $2.75. Throughout its history this College has been a special place, not least because of all the faculty members and dedicated spouses who contributed without praise or recognition but who in their own way made the College possible and helped to shape the lives of its many students, my own included.

2   Four virtues have, in my judgment, shaped the quality and character of Messiah College. These are virtues which should be reflected in all academic venues, but have been especially true of this College. In each regard countless colleges and universities across America would be well served by following the model so effectively engaged on this campus.

3   First, as I read the history of Messiah College, and as I remember my four years at this institution, I am impressed that the College has

sought to broaden education, not restrict it. In 1909, this newly mint-
ed institution was called a Bible school, and indeed it was. Bible pen-
etrated the institution from top to bottom and yet the curriculum,
that very first curriculum, included arithmetic, grammar, literature,
history, science, and vocal music. These are subjects that we today
would call the liberal arts.

4   I find it quite remarkable that in his 1915 baccalaureate address President S. R. Smith addressed the students of this college, Messiah Bible
School, and asked them whether they had ever seen a painting the
equal of Michelangelo's who painted the Sistine Chapel. President
Smith also asked them whether it had been their privilege ever to
gaze upon the face of a woman as beautiful as the statue of the Venus
of Milo, the magnificent Greek sculpture that stands in the Louve in
Paris.

5   It was 1915, and the first president was speaking. This was not easy
for some of the brethren and perhaps sisters to take; this business of
wandering from the Bible, or so they thought. One critic wrote caus-
tically of this broader curriculum and he said, "I may be counted
dense, if I fail to find connections between Bible subjects and
trigonometry and geometry and Virgil and of all things the history of
the United States." But then Peter Wiebe, an advocate and a defend-
er of the school, a brilliant early leader, countered, in my judgement,
in a marvelously gentle but pointed way: he recalled Frances David-
son who had studied geometry at Messiah. When she went to Africa
as a missionary, she was able to draw upon the breadth of her knowledge gained at this College to survey the first mission station at
Matopa. I wonder, how many times since has a baccalaureate speaker at this College, at any college, cited Michelangelo and the Venus of
Milo as an inspiration to the students?

6   Nearly forty years ago, a marvelous poet/philosopher, Mark Van
Doren, said the connectedness of things is what educators contemplate to the limit of their capacity. He wrote, "No human capacity is
great enough to permit a vision of the world as simple." But he went
on to say that if educators do not aim at the vision of connectedness,
no one else will. And the consequences are dire when no one does.
Van Doren concluded by saying that the student who can begin early
in life to think of things as connected are those who will understand

life and live it well. This too, is the vision of Messiah College. Unity, not fragmentation, must be the aim of education, and most especially what one calls Christian education. In the Christian world view the so-called secular and sacred are distinctions without meaning since all truth should ultimately be considered sacred.

7 The search for connections was a conviction at Messiah College from the very first. Why else would S. R. Smith seek to find connections between Michelangelo and King David? Their inspirations were, in some respects, the same.

8 Also from the very first Messiah College has been not just a campus but a community as well. In the early 1940s I traveled from Dayton, Ohio, an outpost to the west, to Grantham, Pennsylvania. Here faculty and students worked and played together. They were supportive of each other. We believed, somewhat naively to be sure, that the College had a special mission. A sense of community prevailed, a feeling that we were dependent on each other. The College was a small college, but I still recall those days in which people met not only with cordiality but occasionally with compassion. It was community at its best.

9 Now if you will, I'd like to contrast that picture with the mighty United States Office of Education in Washington, DC, with its 3000 employees and its twelve-billion dollar budget. Here I've found people who have lost their zest for living, at least between the hours of nine to five. People, incidentally, who were not lazy or evil as the critics like to say, but people who lacked a larger vision. In fact, soon after I arrived in the Commissioner's office, the head of the employees' union walked in one day and asked if we could meet. I agreed, clearly expecting a confrontation, a debate over salaries and benefits and the like. I can tell you I was absolutely stunned when the first question I received was, "Mr. Commissioner, can you tell us why we're here?" The employees of government had money and had security but they were searching for a larger purpose. If it has any failing, the failing of government is its incapacity to be inspired and to be driven by compassion.

10 This came home to me in quite a different way several weeks after I was there. I hired a young recruit from the State Department to work as my assistant. She said that the first day on the job in the State Department she was asked by an assistant secretary if she would

draft his letters in response to the pile of mail that, like the sewers of Paris, keeps flowing in and in. And so she did. She took them home and worked conscientiously. She began one by saying, "We were delighted to receive your letter of September 23," and then went on to work out the details of the response. The next day her boss called her in and very soberly announced, "I read over your drafts and I want you to know right at the beginning that the State Department is never delighted."

11 There's a point. The government's organizations have an inclination to lose compassion. They carry on the tasks but the connections between the people all too frequently are snapped. I'm suggesting that if education is to exercise a moral force in society, the process must take place in a moral context. It must occur in communities that are held together not by pressure or coercion, not by the accident of history, but by shared purposes and goals, by simple acts of kindness, and by the respect group members have for one another. I believe a sense of community has been a hallmark of Messiah College, but the institution is not the walls. It's the human spirit in this room. And this tradition and conviction will be maintained only as there is a continuing commitment to community here today.

12 Third, in reflecting on this institution, I realize that Messiah College has been a place where dedicated teachers are also good and trusted friends. About eighteen months ago I walked unannounced into a sixth grade inner-city classroom in New Haven. About thirty students were clustered around the teacher's desk, and as I moved closer I discovered they were completely absorbed in reading Charles Dickens' Oliver Twist. Every child in that room knew the good guys from the bad guys, and they were cheering little Oliver on as he was trying to survive in an urban jungle. Every student knew the story because each one lived it every day. I've concluded that in that classroom a miracle had occurred. The teacher had quite literally brought nineteenth-century London to New Haven, and she had inspired students to reflect on a larger meaning in their lives.

13 Several years ago, I couldn't go to sleep so instead of counting sheep I counted all the teachers I'd had. It's an exercise I highly commend. There were a few nightmares in the bunch which I recalled, but then sanity drove me quickly to think about the great ones. I thought of my first-grade teacher, Miss Rice, who on the first day of school said,

"Good morning, class, today we learn to read." She inspired me to think that learning and language were connected, a conviction that I carry with me to this very day.

14   Teachers have a message to convey, and so they must communicate with care. But above all, good teachers become great teachers when they reveal themselves, when they are willing to be sensitive and self-revealing, and when they have the capacity not only to teach their subject but to teach themselves as well. They must be capable of laughing and crying and once in a while saying, "I don't know" or, "I believe you're smarter than I am on that point."

15   During my first year as an undergraduate at Messiah College, President C. N. Hostetter, Jr., taught me Bible. That term he was also holding a three-week revival meeting away from campus, and in a burst of carelessness one day he asked if I would teach the class next Friday. It blew my mind, to say nothing of my fellow students. I don't remember how I did; I'm afraid to ask. But I do know that that simple act of confidence, expressed perhaps almost unwittingly by a teacher, profoundly changed my life. The simple truth is that teachers do change a life forever if they teach not only what they know but how they live as well.

16   About three months ago I taped a television program in Los Angeles. The cameraman came bursting around as soon as the red light had gone off and he said, "I want to tell you about my first grade teacher." I said, "All right, go ahead." He began, "During Christmas recess she sent me a picture postcard. I don't remember the picture on the card and I don't remember the message that she wrote, but I'll never forget that she addressed it to Mr. Andy Johnson." This man's eyes got glazed over; he is a fifty-year-old duffer and he is still basking in the glow of a picture postcard sent to him by his first grade teacher. At first I worried, but then I realized that's what education is all about. For fifty years this man has been drawing strength and inspiration from a teacher who said you are somebody. You're a "Mr." These comments, inadvertently conveyed in my judgement, mark the centrality of this institution, and I'm suggesting that throughout its history, Messiah College has been a place where dedicated teachers have profoundly shaped the lives of students.

17   Finally, as I think about this institution, I realize that Messiah College is something special because it has helped students seek connections

between what they learn and how they live. John Gardner said on one occasion that the deepest threat to the integrity of any community is an incapacity on the part of its citizens to any worthy common purpose. And then Gardner went on to reflect on the barrenness of a life that encompasses nothing beyond itself.

18   One of the projects I directed at the Carnegie Foundation was a study of the American high school. For this project we visited high schools from coast to coast. We spent over 2000 hours talking with faculty and students, and with parents. I must confess that during that study I became deeply troubled by what can only be characterized as malaise among the students. I concluded that we not only have a school problem in this nation, we have a youth problem that's perhaps more fundamental and more serious. I was troubled that it's possible for teenagers to finish high school and yet never be asked to participate responsibly in life, never be encouraged to spend time with older people who are lonely, never help a child who hasn't learned to read or even to help clean up litter on the street. One student told us during our interview that she had a job working at McDonald's, and then she went on to say, "It's not very exciting but at least I'm feeling useful." I thought, it's a sad comment on our culture that being useful means pushing Big Macs at McDonald's.

19   In the report we suggest a Carnegie unit, a service term, for every student. We suggest that students do voluntary work in nursing homes, in public parks, in churches, in schools throughout the country. I'm suggesting that it is urgently important that students seek connections between the classroom and the needs of the people. I worry about the generation gap, in which the older and the younger somehow do not communicate with one another.

20   In the summer of 1922, two students of this College, C. N. Hostetter, Jr., and Albert Engle, went to Iron Springs, about thirty-five miles from the College. They walked the last seven miles. They ate berries on the way. They preached in the local store. They prayed in the stone quarry close by, and they attracted the attention of the moonshiners and the bootleggers in the region. The revival that these teenage boys started ran for several weeks and the work continues to this day.

21   In 1967 Messiah College students formed what they called a "committee for the inner city." The goal was to share Christ and His love

to those who may be passed by on the other side. These students donated blood to two hemophiliacs for several years, they helped build houses for unsheltered people in Kentucky, they worked with ex-convicts at Yokecrest Half-Way House. This kind of work in Harrisburg continues today through Messiah College; some of it is linked to courses, some is focused on service-learning, some is expressed through Spring Break student service projects.

22   One of my favorite verse writers is Vachel Lindsay who wrote on one occasion that it is the world's one crime for its babes to grow dull. Not that they sow but that they seldom reap. Not that they serve but that they have no God to serve, not that they die but that they die like sheep. The tragedy of life is not death, it is destined for us all. The tragedy of life is to die with convictions undeclared, and service unfulfilled.

23   It was in 1909 that a small band of church leaders had a large audacious vision. They would build a school, they said, which would, according to its charter, educate students for missions, provide a knowledge of the Bible, and give men and women the opportunity to prepare themselves for work. This vision has prevailed. Messiah College has sought to expand knowledge rather than restrict it. Messiah College has been not just a campus but a community as well. Messiah College has had teachers who were also warm and trusted friends. And Messiah College has been a Christian college in which students have clearly understood that to be truly human, one must serve. This has been the history of Messiah College.

24   It is our special challenge to see that we retain the trust and also leave a legacy for those who will come after.

Vocation

In the Parable of the Good Samaritan, Jesus outlines a crucial concept of Christian vocation. Not only is it our job to love and worship God, but we are also to treat each of his people as our neighbor and care for them accordingly. Furthermore, Jesus outlines an expansive vision for neighbor. No matter the dimension of Christian vocation—paid work, service, relationships—our actions should reflect a commitment to this responsibility.

Luke 10:25–37 (NRSV)

The Parable of the Good Samaritan

25 Just then a lawyer stood up to test Jesus. "Teacher," he said, "what must I do to inherit eternal life?" **26** He said to him, "What is written in the law? What do you read there?" **27** He answered, "You shall love the Lord your God with all your heart, and with all your soul, and with all your strength, and with all your mind; and your neighbor as yourself." **28** And he said to him, "You have given the right answer; do this, and you will live."

29 But wanting to justify himself, he asked Jesus, "And who is my neighbor?" **30** Jesus replied, "A man was going down from Jerusalem to Jericho, and fell into the hands of robbers, who stripped him, beat him, and went away, leaving him half dead. **31** Now by chance a priest was going down that road; and when he saw him, he passed by on the other side. **32** So likewise a Levite, when he came to the place and saw him, passed by on the other side. **33** But a Samaritan while traveling came near him; and when he saw him, he was moved with pity. **34** He went to him and bandaged his wounds, having poured oil and wine on them. Then he put him on his own animal, brought him to an inn, and took care of him. **35** The next day he took out two denarii, gave them to the innkeeper, and said, 'Take care of him; and when I come back, I will repay you whatever more you spend.' **36** Which of these three, do you think, was a neighbor to the man who fell into the hands of the robbers?" **37** He said, "The one who showed him mercy." Jesus said to him, "Go and do likewise."

*F*rederick Buechner (1926–) is an author and Presbyterian minister, who has written prolifically and published over thirty books. His areas of authorship include essays, sermons, fiction, and autobiography, and he has continued to publish throughout his long life. In this short passage, Frederick Buechner addresses the challenge of how we discern God's will for our vocation. He offers two main criteria, which he believes help us to assess whether or not we have reached the vocation that God intends for us.

Vocation

Frederick Buechner

1   It comes from the Latin *vocare*, to call, and means the work a man is called to by God.

2   There are all different kinds of voices calling you to all different kinds of work, and the problem is to find out which is the voice of God rather than of Society, say, or the Superego, or Self-Interest.

3   By and large a good rule for finding out is this. The kind of work God usually calls you to is the kind of work (*a*) that you need most to do and (*b*) that the world most needs to have done. If you really get a kick out of your work, you've presumably met requirement (*a*), but if your work is writing TV deodorant commercials, the chances are you've missed requirement (*b*). On the other hand, if your work is being a doctor in a leper colony, you have probably met requirement (*b*), but if most of the time you're bored and depressed by it, the chances are you have not only bypassed (*a*) but probably aren't help-ing your patients much either.

4   Neither the hair shirt nor the soft berth will do. The place God calls you to is the place where your deep gladness and the world's deep hunger meet.

*J*erry Sittser (1950–) is a professor of theology at Whitworth University. In these two chapters of his book, The Will of God as a Way of Life, *Sittser explores the differences between calling and career, and discusses the factors for determining what God is calling each of us to do. Sittser provides a unique viewpoint on discovering God's will by rejecting the idea that God is playing a cosmic game of hide-and-seek and it is up to humans to figure out what God wants. In contrast, Sittser argues that there are many ways to attain God's calling for our lives if we focus on living our day-to-day lives for God.*

Distinguishing Between Calling and Career

Jerry Sittser

1   Choosing a career is one of the weightier decisions we will ever make. Careers demand our time, our energy, and our loyalty, like nothing else can or does, except marriage and parenthood. No wonder, then, that we want to choose the right career, the one God has willed for us. That decision is not always clear, however, which is evidenced by the frequency with which people change their careers. How can we discover the career God wills for us?

2   The language we use might make the decision harder than it has to be. We use the word "career" to describe the nature of our professional work. I would suggest that we replace it with the word "calling."

3   *Career* is a secular word. We use it often, though without giving much thought to it. I define *career* as a particular line of work one does to earn an income. Most careers require formal education or training. They allow us to contribute to the order and welfare of society. A career usually provides power and status of some kind and helps us to feel as if we fit into society as contributing members.

4   *Calling* is a theological word, perhaps less familiar to us, and its meaning is more ambiguous. I define *calling* as a specific vision of how God wants to use our time, energy, and abilities to serve him in the world.

5 There is obviously overlap between the two words. Many people fulfill their calling in life through a job or career. Nevertheless, a calling is different from a career in at least four ways. We will explore these differences in more detail in the next three chapters, so I will only mention them briefly here at the outset.

6 First, a calling transcends a career in the same way an athlete transcends the sport he or she plays. One simply *is* an athlete, by nature and ability; one *plays* a sport. The primary calling of every Christian is to follow God, regardless of ability, position, opportunity, or background. Whether young or old, ordinary or extraordinary, poverty-stricken or pampered, everyone is called by God to trust, serve, and obey him. This is our primary calling. As Os Guinness, a contemporary Christian author and social critic, argues: "Calling is the truth that God calls us to himself so decisively that everything we are, everything we do, and everything we have is invested with a special devotion, dynamism, and direction lived out as a response to his summons and service."[1]

7 Second, a calling often uses a career, though it should never be reduced to a career. I have a friend who teaches pathology in a local medical residency program. He is a career doctor, but his calling is bigger than his career. He uses his position in medicine to accomplish goals that most secular doctors overlook. My former nanny, Monica, works as a first grade teacher in a public school. What she does with students in the classroom and how she relates to parents outside the classroom, to say nothing about the way she prays for her school, sets her apart from most teachers I know.

8 Third, a calling involves work that can send us in directions where traditional careers do not go. Recently I met a woman who has twenty children, six biological and fourteen adopted. Far from looking harried and harassed by the bedlam in her home, she communicates a spirit of calm, joy, and energy, as if she were a dancer gliding across the stage. How she functions as a mother of twenty children seems well matched for who she is as a person. She is fulfilling her calling, though she does not have a traditional career.

9 Finally, a calling for most Christians is not singular but plural, which is why using the word is somewhat misleading. A Christian's calling in life is rarely to a single duty, unless that duty involves something like serving as a monk. Most of us have multiple callings. We must

learn how to do them all, keeping in mind the importance of simplicity, balance, and flexibility.

10   As I reflect on my own life and experiences in the context of my daily professional work, I see that, although I have pursued three careers in succession, not to mention the dozens of jobs I held when I was much younger, I have had one calling. But I also observe that I have had multiple roles to play, too, all of which embody God's will for my life.

11   I intend to use the term *calling*, in spite of its messiness and complexity, because it forces us to recognize how messy and complex life in the world can be. There is nothing neat and tidy about how we discover our calling—or *callings*, as the case may be—nor about how we fulfill them in ordinary life. Rarely does our journey through life follow a straight and clear path from beginning to end.

Three Careers, One Calling

12   [. . .] I decided to attend seminary because I sensed a "calling" to ministry, although I had little idea what that calling really implied. I thought that ministry had something to do with being at church a lot, preaching sermons, running meetings, visiting people, and helping the needy. Ministry was a job. To get to the point where I could do that job, I had to attend seminary first—which, I assumed, would prepare me.

13   So I attended Fuller Seminary in Pasadena, California. The education I received there was superb. I learned to study the Bible, to think theologically, and to hone my skills. But I received another education that was equally valuable. During my first year at Fuller I joined a youth ministry team at a large local church, Lake Avenue Congregational Church. There I learned to establish three "priorities" in ministry—commitment to God, to church, and to world—and to organize a ministry so that I would do the "work of God without sacrificing the people of God." My experience at that church changed my view of ministry, it became less a job and more a genuine calling to help people grow in Christ.

14   When I graduated from Fuller, I became an associate pastor of a Reformed church in Paramount, California. My job description was outrageously demanding. I was supposed to develop a youth ministry program for junior high, senior high, and college students, to oversee the Christian education program of the church, to develop a practical

plan for evangelism, and to provide pastoral care for the young married couples at the church.

15 The senior pastor, Harold Korver, was a masterful pastor and leader. He was also a superb mentor for me. I arrived shortly after the church had lost its third youth pastor in four years. Suspicion was high and expectations were low among church members. I added to the problem because I was young, brash, and immature. The church was wary of starting all over again with still another youth pastor. Thus Harold gave me some direct advice. "Sittser," he said sharply, "cut the mustard or get out. You have a job to do. So do it." Using what I had learned during my years in seminary, I started to invest in people, especially the youth, many of whom became committed Christians. I look back on those years with deep appreciation for what I learned and for how the church supported me.

16 Four years later I received a call from the president of Northwestern College, a small Christian liberal arts college in Orange City, Iowa, who invited me to apply for an opening in the chaplain's office. I applied for the position and was offered it. So I changed institutions, job descriptions, and locations and went to work as a college chaplain. I stayed there for six years. I discovered that the college setting suited me well. I loved working with students, and I developed deep friendships with faculty as well.

17 It was Lynda who first encouraged me to think about enrolling in a graduate program. She thought that being a college professor would allow me to express my deepest interests and convictions—exploring the "big questions," reading great books, teaching, and mentoring students. So I started a course of study at the University of Chicago and earned my Ph.D. in the history of Christianity. During my final year there I applied for a position at Whitworth College in Spokane, Washington. I have been working at Whitworth for over ten years now.

18 When I view this journey in retrospect, I see a pattern emerge. Without always knowing it, I was operating according to an intuitive sense of calling. Though I have had three careers—pastor, chaplain, and professor—I have had one basic calling: to serve as a bridge between two different worlds—the world of the academy, where ideas rule, and the world of the church, where practical concerns dominate. My calling is to make the academic study of theology

accessible to ordinary people and to help prepare a generation of students for leadership in the church and in the world.

19   We do the will of God when we fulfill our calling in life, a calling that is uniquely ours, like a set of fingerprints. A calling grows out of our temperament, our talents, and our experiences in life, though these are not the only factors that affect a calling, as we will see. Ultimately a calling comes from God. It is part of who we are, of what God has put in us, and of how God wants us to serve his kingdom. Though we have to discover our calling, we should also recognize that it is already in us, very much a part of our identity, waiting to be discovered and expressed, like perennial seeds that, once planted, produce flowers that come up year after year.

20   The process of discovering our calling is as subtle as sign language, where every movement and gesture counts for something. If anything, a calling probably discovers us as much as we discover it. In his sermon "The Calling of Voices," Frederick Buechner, a contemporary novelist and preacher, explores the divine nature of our calling. A calling itself lays claim to us as we discover it. Buechner defines a calling as "the work that [a person] is called to in this world, the thing that he is summoned to spend his life doing." He believes that a calling is like a mandate. It places demands on us. "We can speak of a man's choosing his vocation, but perhaps it is at least as accurate to speak of a vocation's choosing the man, of a call's being given and a man's hearing it, or not hearing it."[2]

21   This idea of a calling was especially important to the leaders of the Reformation in the sixteenth century. John Calvin, for example, believed that God has assigned to each Christian a specific calling in life, which provides a person with a meaningful job to do, a way to serve the world, and a sense of divine purpose. He affirmed that every person is given a calling, and that every calling is unique. "Every individual's sphere of life, therefore, is a post assigned him by the Lord that he may not wander about in uncertainty all the days of his life. . . . Our present life, therefore, will he best regulated if we always keep our calling in mind."

22   Since God is the one who calls us into specific forms of service, every calling has dignity and purpose to it, regardless of what the powerful and famous may think.

And everyone in his respective sphere of life will show more patience, and will overcome the difficulties, cares, miseries and anxieties in his path, when he will be convinced that every individual has his task laid upon his shoulders by God. If we follow our calling we shall receive this unique consolation that there is no work so mean and so sordid that does not look truly respectable and highly important in the sight of God![3]

The Problem with Careers

23 As we have already noted, a calling is not the same thing as a career, though the two are related. A career involves some kind of socially useful work. It usually requires specific education or training, promises advancement, provides compensation, and produces something considered valuable to society.

24 A career serves the needs, welfare, and interests of the larger society. Thus, engineers design cars, which assembly-line workers assemble, executives advertise, car dealers sell, insurance agents insure commuters drive, and mechanics fix, until the cars end up in the junkyard. Then junk dealers sell them for used parts until there is nothing left but rusted metal, which owners of foundries buy and use for scrap metal to make steel for another round of automobiles. Careers, in other words, function symbiotically, creating a circular system that keeps perpetuating itself as if it were a kind of economic ecosystem.

25 There are three possible problems with careers. First, not everyone's calling fits into a specific career. Sometimes people work at jobs because they need the income, though the labor they provide has little to do with their deepest interests and motivations. In my younger years I piled lumber, shoveled coal, flipped burgers, built apartments, and sold shoes because I needed the money. All were productive jobs and now provide me with hilarious stories to tell my kids or use as sermon illustrations, but none embodied my sense of calling. Some people spend their entire lives doing work that offers little satisfaction and little sense of calling because they have families to support and bills to pay. We even have a phrase for that: "dead-end jobs."

26 Second, sometimes a career can actually prevent a person from discovering or pursuing a calling. A career has incredible power to socialize people within its own area. When a professional basketball player justifies a strike by arguing that he simply wants to make

enough income to "provide for his family"—never mind that many professional athletes make more *in one year* than most people do over a lifetime—we see the results of socialization. A career can cause a person to embrace values that advance his or her own interests or those of a social group, not the needs of society.

27 I think of a young student who aspires to be a medical missionary in the Third World. Years later, however, he finds himself settled in a comfortable suburban practice that supports his lavish lifestyle. "I had to think about my own professional security and advancement," he insists. Or a woman is inspired during her college years to pursue a career in law so that she can provide legal services in the inner city. But she ends up handling messy though profitable divorce cases. She excuses her change of direction by saying, "There is no money in justice."

28 I have witnessed this tragedy firsthand in college teaching. A bright student wants to become a college professor and scholar as a way to reach Generation Z, "the lost generation." But graduate school has a deleterious effect on him, and what graduate school starts, his first teaching post finishes. His scholarly interests become increasingly obscure, his writing abstruse and inaccessible. He cares less and less about the ordinary, tedious work of classroom teaching and more and more about research. He spends as little time as possible with students, whom he sees as a distraction. Instead, he attends as many scholarly conferences as he can, where he prances around like a rooster trying to impress and intimidate. His idealism and vision gradually disappear. He has forsaken the calling that once motivated him, and he does not replace that calling with another that reflects his Christian convictions.

29 Third, some callings never translate into formal careers. Our modern obsession with careers, especially with the power, status, and income they provide, has marginalized people who have chosen not to pursue one. Some homemaker fathers and mothers see their parental role as central to their sense of calling and have been deprived of cultural validation because they have no formal careers. Many people, especially retirees, have cut themselves loose from a career in order to devote more time and energy to volunteer service, but they are put on the shelf by a culture that evaluates the worth of people according to a career, not according to their devotion to service. Little do we realize what would happen to our society—what in fact is happening

to our society—without the contributions to the common good that homemakers, retirees, and volunteers make.

30   I am not suggesting that living in suburbs, handling divorce cases, or becoming scholars is wrong. But what should concern us is the subtle and insidious ways that a career can undermine our commitment to serve God. Most careers have enormous infrastructures—graduate schools, professional guilds, bureaucratic institutions (like unions), methods of evaluation, standards of success—that impose values not always compatible with Christian convictions. Careers far too often emphasize competition over cooperation, wealth over generosity, power over service, and ideology over truth. They can become self-serving. Having a career, therefore, runs the risk of subverting our commitment to God.

What It Means to Have a Calling

31   I have been negligent thus far in addressing the critical issue of whether the concept of a "calling" applies only to Christians. I have used (and I will continue to use) examples drawn from the secular world that have nothing to do with Christianity or Christian service—fields such as athletics, sales and service, medicine, and law—that serve the common good. Does every person have a calling? If so, then what is distinctively Christian about a calling?

32   As you will recall, God wills above all that we seek him through his Son, Jesus Christ. God gives us grace not only when we seek him, but even before we seek him. He is the one whom we seek; he is also the one who does the seeking. God gives us the grace of salvation. He wants to make us right with him.

33   But God gives another kind of grace, too. The Reformed tradition calls it "common grace" because it refers to the grace that God gives to all people. It is the grace of creation, not of redemption. Many people, non-Christian as well as Christian, serve God *indirectly* by using their gifts for a worthy cause. People with little or no interest in Christianity can contribute to God's work in the world, even though they do not realize what they are doing and whom they are serving. As we learn from the book of Isaiah, even the pagan king Cyrus served God's greater plan by allowing the Jews to return to their homeland.[4]

34   Non-Christians, therefore, can and do contribute to the common good, whatever their convictions and motivations happen to be. Doctors of all types can heal sick people, lawyers can advocate justice, entrepreneurs can start helpful businesses, and teachers can educate students. God uses all kinds of people to accomplish his purposes.

35   A calling applies to our earthly life. It honors God, however unintentionally, by contributing something positive to the world that God has made, works now to redeem, and plans one day to restore when Jesus returns to establish his earthly kingdom. People in distinctively religious professions, therefore, are not the only ones who have a calling. So do construction workers, architects, seamstresses, artists, government representatives, army officers, and accountants, though their work is not at all devoted to specifically religious activities. This principle applies to everyone, Christian and non-Christian alike, who serve God when they advance the cause of justice, truth, beauty, and goodness.

36   A calling contributes uniquely to God's work in the world. People with a calling have a sense of higher purpose and see the bigger picture. For example:

- Selling insurance is a career, the success of which is determined by the size of policies sold, whether people need the insurance or not; helping people to become good stewards of their resources is a calling.
- Managing a sporting goods store is a career; challenging people to use their leisure time to find refreshment and renewal is a calling.
- Teaching social studies at a junior high is a career; providing instruction, support, and guidance to adolescents going through a difficult passage in life is a calling.
- Functioning as a secretary is a career; organizing an office so that details are handled efficiently, but never at the expense of people, is a calling.

37   A career causes people to think of income, power, position, and prestige. A calling inspires people to consider human need, moral absolutes, and the welfare of society.

38   A career does not define a person, nor does it determine a calling. If anything, the opposite occurs. God defines the person and gives that person a calling. Then he or she is free to use a career for God's kingdom

purpose. As Os Guinness puts it, "A sense of calling should precede a choice of job and career, and the main way to discover calling is along the line of what we are each created and gifted to be. Instead of, 'You are what you do,' calling says: 'Do what you are.'"[5]

39 My two boys had the same first grade teacher. They have had many good teachers since then, but they still refer to her as their favorite teacher. I have often wondered what makes her so effective. She certainly teaches the basic subject matter well, as evidenced by the skills students develop. She manages the class exceptionally well, too. She maintains order but never dominates the students. She encourages conversation and creativity, but she never permits chaos. There is goodness and kindness in her as well. She loves her students, and they know it and feel it. Teaching is more than a job to her; it is a calling. It is an extension of who she is, how she sees the world, what drives her.

40 A calling is a way of seeing the world with the eyes of the heart. No two people see the world in exactly the same way. Imagine ten people arriving at the scene of a terrible accident. Though they witness the same event, they all see something different and respond in different ways. One man sees confused motorists unsure of what to do, so he begins to direct traffic. A woman sees the details of the accident, immediately calls 911 on her cell phone, and describes the scene with astonishing accuracy. A retired teacher sees two traumatized children whose mother is lying lifeless on the side of the road; she wraps her arms around them to comfort them. A nurse sees catastrophic injury and immediately checks vital signs. A pastor sees a witness to the accident sobbing uncontrollably and tries to calm her down. A young woman, still in her teens, sees a spiritual battle unfolding and prays. Other people see chaos, so they get blankets, flares, and emergency supplies out of their cars and put them to good use. Everyone responds differently to the accident because they see differently. What they see is determined by something deep within them.

41 How we see the world around us points the way to our calling. Some people see poor organization wherever they go. They join an institution and make it run more efficiently. Other people see poor health, whether in body, mind, or spirit, and pursue careers to bring physical, psychological, or spiritual healing to people. Still others see poor housing, and they work at nonprofit organizations like Habitat for Humanity to alleviate the problem.

42   I know in my head that there is much that is wrong in the world, yet I do not see it with the eyes of my heart. For example, I do not concern myself much with inept government, although I read about it in the newspaper almost every day. I do not respond with alarm to national health-care problems, nor do I lie awake at night tossing and turning about global warming and the pollution of our oceans, about illiteracy in our inner cities, or about refugees in eastern Europe, although I am aware of these problems and occasionally contribute money to remedy them.

43   But there are things I do see with the eyes of my heart. I see Christians who have at their disposal a legacy of two thousand years of faith but live as if they were spiritual orphans. I see churches filled with immature Christians who do not know how to connect Christian faith to life experience. I see college students who have four or five precious years to make important decisions about what they want to become and to accomplish in life, and who need guidance as they lay a foundation for future success.

44   How do we discover our calling? Or how does our calling discover us? We discover it by embarking on a journey. The journey to get there is a necessary part of the calling itself. Many of us will not know at an early age what our calling is. That does not mean we have no calling. It is already in us, like a bulb lying dormant in the frozen ground, waiting for spring to arrive, so that it can burst through the ground. Our deep sense of calling should send us on a journey of discovery. We have to travel to get where God wants us to go. It is not an easy path we must follow.

Notes

[1] Os Guinness, *The Call: Finding and Fulfilling the Central Purpose of Your Life* (Nashville: Word, 1998), 29.

[2] Frederick Buechner, "The Calling of Voices," *The Hungering Dark* (New York: Seabury, 1981), 27.

[3] John Calvin, *Golden Booklet of the True Christian Life* (Grand Rapids: Baker, 1952), 94–96.

[4] See Isaiah 44:24–45:7.

[5] Guinness, *The Call*, 46.

Discovering What We're Supposed to Do

Jerry Sittser

1 I did not intend to become a writer. I did not even want to be writer. The very idea made me feel as insecure as a stage actor with a had memory. How I fell into writing—and it was about as accidental as a fall—says something important about how we discover our calling, or perhaps how our calling discovers us.

2 I served as a college chaplain in my late twenties. Soon after arriving on the campus of Northwestern College, I initiated a discipleship seminar for Christian students. The students who attended the weekly seminar became leaders of small discipleship groups on campus. To prepare them to lead the groups, I decided to write weekly study guides they could use. The resource I provided had an immediate and practical purpose. I did not consider what I wrote each week as real "writing" because I did not intend it for formal publication. I was like a weekend gardener trying to raise enough food to provide for the family. The suggestion that I was a farmer would have been ridiculous to me.

3 The college occasionally invited speakers to visit the campus for a few days to address students, faculty, and members of the community. One of those speakers was Leighton Ford, an evangelist with the Billy Graham Evangelistic Association. He conducted several evangelistic rallies at the college and in the community. One morning, while sitting in my office, he picked up a few copies of the study guides I had written and perused them. He liked what he read and suggested I try to get them published. He even recommended a publisher he thought would he appropriate.

4 "That sounds wonderful," I said politely, "But who am I to them?"

5 He smiled, "It doesn't matter who you are. It matters who I am." Then, on his initiative and without my knowledge, he wrote friends at the publishing house and told them about me. One of the editors contacted me and asked me to send my study guides to him. They

became the foundation for my first book, *The Adventure: Putting Energy into Your Walk with God.*

6 Leighton Ford took the initiative—it was an act of pure generosity on his part. But I had laid the groundwork for years by writing material that had an immediate and practical purpose, and nothing more. I was fulfilling my calling as a writer long before I published anything. I became a *published* author by writing before there was any thought or possibility of publication.

7 Discovering our calling can be like going on a journey. The experiences we have along the road have a cumulative effect, preparing us for future service. In other words, knowing God's will requires more than mere information about what we might be doing in the future, as if we were soldiers being given orders for our next tour of duty. We come to know the will of God as a life calling through experience itself. We discover what our calling is in the same way an artist paints on a canvas or a person falls in love. We learn by trying, by experimenting, by doing. Our calling is inseparable from the journey. In one sense, it *is* the journey.

8 Experience teaches us, prepares us, and seasons us for what lies ahead. If we are attentive to God in this present moment—which, as we have already learned, *is* the primary will of God for our lives—we will begin the glorious process of that discovery. We will learn as we go and become ready for what lies ahead. We will grow in character and conviction, gain necessary skills, and become mature. In due time our sense of calling will emerge, unfolding like a glorious landscape that we see on a road trip across America.

9 If I had tried to divine the future as I imagined it would be or thought it should be—or as I thought God had "willed" it for me—I would not have been able to see with any degree of clarity what I ended up doing. Where I have arrived is a far different place from where I had planned to be. As I now look back, however, I see a pattern that makes sense to me. What I did at one stage anticipated what came later on, even though I could not see it at the time.

Not What We Expect

10 Imagine standing in a room with an open door. As you look through that door, you see another room with an open door, which opens up

to still another room with an open door, and so on. You can see through open doors into at least ten successive rooms. Let's say that you are convinced that your calling is in that tenth room, which you can see clearly from where you are standing. You want to get there as quickly and directly as you can, traveling through those ten open doors like an arrow flying fast and straight to its target. But what you do not realize is that once you walk through just one open door and enter another room, you will see other open doors in that room that you could not have seen before entering it. Going through one of those doors may lead you in an entirely different direction.

11   We cannot predict the future. We will go places, do things, meet people, face challenges, accomplish goals, and pursue careers that fall outside our present field of vision. We can see only a little ways ahead of us. But as we proceed, there will be strange twists and turns along the way. There will be surprises that we did not and could not anticipate.

12   I am not suggesting that it is impossible to know our calling at a young age. I know people who discerned their calling when they were still in elementary school. They knew beyond a shadow of a doubt that God was calling them to be a doctor or a teacher or a scientist. Still, how they fulfilled that calling did not always line up with their expectations. They ended up doing what they wanted to do, but not necessarily in the way they expected to do it. They planned to practice medicine, but perhaps not in an inner city clinic. Or they planned to teach elementary school, only in the United States, not in Cairo, where they eventually landed.

Shackleton's Historic Feat

13   Take Ernest Shackleton as an example. He wanted to be a great explorer during "the heroic age" of exploration in the late nineteenth and early twentieth centuries. He aimed to be the first to reach the South Pole, but bad weather and short supplies turned him back. So he tried instead to be the first to cross the entire Antarctic continent by dogsled. He had a special ship built that would get him to his point of departure, and he carefully selected twenty-eight men and fifty-five dogs to accompany him on the perilous journey. The ship got within eighty miles of where his party planned to begin the expedition. Then pack ice moved in and encircled the ship, preventing

further progress. When the ice began to move, the ship with its crew and cargo drifted north for hundreds of miles until all hope of starting the expedition was lost.

14 Shackleton found himself in dire circumstances. His ship had broken apart and sunk. His crew was stranded on a frozen sea. They had supplies to last, and they had three lifeboats, but they were hundreds of miles from the open ocean and hundreds more from land. So they waited. Finally, spring arrived and the ice broke up. They launched their small lifeboats and headed for land. They landed on Elephant Island, a small, uninhabited wasteland of an island that had nothing on it but rock, glaciers, penguins, and seals.

15 They built a shelter, hunted for food, and passed the time. Shackleton knew, however, that someone would have to make a run to an island with a human settlement, or they would all perish on Elephant Island. So he launched one of the lifeboats and, accompanied by five men, sailed for some twenty days through wild seas and in horrible weather until they reached South Georgia Island. Unfortunately, they landed on the wrong side of the island. So Shackleton and two of his men took thirty-six hours to cross an uncharted island covered with huge glaciers and mountains rising as high as ten thousand feet. Finally, they reached a whaling station. It took them four more months before they could reach the rest of the crew stranded on Elephant Island. Not one man, however, was lost, though they had been cut off from all contact with civilization for twenty-two months.

16 Shackleton did accomplish his lifelong ambition, though not in the way he had expected or planned. He never crossed the Antarctic, but he did cross a massive ice pack, a stretch of treacherous ocean, and an uncharted island. Amazingly, he survived it all. He faced obstacles and odds that few other explorers ever dreamed of facing, to say nothing of conquering.

17 Shackleton knew that he had accomplished something extraordinary. He realized after it was all over that his ambition in life had been fulfilled, however strangely and circuitously. He had achieved greatness as an explorer, only a different greatness from what he had expected. "In memories we were rich," he wrote in his journal after they had reached South Georgia Island. "We had pierced the veneer of outside things. We had 'suffered, starved, and triumphed, groveled down yet

grasped at glory, grown bigger in the bigness of the whole.' We had seen God in His splendors, heard the text that Nature renders. We had reached the naked soul of man."[1]

An Unfolding Discovery

18 We discover our calling, then, not by trying to plan our life out ten years in advance but by being attentive to what God is doing through immediate circumstances and in the present moment. Over time our sense of calling will unfold simply and naturally, as scenery unfolds to backpackers hiking their way through the mountains. Rarely will we be able to see the whole pathway stretched out before us at any one time. Sometimes we will only be able to see far enough ahead to keep going.

19 In *Traveling Mercies*, an autobiography telling the story of her conversion, writer Anne Lamott recalls a sermon she heard that underscored the importance of paying attention to what is immediately at hand, not what is in the distant future, and to what God is doing now, not what God might do someday.

> Pastor Veronica said that when she prays for direction, one spot of illumination always appears just beyond her feet, a circle of light into which she can step. She moved away from the pulpit to demonstrate, stepping forward shyly . . . and then, after standing there looking puzzled, she moved another step forward to where the light had gone, two feet ahead of where she had been standing, and then again, "We in our faith work," she said, "stumble along toward where we think we're supposed to go, bumbling along, and here is what's so amazing—we end up getting exactly where we're supposed to be."[2]

20 Lamott's pastor is right. The pathway will continue to appear, no matter how confusing the route might be. We will be given just enough light to know where our next step should be. It is all a journey, as Shackleton discovered. The journey itself is a glorious thing. Failure will serve us as well as success, hard times will show us the way as readily as easy times. According to Elisabeth Elliot, God calls us within our own frame of reference and in ways that are appropriate, given our journey through life. "God leads me, I believe, within my own frame of reference. What I am, where I am, and how I got there, all have a great deal to do with what my frame of reference is. God can be counted on to choose the right avenue of approach."[3]

21   Discovering our calling is as much an art as it is a science. It is an intuitive process that defies simple steps and easy formulas. We need to be attentive to the signs, which provide hints and impressions and give us a sense of direction. We will undoubtedly face subtlety, ambiguity, and confusion along the way. But we must keep going and keep seeking as we keep doing.

Our Deepest Motivation

22   There are six signs to look for in this process. First, we should look within ourselves to see what motivates us. We must come to know our deepest and truest self—what captures our interest, what gives us energy. For whatever reason, some people seem to have an inner compulsion or drive that propels them toward a calling. Something deep within motivates them to start a new business or to compose a symphony or to teach in an inner city school, as if they *have* to do it, not only because they have the talent for it, which every calling requires, but also because they have the interest, energy, and passion for it. It is simply *in* them.

23   Mozart, for example, had music in him from the moment he was born. He was so precocious that he achieved fame as a performer and composer while he was still a young boy. Picasso painted brilliantly as a teenager. Francis of Assisi had a magnetic personality that attracted a following even before he became a Christian. That quality served him well when he founded the most influential religious order of the Middle Ages, the Friars Minor (better known as the Franciscans). Thomas Edison did not choose to become an inventor. He simply *was* an inventor. His basic orientation in life was imaginative and inventive. Jonathan Edwards, the most brilliant theologian America has ever produced, was driven to ponder deep theological questions and to formulate new ways of thinking about God. These people could no more *not* do their callings than cows could not chew their cud or geese could not fly south.

Talent

24   A second critical element in discovering our calling is talent. Proper talent is obviously necessary. Good intentions are not enough; we must have the gifts to get the job done. Still, the intersection between inner motivation and talent is complex, as we will see.

25 As portrayed in the film *Amadeus*, Salieri, a music composer of modest ability, spent his later years burning with jealousy over the work of a younger and better composer, Mozart. After hearing Mozart's music, Salieri discovered how pedestrian his own music was. He prayed (what is probably a fictional prayer), "O Lord, if you had to give me the calling, why could you not have given me the gift to go with it?"

26 At least Salieri understood his limits. Not everyone does. My wife, Lynda, was a professional musician, a soloist, and a choir director. She usually had someone in one of her choirs convinced that he (or she) was called by God to be a soloist, though without having the voice for it. "If God calls someone," Lynda often said to me, "one would think that God would have given that person the ability to do it." It is painful to learn that what we want to do might not be what we can do because we lack the talent. If we fail to learn this lesson, we will try to do things that would have been better left undone. We will try to preach sermons that would have been better filed away, to lead organizations that would have been better led by someone else, or to teach students who would have been better taught by someone with a higher aptitude for teaching.

27 Of course, talent alone is not enough. It provides a clue, but it falls short of being the *sine qua non* of a calling. On the one hand, some people will never be able to use all the talent they have. Some athletes could play more than one sport professionally, though the demands of competition force them to stick to only one. Some students could master any subject they care to study, but time does not allow it. So how can talented people decide what to use of their sizable reservoir? A sense of calling will help them sort it out.

28 On the other hand, some people excel in lines of work for which they appear to have only modest ability. Steve Largent was for many years the Seattle Seahawks' most successful receiver. He never claimed to have great ability, and opponents agreed. But Largent had drive and savvy and love for the sport, which compensated for his average talent and turned him into an accomplished professional football player. The same is true of John Stockton, point guard for the Utah Jazz. He is barely six feet tall, a virtual midget for a professional basketball player. He is not particularly fast or strong. Yet he has set the NBA record for assists and steals, and he has helped to lead the Jazz into

the NBA Playoffs almost every year he has played. His mastery of the sport surpasses what his modest abilities would seem to allow.

29   We note the same phenomenon in the Scriptures. Paul admitted that his ability as an orator was inadequate for the task, that his presence as a speaker was anything but impressive.[4] If we were to reduce Paul's abilities to a resumé, we would not have considered him for the job. But Paul was dogged and determined. He worked harder than all the other apostles and endured suffering of every kind.[5] He refused to give up. How do we explain someone like the apostle Paul? Abilities and background alone do not tell the whole story. His power came from another source. It came from God.

Life Experience

30   Third, life experiences can have a similar effect. Sometimes what happens *to* us pushes us toward a calling. A young widow whose husband dies of cancer goes to work for Hospice. A college student who hated junior high becomes a popular and effective counselor in a junior high school. A woman who endured years of abuse opens a clinic for battered women. A man who grew up in a lukewarm church becomes a successful evangelist. In each case, life experience awakened them to their life calling.

31   Sometimes the propelling event can be an insignificant experience that happens at just the right time. *Masterpiece Theater*, a PBS program, recently ran a dramatic presentation of the true story of British actress Coral Atkins. While attending a charity event for a children's home, Atkins met a little girl whose painful past and obvious need for love awakened terrible memories of Atkins' childhood. She was so moved by the experience that she gave up her glamorous career as an actress to start a home for disturbed children, a venture that turned out to be both wonderful and harrowing. The course her life took turned on that one ordinary experience of attending a charity event.

32   The experience of suffering can have a similar effect, as Anthony Storr, lecturer in clinical psychiatry at Oxford, argues in *Solitude: A Return to the Self*. He recounts stories of people whose suffering in prison set them on a course of writing or gave them insight that they would not otherwise have had. Their confinement isolated them, stirred their creativity, and enlarged their perspective on life. It inspired them to write on the human condition.

33   John Bunyan, for example, wrote his autobiography, *Grace Abounding* (1666), and began his classic work, *The Pilgrim's Progress*, during the twelve years he spent in the Bedford county jail for his Nonconformist beliefs. His works convey profound insight into temptation and suffering. His experience in jail helped him perceive the depths of human sin and to explore the wonder of God's plan of salvation. Dostoyevsky developed his philosophy of life and laid out plots for several of his stories and novels during the years he spent in a Siberian prison camp. His suffering became like a voice, calling him to ask and answer the most profound questions in life. Dostoyevsky would have been a writer whether or not he spent time in prison. He would not have written, however, with the same insight and power.[6]

Open and Closed Doors

34   A fourth factor in discovering our calling is opportunity. They constitute what Elisabeth Elliot categorizes as "circumstances." She believes that God can and does use circumstances to lead us. "Circumstances are without question a part of God's will. . . . It is a normal assumption of faith that he will use circumstances to nudge me in the right direction."[7]

35   Opportunities represent the proverbial "open door" that comes along every so often. The apostle Paul uses this expression to refer to opportunities he was given—or opportunities he prayed for—to preach the gospel in regions previously closed to him.[8] He had doors opened to continue his apostolic calling even in such odd and odious places as a prison, where he inspired fearful believers and witnessed to pagan prison guards.[9]

36   Experiences during one's college years provide opportunities that sometimes engender a sense of calling. Some Whitworth students who have worked as counselors at summer camps later become directors of youth programs. Other students who have spent a semester in Latin America return to do economic development work. Still other students who have enrolled in semester-long internships in nonprofit organizations go to work for the same organization after graduation. Colleges like Whitworth excel in providing such opportunities for students to test their gifts and discover their calling.

37   Opportunities can also result from a benefactor's generosity. I did not ask Leighton Ford to write a letter on my behalf. It never even occurred to me that I might have publishable material until he mentioned it. He took the initiative to open the door for me, as he has done for many others. He considers it a part of his own calling to use his vast network of contacts to give young Christian leaders a chance to get started. He communicates with these leaders by phone and through e-mail, suggests their names when churches and organizations are looking for fresh leadership, and offers them advice when they need it.

38   Some opportunities appear to be a matter of pure chance. John Calvin, a lawyer by training, was converted to Christ and embraced the Reformation faith sometime in the early 1530s. He had already published a commentary on the philosopher Seneca, so he was already known for his brilliance.

39   While traveling to Strasbourg in 1536, he was forced by unforeseen circumstances to take a detour through Geneva. At that time Geneva was facing tremendous upheaval, for the city council had just voted to make Geneva a Reformation city, though they had little idea what it meant. When William Farel, one of the leaders of the fledgling movement, heard that Calvin was passing through, he paid him a visit at the hotel and asked him to stay in Geneva to help organize the new church. By nature a reserved man, Calvin wanted nothing to do with such leadership. He felt committed to pursuing a life of solitude and scholarship, so he refused Farel's request.

40   But Farel would not be put off so easily, in words now famous, Farel told Calvin that if he did not remain in Geneva and help lead the movement, "God will condemn you." It was hardly a welcomed opportunity, but Calvin knew that he was supposed to stay. "I felt as if God from heaven had laid his mighty hand upon me to stop me in my course . . . and I was so terror-stricken that I did not continue my journey."

41   As a result, Calvin stayed in Geneva until he died, except for a brief three years when opponents on the city council ordered him to leave. During his twenty-five years in that city, Calvin preached thousands of sermons, provided pastoral care for a large congregation, published his *Institutes of the Christian Religion*, and wrote commentaries on almost every book of the Bible. He helped to organize a church that became

a model for other Reformation leaders in Europe. He participated in important meetings with church leaders from all over Europe. Yet his entire career as a pastor and church leader in Geneva resulted from a chance detour and a brief encounter with William Farel.[10]

42 Closed doors can give us clues about our calling, too. Parker Palmer, an educator, speaker, and author, argues that a calling implies *limits*. In choosing to pursue one calling, we eliminate other possible callings. We have to make choices, bypassing options that may look good to us. We must therefore discern what we are *not* supposed to do. As Palmer writes, "The truth is that I cannot be anything I want to be or do anything I want to do."

43 Thus, we must discern what is in us, recognize our limits, and allow doors to close as well as open. "The God who created us does not ask us to conform to some abstract norm for the ideal self. The God who created us asks us to honor the nature that is our birthright from God, which means both our potentials and our limits. When we fail to do so, reality happens—God happens—and the way closes behind us."[11]

44 A friend of mine left the parish ministry in the mid 1980s to pursue a doctorate in New Testament. He felt that God was calling him to teach in a Christian college or seminary. In order to help support his growing family during this time, he began to work part-time in a major Christian publishing house. As the completion of his program approached, he sent out numerous applications to Christian colleges and seminaries. But every door he tried to open was locked, whereas a full-time position opened up in that publishing company, where he could use his skills and expertise. That is where he is working to this day.

The Voice of People

45 The fifth factor that can assist us in discovering our calling is participation in a community. Rarely does a person discover a calling in isolation from a community. Only friends know us well enough to size up our gifts, to listen to our dreams, to challenge our thinking, and to encourage or discourage our plans. They help us recognize our strengths and weaknesses and discover who we are and what we ought to do with our lives. Though God is Lord of the universe, he does not work in a vacuum. He uses people as well as circumstances to help us discern our calling.

46   Elisabeth Elliot suggests that advice from the community of faith
      embodies one of the "natural means" God uses to guide us and to
      help us discover our calling. "The times when we find ourselves
      entirely alone in the making of a decision are rare," she writes.
      Friends can give us particularly good advice, though we must be sure
      to discern their motivation and perspective.

> A person who loves God and has had some experience in finding his
> will is the kind we should look for. I have been . . . blessed in having sev-
> eral friends of my own age who have helped me often. But I have been
> especially blessed through the advice of men and women much older
> than I. They see things I don't see. They've been over roads I've never
> traveled. They have perspective I couldn't possibly have.[12]

47   Many Whitworth students majoring in religion have found such a
      community in our religion department. I am surprised by how honest
      they are with each other. "I just can't see you doing youth ministry,"
      one student will say to another. "I think you have all the gifts to be a
      senior pastor." "I think you would make an excellent teacher or college
      professor." Not that these students exercise absolute authority. They do
      not speak for God, and they have on occasion been wrong. But they
      can and do provide perspective. They are "signs" that point the way.

48   Mentors often fulfill a similar purpose. The apostle Paul challenged
      several of his protégés to pursue a particular calling. Timothy, for
      example, grew up in a believing home. Both his mother and grand-
      mother nurtured him in the faith. While still a young man he met the
      apostle Paul, who became his mentor. When Timothy began to strug-
      gle in his pastoral work, Paul charged him to carry out his duties
      with courage and conviction, in spite of his youthfulness, inex-
      perience, and timidity:

> Let no one despise your youth, but set the believers an example in speech
> and conduct, in love, in faith, in purity. Until I arrive, give attention to the
> public reading of scripture, to exhorting, to teaching. Do not neglect the
> gift that is in you, which was given to you through prophecy with the lay-
> ing on of hands by the council of elders. Put these things into practice,
> devote yourself to them, so that all may see your progress.[13]

Joyful Service

49   There is one final sign—the sign of joy. Some people believe mis-
      takenly that we discover our calling by identifying the one thing we
      would least like to do, as if misery was *the* infallible sign of a calling.

I disagree with that perspective. God wants us to live joyfully. He calls us to serve him with gladness of heart. We will know our calling not only if we feel driven to it but also if we find joy in it. God loves a cheerful giver, wrote Paul. He also loves a cheerful servant.

50 Once again, Elisabeth Elliot offers sound advice. She admits that she used to think God's calling would require her to do the thing she least wanted to do. But then she reconsidered that negative perspective. "A better understanding of Scripture has shown me that even I, chief of miserable offenders that I know myself to be, may now and then actually want what God wants. This is likely to be the case more and more as I practice obedience, but it can also be a very simple and natural thing."[14]

51 We should not confuse happiness and joy. We will never experience complete happiness on earth. The world is a tormented place. Farmers must deal with tenacious weeds, entrepreneurs with fickle consumers, teachers with unruly students, ministers with lukewarm church members. However much we take pleasure in our calling, we will grow weary with the work, feel irritation with colleagues and coworkers, endure periods of boredom, and fight structures that make our work unnecessarily complicated. We live in a fallen world.

52 I have been a college professor for ten years. I have graded upward of 15,000 papers. Some of them were a pleasure to read. Some were not. But I learned early on that if I wanted to be a good college professor, I would have to assign and grade lots of papers, because students learn best by writing. Grading papers is by no means the most fulfilling part of college teaching. Duty drives me to do it, however tedious and boring and hard.

53 Hard is one thing; miserable is another. We might not always be happy doing our work, but we can nevertheless be joyful, taking "pleasure in our toil," as the book of Ecclesiastes charges us to do. Such joy will come from knowing that we are doing something that is suitable to our nature and fruitful for God's kingdom work. Frederick Buechner argues that amidst all the voices that are trying to get our attention and to give us direction in discerning God's call, the voice we should listen to most attentively "is the voice that we might think we should listen to least, and that is the voice of our own gladness." This voice of gladness, which reminds us of the joy we find in the work we do, may turn out to be the most reliable sign of all.[15]

What God Considers Great

54   These, then, are six signs we should look for; they are not easy steps to take. The discovery of a calling is not a simple process, nor should it be. It is rare that a person hears a voice from heaven. The apostle Paul did, but Timothy did not, nor did most of Paul's companions in the faith. I have not yet met a person who has heard God speak to him or her as one person speaks to another. For most of us our calling will emerge over time and through experience. We will discover it by simply living and learning, failing as well as succeeding, experimenting, and, above all, listening. What we should listen for is not so much a voice *from* God but the voice *of* God as he speaks to us through reflection, talents, experience, opportunity, community, and the gladness of our own hearts.

55   Mother Teresa recognized that assuming a posture of silence is the proper way to begin praying, for silence helps us to listen to God. "I always begin my prayer in silence, for it is in the silence of the heart that God speaks. God is the friend of silence—we need to listen to God because it's not what we say but what He says to us and through us that matters."[16]

56   God assures us that we will discover our calling. He is the one who calls; he will enable us to hear, understand, and accomplish our calling. We will succeed, though we might not succeed as the world defines success. Earlier in the chapter I mentioned a number of well-known people—Mozart, Dostoyevsky, Bunyan, Edwards—to illustrate how we may discover our calling. Few of us will succeed as they did. Unlike them, most of us will not be remembered long after we die. If anything, our calling might lead us into obscurity rather than fame. We might receive little acclaim for what we do. But why should we even want that? Laying up "treasures in heaven," as Jesus called it, does not leave much capital left over for investments on earth. Though our calling may have earthly value, it may not receive much earthly applause.

57   Heaven judges success differently from earth. If we fulfill our callings with integrity, faithfulness, and love, we will bear fruit for God's kingdom. God will honor us in heaven, whether or not people recognize our service here on earth. In *The Great Divorce* C. S. Lewis describes a procession in heaven to honor a great saint who has just

died. The narrator of the story wonders if it is someone he would have heard of on earth. By the sight of the magnificent procession, that would appear to be likely. But the narrator's guide responds, "It's someone ye'll never have heard of. Her name on earth was Sarah Smith and she lived on Golders Green."

58 The narrator comments, "She seems to be . . . well, a person of particular importance?"

59 His guide responds, "Aye. She is one of the great ones. Ye have heard that fame in this country and fame on Earth are two quite different things."[17]

60 Sarah Smith was great in the eyes of heaven because she fulfilled her calling without regard to earthly honors. She did the will of God for God's sake and for the world's good. Though the world forgot, God did not. He honored her for it.

Notes

[1] Caroline Alexander, *The Endurance: Shackleton's Legendary Antarctic Expedition* (New York: Alfred A. Knopf, 1998), 165.

[2] Anne Lamott, *Traveling Mercies* (New York: Pantheon, 1999), 84.

[3] Elisabeth Elliot, *A Slow and Certain Light* (Nashville: Abingdon, 1973), 101.

[4] 1 Corinthians 2:1–5; 2 Corinthians 10:10–11.

[5] 1 Corinthians 15:10; 2 Corinthians 11.

[6] Anthony Storr, *Solitude: A Return to the Self* (New York: Free Press, 1988), 56–59.

[7] Elliot, *A Slow and Certain Light*, 104.

[8] Colossians 4:3–4.

[9] Philippians 1:12–14.

[10] T. H. L. Parker, "The Life and Times of John Calvin," *Christian History* 4 (No. 4, 1986): 11.

[11] Parker Palmer, "On Minding Your Call—When No One Is Calling," *Weavings* 11 (May/June 1996): 20.

[12] Elliot, *A Slow and Certain Light*, 108–9.

[13] 1 Timothy 4:12–15.

[14] Elliot, *A Slow and Certain Light*, 99.

[15] Frederick Buechner, "The Calling of Voices," *The Hungering Dark* (New York: Seabury, 1981), 31.

[16] Mother Teresa, *A Simple Path* (New York: Ballantine, 1995), 7.

[17] C. S. Lewis, *The Great Divorce* (New York: Macmillan, 1946), 107.

*D*orothy L. Sayers (1893–1957) was a famous English writer who wrote poems, plays, essays, and mystery stories. She was also known for being a Christian humanist, who believed that human freedom and creativity are important aspects of the Christian life. Her Christian humanism shaped her beliefs about work and how Christians should approach it, as seen in her essay "Why Work?"

Why Work?

Dorothy L. Sayers

1   I have already, on a previous occasion, spoken at some length on the subject of Work and Vocation.[1] What I urged then was a thoroughgoing revolution in our whole attitude to work. I asked that it should be looked upon—not as a necessary drudgery to be undergone for the purpose of making money, but as a way of life in which the nature of man should find its proper exercise and delight and so fulfill itself to the glory of God. That it should, in fact, be thought of as a creative activity undertaken for the love of the work itself; and that man, made in God's image, should make things, as God makes them, for the sake of doing well a thing that is well worth doing.

2   It may well seem to you—as it does to some of my acquaintances— that I have a sort of obsession about this business of the right attitude to work. But I do insist upon it, because it seems to me that what becomes of civilization after this war is going to depend enormously on our being able to effect this revolution in our ideas about work. Unless we do change our whole way of thought about work. I do not think we shall ever escape from the appalling squirrel cage of economic confusion in which we have been madly turning for the last three centuries or so, the cage in which we landed ourselves by acquiescing in a social system based upon Envy and Avarice.

3   A society in which consumption has to be artificially stimulated in order to keep production going is a society founded on trash and waste, and such a society is a house built upon sand.

4   It is interesting to consider for a moment how our outlook has been forcibly changed for us in the last twelve months by the brutal presence

of war. War is a judgment that overtakes societies when they have been living upon ideas that conflict too violently with the laws governing the universe. People who would not revise their ideas voluntarily find themselves compelled to do so by the sheer pressure of the events which these very ideas have served to bring about.

5 Never think that wars are irrational catastrophes: they happen when wrong ways of thinking and living bring about intolerable situations; and whichever side may be the more outrageous in its aims and the more brutal in its methods, the root causes of conflict are usually to be found in some wrong way of life in which all parties have acquiesced, and for which everybody must, to some extent, bear the blame.

6 It is quite true that false Economics is one of the root causes of the present war; and one of the false ideas we had about Economics was a false attitude both to Work and to the goods produced by Work. This attitude we are now being obliged to alter, under the compulsion of war—and a very strange and painful process it is in some ways. It is always strange and painful to have to change a habit of mind: though, when we have made the effort, we may find a great relief, even a sense of adventure and delight, in getting rid of the false and returning to the true.

7 Can you remember—it is already getting difficult to remember—what things were like before the war? The stockings we bought cheap and threw away to save the trouble of mending? The cars we scrapped every year to keep up with the latest fashion in engine design and streamlining? The bread and bones and scraps of fat that littered the dustbins—not only of the rich, but of the poor? The empty bottles that even the dustman scorned to collect, because the manufacturers found it cheaper to make new ones than to clean the old? The mountains of empty tins that nobody found it worthwhile to salvage, rusting and stinking on the refuse dumps? The food that was burnt or buried because it did not pay to distribute it? The land choked and impoverished with thistle and ragwort, because it did not pay to farm it? The handkerchiefs used for paint rags and kettle-holders? The electric lights left blazing because it was too much trouble to switch them off? The fresh peas we could not be bothered to shell, and threw aside for something out of a tin? The paper that cumbered the shelves, and lay knee-deep in the parks, and littered the seats of railway trains? The scattered hairpins and smashed crockery, the cheap knickknacks of steel and wood and rubber and glass and tin that we bought to fill in an odd half hour at Woolworth's and forgot

as soon as we had bought them? The advertisements imploring and exhorting and cajoling and menacing and bullying us to glut ourselves with things we did not want, in the name of snobbery and idleness and sex appeal? And the fierce international scramble to find in helpless and backward nations a market on which to fob off all the superfluous rubbish which the inexorable machines ground out hour by hour, to create money and to create employment?

8   Do you realize how we have had to alter our whole scale of values, now that we are no longer being urged to consume but to conserve? We have been forced back to the social morals of our great-grandparents. When a piece of lingerie costs three precious coupons, we have to consider, not merely its glamour value, but how long it will wear. When fats are rationed, we must not throw away scraps, but jealously use to advantage what it cost so much time and trouble to breed and rear. When paper is scarce we must—or we should—think whether what we have to say is worth saying before writing or printing it. When our life depends on the land, we have to pay in short commons for destroying its fertility by neglect or overcropping. When a haul of herrings takes valuable manpower from the forces, and is gathered in at the peril of men's lives by bomb and mine and machine gun, we read a new significance into those gloomy words which appear so often in the fishmonger's shop: NO FISH TODAY. . . . We have had to learn the bitter lesson that in all the world there are only two sources of real wealth: the fruit of the earth and the labor of men; and to estimate work not by the money it brings to the producer, but by the worth of the thing that is made.

9   The question that I will ask you to consider today is this: When the war is over, are we likely, and *do we want* to keep this attitude to work and the results of work? Or are we preparing and *do we want* to go back to our old habits of thought? Because I believe that on our answer to this question the whole economic future of society will depend.

10 Sooner or later the moment will come when we have to make a decision about this. At the moment, we are not making it—don't let as flatter ourselves that we are. It is being made for us. And don't let us imagine that a wartime economy has stopped waste. It has not. It has only transferred it elsewhere. The glut and waste that used to clutter our own dustbins have been removed to the field of battle. That is where all the surplus consumption is going. The factories are roaring more loudly than ever, turning out night and day goods that are of no conceivable value for the maintenance of life; on the contrary, their

sole object is to destroy life, and instead of being thrown away they are being blown away—in Russia, in North Africa, over Occupied France, in Burma, China, and the Spice Islands, and on the Seven Seas.

11 What is going to happen when the factories stop turning out armaments? No nation has yet found a way to keep the machines running and whole nations employed under modern industrial conditions without wasteful consumption. For a time, a few nations could contrive to keep going by securing a monopoly of production and forcing their waste products onto new and untapped markets. When there are no new markets and all nations are industrial producers, the only choice we have been able to envisage so far has been that between armaments and unemployment. This is the problem that some time or other will stare us in the face again, and this time we must have our minds ready to tackle it. It may not come at once—for it is quite likely that after the war we shall have to go through a further period of managed consumption while the shortages caused by the war are being made good. But sooner or later we shall have to grapple with this difficulty, and everything will depend on our attitude of mind about it.

12 Shall we be prepared to take the same attitude to the arts of peace as to the arts of war? I see no reason why we should not sacrifice our convenience and our individual standard of living just as readily for the building of great public works as for the building of ships and tanks—but when the stimulus of fear and anger is removed, shall we be prepared to do any such thing? Or shall we want to go back to that civilization of greed and waste which we dignify by the name of a "high standard of living"? I am getting very much afraid of that phrase about the standard of living. And I am also frightened by the phrase "after the war"—it is so often pronounced in a tone that suggests: "After the war, we want to relax, and go back, and live as we did before." And that means going back to the time when labor was valued in terms of its cash returns, and not in terms of the work.

13 Now the answer to this question, if we are resolute to know what we are about, will not be left to rich men—to manufacturers and financiers. If these people have governed the world of late years it is only because we ourselves put the power into their hands. The question can and should be answered by the worker and the consumer.

14 It is extremely important that the worker should really understand where the problem lies. It is a matter of brutal fact that in these days

labor, more than any other section of the community has a vested interest in war. Some rich employers make profit out of war—that is true; but what is infinitely more important is that for all working people war means full employment and high wages.

15 When war ceases, then the problem of employing labor at the machines begins again. The relentless pressure of hungry labor is behind the drive toward wasteful consumption, whether in the destruction of war or in the trumpery of peace.

16 The problem is far too much simplified when it is presented as a mere conflict between labor and capital, between employed and employer. The basic difficulty remains, even when you make the State the sole employer, even when you make Labor into the employer. It is not simply a question of profits and wages or living conditions—but of what is to be done with the work of the machines, and what work the machines are to do.

17 If we do not deal with this question now, while we have time to think about it, then the whirligig of wasteful production and wasteful consumption will start again and will again end in war. And the driving power of labor will be thrusting to turn the wheels, because it is to the financial interest of labor to keep the whirligig going faster and faster till the inevitable catastrophe comes.

18 And so that those wheels may turn, the consumer—that is you and I, including the workers, who are consumers also—will again be urged to consume and waste; and unless we change our attitude—or rather unless we keep hold of the new attitude forced upon us by the logic of war—we shall again be bamboozled by our vanity, indolence, and greed into keeping the squirrel cage of wasteful economy turning. We could—you and I—bring the whole fantastic economy of profitable waste down to the ground overnight, without legislation and without revolution, merely by refusing to cooperate with it. I say, we could—as a matter of fact, we have; or rather, it has been done for us. If we do not want it to rise up again after the war, we can prevent it—simply by preserving the wartime habit of valuing work instead of money. The point is: do we *want* to? . . .

19 Whatever we do, we shall be faced with grave difficulties. That cannot be disguised. But it will make a great difference to the result if we are genuinely aiming at a real change in economic thinking. And by that I mean a radical change from top to bottom—a new system; not a mere adjustment of the old system to favor a different set of people.

20   The habit of thinking about work as something one does to make
money is so ingrained in us that we can scarcely imagine what a
revolutionary change it would be to think about it instead in terms of
the work done. To do so would mean taking the attitude of mind we
reserve for our unpaid work—our hobbies, our leisure interests, the
things we make and do for pleasure—and making *that* the standard
of all our judgments about things and people. We should ask of an
enterprise, not "will it pay?" but "is it good?"; of a man, not "what
does he make?" but "what is his work worth?"; of goods, not "can we
induce people to buy them?" but "are they useful things well
made?"; of employment, not "how much a week?" but "will it exercise my faculties to the utmost?" And shareholders in—let us say—
brewing companies, would astonish the directorate by arising at
shareholders' meetings and demanding to know, not merely where
the profits go or what dividends are to be paid, not even merely
whether the workers' wages are sufficient and the conditions of labor
satisfactory, but loudly, and with a proper sense of personal responsibility: "What goes into the beer?"

21   You will probably ask at once: How is this altered attitude going to
make any difference to the question of employment? Because it
sounds as though it would result in not more employment, but less.
I am not an economist, and I can only point to a peculiarity of war
economy that usually goes without notice in economic textbooks. In
war, production for wasteful consumption still goes on; but there is
one great difference in the goods produced. None of them is valued
for what it will fetch, but only for what it is worth in itself. The gun
and the tank, the airplane and the warship have to be the best of their
kind. A war consumer does not buy shoddy. He does not buy to sell
again. He buys the thing that is good for its purpose, asking nothing
of it but that it shall do the job it has to do. Once again, war forces the
consumer into a right attitude to the work. And, whether by strange
coincidence, or whether because of some universal law, as soon as
nothing is demanded of the thing made but its own integral perfection, its own absolute value, the skill and labor of the worker are
fully employed and likewise acquire an absolute value.

22   This is probably not the kind of answer that you will find in any theory of economics. But the professional economist is not really trained
to answer, or even to ask himself questions about absolute values.
The economist is inside the squirrel cage and turning with it. Any
question about absolute values belongs to the sphere, not of economics, but of religion.

23 And it is very possible that we cannot deal with economics at all, unless we can see economy from outside the cage; that we cannot begin to settle the relative values without considering absolute values. And if so, this may give a very precise and practical meaning to the words: "Seek ye first the kingdom of God, and his righteousness: and all these things shall be added unto you."[2] . . . I am persuaded that the reason why the Churches are in so much difficulty about giving a lead in the economic sphere is because they are trying to fit a Christian standard of economics to a wholly false and pagan understanding of work.

24 What is the Christian understanding of work? . . . I should like to put before you two or three propositions arising out of the doctrinal position which I stated at the beginning: namely, that work is the natural exercise and function of man—the creature who is made in the image of his Creator. You will find that any one of them, if given in effect everyday practice, is so revolutionary (as compared with the habits of thinking into which we have fallen), as to make all political revolutions look like conformity.

25 The first, stated quite briefly, is that work is not, primarily, a thing one does to live, but the thing one lives to do. It is, or it should be, the full expression of the worker's faculties, the thing in which he finds spiritual, mental, and bodily satisfaction, and the medium in which he offers himself to God.

26 Now the consequences of this are not merely that the work should he performed under decent living and working conditions. That is a point we have begun to grasp, and it is a perfectly sound point. But we have tended to concentrate on it to the exclusion of other considerations far more revolutionary.

27 (a) There is, for instance, the question of profits and remuneration. We have all got it fixed in our heads that the proper end of work is to be paid for—to produce a return in profits or payment to the worker which fully or more than compensates the effort he puts into it. But if our proposition is true, this does not follow at all. So long as Society provides the worker with a sufficient return in real wealth to enable him to carry on the work properly, then he has his reward. For his work is the measure of his life, and his satisfaction is found in the fulfillment of his own nature, and in contemplation of the perfection of his work.

28 That, in practice, there is this satisfaction, is shown by the mere fact that a man will put loving labor into some hobby which can never bring him any economically adequate return. His satisfaction comes,

in the godlike manner, from looking upon what he has made and finding it very good. He is no longer bargaining with his work, but serving it. It is only when work has to be looked on as a means to gain that it becomes hateful; for then, instead of a friend, it becomes an enemy from whom tolls and contributions have to be extracted. What most of us demand from society is that we should always get out of it a little *more* than the value of the labor we give to it. By this process, we persuade ourselves that society is always in our debt—a conviction that not only piles up actual financial burdens, but leaves us with a grudge against society.

29 (b) Here is the second consequence. At present we have no clear grasp of the principle that every man should do the work for which he is fitted by nature. The employer is obsessed by the notion that he must find cheap labor, and the worker by the notion that the best-paid job is the job for him. Only feebly, inadequately, and spasmodically do we ever attempt to tackle the problem from the other end, and inquire: What type of worker is suited to this type of work? People engaged in education see clearly that this is the right end to start from, but they are frustrated by economic pressure, and by the failure of parents on the one hand and employers on the other to grasp the fundamental importance of this approach. And that the trouble results far more from a failure of intelligence than from economic necessity is seen clearly under war conditions, when, although competitive economics is no longer a governing factor, the right men and women are still persistently thrust into the wrong jobs, through sheer inability on everybody's part to imagine a purely vocational approach to the business of fitting together the worker and his work.

30 (c) A third consequence is that, if we really believed this proposition and arranged our work and our standard of values accordingly, we should no longer think of work as something that we hastened to get through in order to enjoy our leisure; we should look on our leisure as the period of changed rhythm that refreshed us for the delightful purpose of getting on with our work. And, this being so, we should tolerate no regulations of any sort that prevented us from working as long and as well as our enjoyment of work demanded. We should resent any such restrictions as a monstrous interference with the liberty of the subject. How great an upheaval of our ideas that would mean I leave you to imagine. It would turn topsy-turvy all our notions about hours of work, rates of work, unfair competition, and all the rest of it. We should all find ourselves fighting, as now only artists and the members of certain professions fight, for precious time

in which to get on with the job—instead of fighting for precious hours saved from the job.

31   (d) A fourth consequence is that we should fight tooth and nail, not for mere employment, but for the quality of the work that we had to do. We should clamor to be engaged in work that was worth doing, and in which we could take pride. The worker would demand that the stuff he helped to turn out should be good stuff—he would no longer be content to take the cash and let the credit go. Like the shareholders in the brewery, he would feel a sense of personal responsibility and clamor to know, and to control, what went into the beer he brewed. There would be protests and strikes—not only about pay and conditions, but about the quality of the work demanded and the honesty, beauty, and usefulness of the goods produced. The greatest insult which a commercial age has offered to the worker has been to rob him of all interest in the end product of the work and to force him to dedicate his life to making badly things which were not worth making.

32   This first proposition chiefly concerns the worker as such. My second proposition directly concerns Christians as such, and is this: it is the business of the Church to recognize that the secular vocation, as such, is sacred. Christian peoples and particularly perhaps the Christian clergy, must get it firmly into their heads that when a man or woman is called to a particular job of secular work, that is as true vocation as though he or she were called to specifically religious work. The Church must concern Herself not only with such questions as the just price and proper working conditions: She must concern Herself with seeing that the work itself is such as a human being can perform without degradation—that no one is required by economic or any other considerations to devote himself to work that is contemptible, soul destroying, or harmful. It is not right for Her to acquiesce in the notion that a man's life is divided into the time he spends on his work and the time he spends in serving God. He must he able to serve God *in* his work, and the work itself must be accepted and respected as the medium of divine creation.

33   In nothing has the Church so lost Her hold on reality as in Her failure to understand and respect the secular vocation. She has allowed work and religion to become separate departments, and is astonished to find that, as a result, the secular work of the world is turned to purely selfish and destructive ends, and that the greater part of the world's intelligent workers have become irreligious, or at least, uninterested in religion.

34   But is it astonishing? How can anyone remain interested in a religion which seems to have no concern with nine-tenths of his life? The Church's approach to an intelligent carpenter is usually confined to exhorting him not to be drunk and disorderly in his leisure hours, and to come to church on Sundays. What the Church *should* be telling him is this: that the very first demand that his religion makes upon him is that he should make good tables.

35   Church by all means, and decent forms of amusement, certainly— but what use is all that if in the very center of his life and occupation he is insulting God with bad carpentry? No crooked table legs or ill-fitting drawers ever, I dare swear, came out of the carpenter's shop at Nazareth. Nor, if they did, could anyone believe that they were made by the same hand that made Heaven and earth. No piety in the worker will compensate for work that is not true to itself; for any work that is untrue to its own technique is a living lie.

36   Yet in Her own buildings, in Her own ecclesiastical art and music, in Her hymns and prayers, in Her sermons and in Her little books of devotion, the Church will tolerate, or permit a pious intention to excuse work so ugly, so pretentious, so tawdry and twaddling, so insincere and insipid, so *bad* as to shock and horrify any decent draftsman.

37   And why? Simply because She has lost all sense of the fact that the living and eternal truth is expressed in work only so far as that work is true in itself, to itself, to the standards of its own technique. She has forgotten that the secular vocation is sacred. Forgotten that a building must be good architecture before it can be a good church; that a painting must be well painted before it can be a good sacred picture; that work must be good work before it can call itself God's work.

38   Let the Church remember this: that every maker and worker is to serve God *in* his profession or trade—not outside it. The Apostles complained rightly when they said it was not meet they should leave the word of God and serve tables; their vocations was to preach the word.[3] But the person whose vocation it is to prepare the meals beautifully might with equal justice protest: It is not meet for us to leave the service of our tables to preach the word.

39   The official Church wastes time and energy, and, moreover, commits sacrilege, in demanding that secular workers should neglect their proper vocation in order to do Christian work—by which She means ecclesiastical work. The only Christian work is good work well done.

Let the Church see to it that the workers are Christian people and do their work well, as to God: then all the work will be Christian work, whether it is church embroidery, or sewage farming. As Jacques Maritain says: "If you want to produce Christian work, be a Christian, and to make a work of beauty into which you have put your heart; do not adopt a Christian pose."[4] He is right.

40 And let the Church remember that the beauty of the work will be judged by its own, and not by ecclesiastical standards.

41 Let me give you an illustration of what I mean. When my play *The Zeal of Thy House* was produced in London, a dear old pious lady was much struck by the beauty of the four great archangels who stood throughout the play in their heavy, gold robes, eleven feet high from wingtip to sandal-tip. She asked with great innocence "whether I selected the actors who played the angels for the excellence of their moral character?"

42 I replied that the angels were selected, to begin with, not by me but by the producer, who had the technical qualifications for selecting suitable actors—for that was part of his vocation. And that he selected, in the first place, young men who were six feet tall so that they would match properly together. Secondly angels had to be of good physique, so as to be able to stand stiff on the stage for two and a half hours, carrying the weight of their wings and costumes, without wobbling, or fidgeting, or fainting. Thirdly, they had to be able to speak verse well, in an agreeable voice and audibly. Fourthly, they had to be reasonably good actors. When all these technical conditions had been fulfilled, we might come to the moral qualities, of which the first would be the ability to arrive on the stage punctually and in a sober condition, since the curtain must go up on time, and a drunken angel would be indecorous.

43 After that, and only after that, one might take character into consideration, but that, provided his behavior was not so scandalous as to cause dissension among the company, the right kind of actor with no morals would give a far more reverent and seemly performance than a saintly actor with the wrong technical qualifications. The worst religious films I ever saw were produced by a company which chose its staff exclusively for their piety. Bad photography, bad acting, and bad dialogue produced a result so grotesquely irreverent that the pictures could not have been shown in churches without bringing Christianity into contempt.

44   God is not served by technical incompetence; and incompetence and untruth always result when the secular vocation is treated as a thing alien to religion. . . .

45   And conversely: when you find a man who is a Christian praising God by the excellence of his work—do not distract him and take him away from his proper vocation to address religious meetings and open church bazaars. Let him serve God in the way to which God has called him. If you take him away from that, he will exhaust himself in an alien technique and lose his capacity to do his dedicated work. It is your business, you churchmen, to get what good you can from observing his work—not to take him away from it, so that he may do ecclesiastical work for you. But, if you have any power, see that he is set free to do his own work as well as it may be done. He is not there to serve you; he is there to serve God by serving his work.

46   This brings me to my third proposition; and this may sound to you the most revolutionary of all. It is this: the worker's first duty is to *serve the work*. The popular catchphrase of today is that it is every-body's duty to serve the community. It is a well-sounding phrase, but there *is* a catch in it. It is the old catch about the two great command-ments. "Love God and your neighbor: on those two commandments hang all the Law and the Prophets."[5]

47   The catch in it, which nowadays the world has largely forgotten, is that the second commandment depends upon the first, and that with-out the first, it is a delusion and a snare. Much of our present trouble and disillusionment have come from putting the second command-ment before the first.

48   If we put our neighbor first, we are putting man above God, and that is what we have been doing ever since we began to worship human-ity and make man the measure of all things. Whenever man is made the center of things, he becomes the storm center of trouble—and that is precisely the catch about serving the community. It ought perhaps to make us suspicious of that phrase when we consider that it is the slogan of every commercial scoundrel and swindler who wants to make sharp business practice pass muster as social improvement.

49   "Service" is the motto of the advertiser, of big business, and of fraud-ulent finance. And of others, too. Listen to this. "I expect the judiciary to understand that the nation does not exist for their convenience, but that justice exists to serve the nation." That was Hitler yesterday—

and that is what becomes of "service," when the community, and not the work, becomes its idol. There is, in fact, a paradox about working to serve the community, and it is this: that to aim directly at serving the community is to falsify the work; the only way to serve the community is to forget the community and serve the work. There are three very good reasons for this:

50   The first is that you cannot do good work if you take your mind off the work to see how the community is taking it—any more than you can make a good drive from the tee if you take your eye off the ball. "Blessed are the singlehearted" (for that is the real meaning of the word we translate "the pure in heart"[6]). If your heart is not wholly in the work, the work will not be good—and work that is not good serves neither God nor the community; it only serves mammon.

51   The second reason is that the moment you think of serving other people, you begin to have a notion that other people owe you something for your pains; you begin to think that you have a claim on the community. You will begin to bargain for reward, to angle for applause, and to harbor a grievance if you are not appreciated. But if your mind is set upon serving the work, then you know you have nothing to look for; the only reward the *work* can give you is the satisfaction of beholding its perfection. The work takes all and gives nothing but itself; and to serve the work is a labor of pure love.

52   And thirdly, if you set out to serve the community, you will probably end by merely fulfilling a public demand—and you may not even do that. A public demand is a changeable thing. Nine-tenths of the bad plays put on in theaters owe their badness to the fact that the playwright has aimed at pleasing the audience, instead of at producing a good and satisfactory play. Instead of doing the work as its own integrity demands that it should be done, he has falsified the play by putting in this or that which he thinks will appeal to the groundlings[7] (who by that time have probably come to want something else), and the play fails by its insincerity. The work has been falsified to please the public, and in the end even the public is not pleased. As it is with works of art, so it is with all work.

53   We are coming to the end of an era of civilization which began by pandering to public demand, and ended by frantically trying to create public demand for an output so false and meaningless that even a doped public revolted from the trash offered to it and plunged into war rather than swallow any more of it. The danger of "serving the community" is that one is part of the community; and that in serving it one may only be serving a kind of communal egotism. The only

true way of serving the community is to be truly in sympathy with the community, to be oneself part of the community, and then to serve the work, without giving the community another thought. Then the work will endure, because it will be true to itself. It is the work that serves the community; the business of the worker is to serve the work.

54 Where we have become confused is in mixing up the ends to which our work is put with the *way* in which the work is done. The end of the work will be decided by our religious outlook: as we *are* so we *make*. It is the business of religion to make us Christian people, and then our work will naturally be turned to Christian ends, because our work is the expression of ourselves. But the *way* in which the work is done is governed by no sanction except the good of the work itself, and religion has no direct connection with that, except to insist that the workman should be free to do his work well according to its own integrity. Jacques Maritain, one of the very few religious writers of our time who really understands the nature of creative work, has summed the matter up in a sentence:

> What is required is the perfect practical discrimination between the end pursued by the workman (*finis operantis*, said the Schoolmen) and the end to be served by the work (*finis operis*), so that the workman may work for his wages but the work be controlled and set in being only in relation to its own proper good and nowise in relation to the wages earned; so that the artist may work for any and every human intention he likes, but the work taken by itself be performed and constructed for its own proper beauty alone.[8]

55 Or perhaps we may put it more shortly still: If work is to find its right place in the world, it is the duty of the Church to see to it that the work serves God, and that the worker serves the work.

Notes

[1] These topics were covered in a speech at Brighton in March 1941. The major part of that speech was published in *A Christian Basis for the Post-War World* (S.C.M. Press). "Why Work?" was first presented as a speech at Eastbourne, England, April 23, 1942.

[2] Matt. 6:33.

[3] Acts 6:2.

[4] Ch. 8, "Christian Art." sect. 2, in Jacques Maritain, *Art and Scholasticism with Other Essays*, trans. J. F. Scanlon (New York: Charles Scribner's Sons, 1930), 70.

5 Cf. Matt. 22:37–40.

6 Matt. 5:8.

7 An English slang term that originally referred to spectators in the cheapest seats in a theater. It came to refer to "those of ordinary or unsophisticated taste or critical judgment."

8 Ch. 9. "Art and Morality," sect. 2, in Maritain, *Art and Scholasticism.* 77–78.

In the "Allegory of the Cave," Plato (429–347 BCE) writes in the form of a dia-log in order to emphasize the discourse that must take place between learner and educator. This allegory is the vehicle through which Plato chooses to reveal several of his major philosophical beliefs, especially those pertaining to education and purpose. This fictional dialogue between Socrates and Plato's brother Glau-con illustrates Plato's belief that we cannot fully appreciate the world with our physical senses, but can only truly grasp its reality through our intellect. The allegory also emphasizes the necessity of those who have reached intellectual enlightenment to reach out and help those who have yet to achieve it.

from Allegory of the Cave

Plato

Book VII: On Shadows and Realities in Education

(Socrates, Glaucon.)

1   And now, I said, let me show in a figure how far our nature is enlight-ened or unenlightened: Behold! human beings living in an under-ground den, which has a mouth open toward the light and reaching all along the den; here they have been from their childhood, and have their legs and necks chained so that they cannot move, and can only see before them, being prevented by the chains from turning round their heads. Above and behind them a fire is blazing at a distance, and between the fire and the prisoners there is a raised way; and you will see, if you look, a low wall built along the way, like the screen which marionette-players have in front of them, over which they show the puppets.

2   I see.

3   And do you see, I said, men passing along the wall carrying all sorts of vessels, and statues and figures of animals made of wood and stone and various materials, which appear over the wall? Some of them are talking, others silent.

4   You have shown me a strange image, and they are strange prisoners.

5   Like ourselves, I replied; and they see only their own shadows, or the shadows of one another, which the fire throws on the opposite wall of the cave?

6   True, he said; how could they see anything but the shadows if they were never allowed to move their heads?

7   And of the objects which are being carried in like manner they would only see the shadows?

8   Yes, he said.

9   And if they were able to converse with one another, would they not suppose that they were naming what was actually before them?

10 Very true.

11 And suppose further that the prison had an echo which came from the other side, would they not be sure to fancy when one of the passers-by spoke that the voice which they heard came from the passing shadow?

12 No question, he replied.

13 To them, I said, the truth would be literally nothing but the shadows of the images.

14 That is certain.

15 And now look again, and see what will naturally follow if the prisoners are released and disabused of their error. At first, when any of them is liberated and compelled suddenly to stand up and turn his neck round and walk and look toward the light, he will suffer sharp pains; the glare will distress him, and he will be unable to see the realities of which in his former state he had seen the shadows; and then conceive someone saying to him, that what he saw before was an illusion, but that now, when he is approaching nearer to being and his eye is turned toward more real existence, he has a clearer vision— what will be his reply? And you may further imagine that his instructor is pointing to the objects as they pass and requiring him to name them—will he not be perplexed? Will he not fancy that the shadows which he formerly saw are truer than the objects which are now shown to him?

16 Far truer.

17 And if he is compelled to look straight at the light, will he not have a pain in his eyes which will make him turn away to take refuge in the objects of vision which he can see, and which he will conceive to be in reality clearer than the things which are now being shown to him?

18 True, he said.

19 And suppose once more, that he is reluctantly dragged up a steep and rugged ascent, and held fast until he is forced into the presence of the sun himself, is he not likely to be pained and irritated? When he approaches the light his eyes will be dazzled, and he will not be able to see anything at all of what are now called realities.

20 Not all in a moment, he said.

21 He will require to grow accustomed to the sight of the upper world. And first he will see the shadows best, next the reflections of men and other objects in the water, and then the objects themselves; then he will gaze upon the light of the moon and the stars and the spangled heaven; and he will see the sky and the stars by night better than the sun or the light of the sun by day?

22 Certainly.

23 Last of all he will be able to see the sun, and not mere reflections of him in the water, but he will see him in his own proper place, and not in another; and he will contemplate him as he is.

24 Certainly.

25 He will then proceed to argue that this is he who gives the season and the years, and is the guardian of all that is in the visible world, and in a certain way the cause of all things which he and his fellows have been accustomed to behold?

26 Clearly, he said, he would first see the sun and then reason about him.

27 And when he remembered his old habitation, and the wisdom of the den and his fellow-prisoners, do you not suppose that he would felicitate himself on the change, and pity him?

28 Certainly, he would.

29   And if they were in the habit of conferring honors among themselves
on those who were quickest to observe the passing shadows and to
remark which of them went before, and which followed after, and
which were together; and who were therefore best able to draw con-
clusions as to the future, do you think that he would care for such
honors and glories, or envy the possessors of them? Would he not say
with Homer,

> "Better to be the poor servant of a poor master,"

and to endure anything, rather than think as they do and live after
their manner?

30   Yes, he said, I think that he would rather suffer anything than enter-
tain these false notions and live in this miserable manner.

31   Imagine once more, I said, such a one coming suddenly out of the sun
to be replaced in his old situation; would he not be certain to have his
eyes full of darkness?

32   To be sure, he said.

33   And if there were a contest, and he had to compete in measuring the
shadows with the prisoners who had never moved out of the den,
while his sight was still weak, and before his eyes had become steady
(and the time which would be needed to acquire this new habit of
sight might be very considerable), would he not be ridiculous? Men
would say of him that up he went and down he came without his
eyes; and that it was better not even to think of ascending; and if anyone tried to loose another and lead him up to the light, let them only
catch the offender, and they would put him to death.

34   No question, he said.

35   This entire allegory, I said, you may now append, dear Glaucon, to
the previous argument; the prison-house is the world of sight, the
light of the fire is the sun, and you will not misapprehend me if you
interpret the journey upward to be the ascent of the soul into the
intellectual world according to my poor belief, which, at your desire,
I have expressed—whether rightly or wrongly, God knows. But,
whether true or false, my opinion is that in the world of knowledge
the idea of good appears last of all, and is seen only with an effort;
and, when seen, is also inferred to be the universal author of all
things beautiful and right, parent of light and of the lord of light in

this visible world, and the immediate source of reason and truth in the intellectual; and that this is the power upon which he who would act rationally either in public or private life must have his eye fixed.

36 I agree, he said, as far as I am able to understand you.

37 Moreover, I said, you must not wonder that those who attain to this beatific vision are unwilling to descend to human affairs; for their souls are ever hastening into the upper world where they desire to dwell; which desire of theirs is very natural, if our allegory may be trusted.

38 Yes, very natural.

39 And is there anything surprising in one who passes from divine contemplations to the evil state of man, misbehaving himself in a ridiculous manner; if, while his eyes are blinking and before he has become accustomed to the surrounding darkness, he is compelled to fight in courts of law, or in other places, about the images or the shadows of images of justice, and is endeavoring to meet the conceptions of those who have never yet seen absolute justice?

40 Anything but surprising, he replied. Anyone who has common-sense will remember that the bewilderments of the eyes are of two kinds, and arise from two causes, either from coming out of the light or from going into the light, which is true of the mind's eye, quite as much as of the bodily eye; and he who remembers this when he sees anyone whose vision is perplexed and weak, will not be too ready to laugh; he will first ask whether that soul of man has come out of the brighter life, and is unable to see because unaccustomed to the dark, or having turned from darkness to the day is dazzled by excess of light. And he will count the one happy in his condition and state of being, and he will pity the other; or, if he have a mind to laugh at the soul which comes from below into the light, there will be more reason in this than in the laugh which greets him who returns from above out of the light into the den.

41 That, he said, is a very just distinction.

42 But then, if I am right, certain professors of education must be wrong when they say that they can put a knowledge into the soul which was not there before, like sight into blind eyes.

43 They undoubtedly say this, he replied.

44 Whereas, our argument shows that the power and capacity of learning exists in the soul already; and that just as the eye was unable to turn from darkness to light without the whole body, so too the instrument of knowledge can only by the movement of the whole soul be turned from the world of becoming into that of being, and learn by degrees to endure the sight of being, and of the brightest and best of being, or, in other words, of the good.

45 Very true.

46 And must there not be some art which will effect conversion in the easiest and quickest manner; not implanting the faculty of sight, for that exists already, but has been turned in the wrong direction, and is looking away from the truth?

47 Yes, he said, such an art may be presumed.

48 And whereas the other so-called virtues of the soul seem to be akin to bodily qualities, for even when they are not originally innate they can be implanted later by habit and exercise, the virtue of wisdom more than anything else contains a divine element which always remains, and by this conversion is rendered useful and profitable; or, on the other hand, hurtful and useless. Did you never observe the narrow intelligence flashing from the keen eye of a clever rogue— how eager he is, how clearly his paltry soul sees the way to his end; he is the reverse of blind, but his keen eyesight is forced into the service of evil, and he is mischievous in proportion to his cleverness?

49 Very true, he said.

50 But what if there had been a circumcision of such natures in the days of their youth; and they had been severed from those sensual pleasures, such as eating and drinking, which, like leaden weights, were attached to them at their birth, and which drag them down and turn the vision of their souls upon the things that are below—if, I say, they had been released from these impediments and turned in the opposite direction, the very same faculty in them would have seen the truth as keenly as they see what their eyes are turned to now.

51 Very likely.

52 Yes, I said; and there is another thing which is likely, or rather a necessary inference from what has preceded, that neither the uneducated and uninformed of the truth, nor yet those who never make an end

of their education, will be able ministers of the State; not the former, because they have no single aim of duty which is the rule of all their actions, private as well as public; nor the latter, because they will not act at all except upon compulsion, fancying that they are already dwelling apart in the islands of the blessed.

53 Very true, he replied.

54 Then, I said, the business of us who are the founders of the State will be to compel the best minds to attain that knowledge which we have already shown to be the greatest of all—they must continue to ascend until they arrive at the good; but when they have ascended and seen enough we must not allow them to do as they do now.

55 What do you mean?

56 I mean that they remain in the upper world: but this must not be allowed; they must be made to descend again among the prisoners in the den, and partake of their labors and honors, whether they are worth having or not.

57 But is not this unjust? he said; ought we to give them a worse life, when they might have a better?

58 You have again forgotten, my friend, I said, the intention of the legislator, who did not aim at making any one class in the State happy above the rest; the happiness was to be in the whole State, and he held the citizens together by persuasion and necessity, making them benefactors of the State, and therefore benefactors of one another; to this end he created them, not to please themselves, but to be his instruments in binding up the State.

59 True, he said, I had forgotten.

60 Observe, Glaucon, that there will be no injustice in compelling our philosophers to have a care and providence of others; we shall explain to them that in other States, men of their class are not obliged to share in the toils of politics: and this is reasonable, for they grow up at their own sweet will, and the government would rather not have them. Being self-taught, they cannot be expected to show any gratitude for a culture which they have never received. But we have brought you into the world to be rulers of the hive, kings of yourselves and of the other citizens, and have educated you far better and more perfectly than they have been educated, and you are better able to share in the

double duty. Wherefore each of you, when his turn comes, must go down to the general underground abode, and get the habit of seeing in the dark. When you have acquired the habit, you will see ten thousand times better than the inhabitants of the den, and you will know what the several images are, and what they represent, because you have seen the beautiful and just and good in their truth. And thus our State, which is also yours, will be a reality, and not a dream only, and will be administered in a spirit unlike that of other States, in which men fight with one another about shadows only and are distracted in the struggle for power, which in their eyes is a great good. Whereas the truth is that the State in which the rulers are most reluctant to govern is always the best and most quietly governed, and the State in which they are most eager, the worst.

61   Quite true, he replied.

62   And will our pupils, when they hear this, refuse to take their turn at the toils of State, when they are allowed to spend the greater part of their time with one another in the heavenly light?

63   Impossible, he answered; for they are just men, and the commands which we impose upon them are just; there can be no doubt that every one of them will take office as a stern necessity, and not after the fashion of our present rulers of State.

64   Yes, my friend, I said; and there lies the point. You must contrive for your future rulers another and a better life than that of a ruler, and then you may have a well-ordered State; for only in the State which offers this, will they rule who are truly rich, not in silver and gold, but in virtue and wisdom, which are the true blessings of life. Whereas, if they go to the administration of public affairs, poor and hungering after their own private advantage, thinking that hence they are to snatch the chief good, order there can never be; for they will be fighting about office, and the civil and domestic broils which thus arise will be the ruin of the rulers themselves and of the whole State.

65   Most true, he replied.

66   And the only life which looks down upon the life of political ambition is that of true philosophy. Do you know of any other?

67   Indeed, I do not, he said.

68 And those who govern ought not to be lovers of the task? For, if they are, there will be rival lovers, and they will fight.

69 No question. Who, then, are those whom we shall compel to be guardians? Surely they will be the men who are wisest about affairs of State, and by whom the State is best administered, and who at the same time have other honors and another and a better life than that of politics?

70 They are the men, and I will choose them, he replied.

Albert Schweitzer (1875–1965) was an author, philosopher, theologian, and musician. Schweitzer's philosophy of "Reverence for Life" is an idea for which he is often remembered and commended. This commitment led him to speak out against European colonialism and any worldviews that highlighted power and violence. In "I Resolve to Become a Jungle Doctor," Schweitzer details his decision to leave a promising career as an organist to spend years in medical school training to become a doctor so as to care for people in Africa. His decision, and the response to his decision by friends and family, provides valuable insight into how people discern God's particular vocation in their lives.

I Resolve to Become a Jungle Doctor

Albert Schweitzer

1   On October 13, 1905, I dropped into a letter box on the avenue de la Grande Armée in Paris letters to my parents and to some of my closest friends telling them that at the beginning of the winter term I would embark on the study of medicine with the idea of later going out to equatorial Africa as a doctor. In one letter I submitted my resignation from the post of principal of the Collegium Wilhelmitanum (the theological seminary of St. Thomas) because of the time my studies would require.

2   The plan I hoped to realize had been in my mind for some time. Long ago in my student days I had thought about it. It struck me as inconceivable that I should be allowed to lead such a happy life while I saw so many people around me struggling with sorrow and suffering. Even at school I had felt stirred whenever I caught a glimpse of the miserable home surroundings of some of my classmates and compared them with the ideal conditions in which we children of the parsonage at Günsbach had lived. At the university, enjoying the good fortune of studying and even getting some results in scholarship and the arts, I could not help but think continually of others who were denied that good fortune by their material circumstances or their health.

3 One brilliant summer morning at Günsbach, during the Whitsuntide holidays—it was in 1896—as I awoke, the thought came to me that I must not accept this good fortune as a matter of course, but must give something in return.

4 While outside the birds sang I reflected on this thought, and before I had gotten up I came to the conclusion that until I was thirty I could consider myself justified in devoting myself to scholarship and the arts, but after that I would devote myself directly to serving humanity. I had already tried many times to find the meaning that lay hidden in the saying of Jesus: "Whosoever would save his life shall lose it, and whosoever shall lose his life for My sake and the Gospels shall save it." Now I had found the answer. I could now add outward to inward happiness.

5 What the character of my future activities would be was not yet clear to me. I left it to chance to guide me. Only one thing was certain, that it must be direct human service, however inconspicuous its sphere.

6 I naturally thought first of some activity in Europe. I formed a plan for taking charge of and educating abandoned or neglected children, then making them pledge to help children later on in a similar situation in the same way. When in 1903, as director of the theological seminary I moved into my roomy and sunny official quarters on the second floor of the College of St. Thomas, I was in a position to begin the experiment. I offered help now in one place, now in another, but always to no avail. The charters of the organizations that looked after destitute and abandoned children had made no provisions for accepting volunteers. For example, when the Strasbourg orphanage burned down, I offered to take in a few boys temporarily, but the superintendent did not even let me finish my sentence. I made similar attempts elsewhere also in vain.

7 For a time I thought I would someday devote myself to tramps and discharged convicts. To prepare myself for this I joined the Reverend Augustus Ernst at St. Thomas in an undertaking he had begun. Between one and two in the afternoon he remained at home ready to speak to anyone who came to him asking for help or a night's lodging. He did not, however, give the applicant money, nor did he make him wait until the information about his circumstances could be confirmed. Instead he would offer to look up the applicant in his home

or shelter that very afternoon and verify the information he had been given about the situation. After this, he would give him all necessary assistance for as long as was needed. How many bicycle rides did we make into town or the suburbs, and quite often only to find that the applicant was unknown at the address he had given. In many cases, however, it provided an opportunity for giving appropriate help, with knowledge of the circumstances. I also had friends who kindly contributed money to this cause.

8   As a student, I had been active in social service as a member of the student association known as the Diaconate of St. Thomas, which held its meetings in the St. Thomas seminary. Each of us had a certain number of poor families assigned to him, which he was to visit every week, taking some aid and then reporting about their situation. The funds we thus distributed we collected from members of the old Strasbourg families who supported this undertaking, begun by earlier generations and now carried on by ourselves. Twice a year, if I remember correctly, each of us had to make a fixed number of financial appeals. For me, being shy and rather awkward in society, these visits were a torture. I believe that in this preparatory experience of soliciting funds, which I had to do much more of in later years, I sometimes showed myself extremely unskillful. However, I learned through them that soliciting with tact and restraint is better appreciated than any sort of aggressive approach, and also that correct soliciting methods include the friendly acceptance of refusal.

9   In our youthful inexperience we no doubt often failed, in spite of our best intentions, to use the money entrusted to us in the wisest way. The expectations of the givers were, however, fulfilled with respect to their purpose—that young men should devote themselves to serve the poor. For that reason I think with deep gratitude of those who met our efforts with so much understanding and generosity, and hope that many students may have the privilege of working as recruits in the struggle against poverty.

10   As I worried about the homeless and former convicts it became clear to me that they could only be effectively helped if many individuals devoted themselves to them. At the same time, however, I realized that in many cases individuals could only accomplish their tasks in collaboration with official organizations. But what I wanted was an absolutely personal and independent activity.

11 Although I was resolved to put my services at the disposal of some organization if it should become really necessary, I nonetheless never gave up the hope of finding an activity to which I could devote myself as an individual and as a wholly free agent. I have always considered it an ever renewed grace that I could fulfill this profound desire.

12 One morning in the autumn of 1904 I found on my writing table in the seminary one of the green-covered magazines in which the Paris Missionary Society (La Société Evangélique des Missions à Paris) reported on its activities every month. A Miss Scherdlin used to pass them on to me. She knew that in my youth I had been impressed by the letters from Mr. Casalis, one of the first missionaries of this society. My father had read them to us in his mission services.

13 Without paying much attention, I leafed through the magazine that had been put on my table the night before. As I was about to turn to my studies, I noticed an article with the headline "Les besoins de la Mission du Congo" ("The needs of the Congo Mission," in the *Journal des Missions Evangéliques*, June 1904). It was by Alfred Boegner, the president of the Paris Missionary Society, an Alsatian, who complained in it that the mission did not have enough people to carry on its work in the Gaboon, the northern province of the Congo colony. The writer expressed the hope that his appeal would bring some of those "on whom the Master's eyes already rested" to a decision to offer themselves for this urgent work. The article concluded: "Men and women who can reply simply to the Master's call, 'Lord, I am coming,' those are the people the Church needs." I finished my article and quietly began my work. My search was over.

14 I spent my thirtieth birthday a few months later like the man in the parable who, "desiring to build a tower, first calculates the cost of completion whether he has the means to complete it." The result was a resolve to realize my plan of direct human service in equatorial Africa.

15 Aside from one trustworthy friend, no one knew of my intention. When it became known through the letters I had sent from Paris, I had hard battles to fight with my relatives and friends. They reproached me more for not taking them into my confidence and discussing the decision with them than they did for the enterprise itself.

With this secondary issue they tormented me beyond measure during those difficult weeks. That theological friends should outdo the others in their protests struck me as all the more absurd because they had no doubt all preached a fine sermon—perhaps a very fine one—that quoted Paul's declaration in his letter to the Galatians that he "did not confer with flesh or blood" before he knew what he would do for Jesus.

16   My relatives and friends reproached me for the folly of my enterprise. They said I was a man who was burying the talent entrusted to him and wanted to trade in false currency. I ought to leave work among Africans to those who would not thereby abandon gifts and achievements in scholarship and the arts. Widor, who loved me as a son, scolded me for acting like a general who, rifle in hand, insists on fighting in the firing line (there was no talk about trenches at that time). A lady who was filled with the modern spirit proved to me that I could do much more by lecturing on behalf of medical help for Africans than I could by the course of action I contemplated. The aphorism from Goethe's *Faust*, "In the beginning was the Deed," was now out of date, she said, "Today propaganda is the mother of events."

17   In the many adversarial debates I had to endure with people who passed for Christians, it amazed me to see them unable to perceive that the desire to serve the love preached by Jesus may sweep a man into a new course of life. They read in the New Testament that it can do so, and found it quite in order there.

18   I had assumed that familiarity with the sayings of Jesus would give a much better comprehension of what to popular logic is not rational. Several times, indeed, my appeal to the obedience that Jesus' command of love requires under certain circumstances earned me an accusation of conceit. How I suffered to see so many people assuming the right to tear open the doors and shutters of my inner self!

19   In general, neither allowing them to see that I was hurt nor letting them know the thought that had given birth to my resolution was of any use. They thought there must be something behind it all, and guessed at disappointment with the slow development of my career. For this there were no grounds at all, in that, even as a young man, I had received as much recognition as others usually get only after a whole life of toil and struggle. Unhappy love was another reason alleged for my decision.

20 The attitude of people who did not try to explore my feelings, but regarded me as a young man not quite right in the head and treated me with correspondingly affectionate ridicule, represented a real kindness.

21 I felt it to be quite natural in itself that family and friends should challenge the rationality of my plan. As one who demands that idealists should be sober in their views, I was aware that every venture down an untrodden path is a venture that looks sensible and likely to be successful only under unusual circumstances. In my own case I held the venture to be justified, because I had considered it for a long time and from every point of view, and I thought that I had good health, sound nerves, energy, practical common sense, toughness, prudence, very few wants, and everything else that might be necessary for the pursuit of my idea. I believed, further, that I had the inner fortitude to endure any eventual failure of my plan.

22 As a man of independent action, I have since that time been approached for my opinion and advice by many people who wanted to risk a similar venture. Only in comparatively few cases have I taken the responsibility of giving them encouragement. I often had to recognize that the need "to do something special" was born of a restless spirit. Such people wanted to dedicate themselves to larger tasks because those that lay nearest did not satisfy them. Often, too, it was evident that they were motivated by quite secondary considerations. Only a person who finds value in any kind of activity and who gives of himself with a full sense of service has the right to choose an exceptional task instead of following a common path. Only a person who feels his preference to be a matter of course, not something out of the ordinary, and who has no thought of heroism but only of a duty undertaken with sober enthusiasm, is capable of becoming the sort of spiritual pioneer the world needs. There are no heroes of action—only heroes of renunciation and suffering. Of these there are plenty. But few of them are known, and even they not to the crowd, but to the few.

23 Carlyle's *On Heroes and Hero-Worship* is not a profound book.

24 The majority of those who feel the impulse and are actually capable of devoting their lives to independent action are compelled by circumstances to renounce that course. As a rule they have to provide

for one or more dependents, or they have to stay with their profession in order to earn a living. Only a person who, thanks to his own efforts or the devotion of friends, is free from material needs can nowadays take the risk of undertaking such a personal task.

25   This was not so much the case in earlier times because anyone who gave up remunerative work could still hope to get through life somehow or other, but anyone thinking of doing such a thing in the difficult economic conditions of today runs the risk of coming to grief both materially and spiritually.

26   I know not only by what I have observed but also by experience that there are worthy and capable people who have had to renounce a course of independent action that would have been of great value to the world because of circumstances that made it impossible.

27   Those who are given the chance to embark on a life of independent action must accept their good fortune in a spirit of humility. They must often think of those who, though equally willing and capable, were not in a position to do the same. And as a rule they must temper their own strong determination with humility. Almost always they must search and wait until they find a path that will permit the action they long to take. Fortunate are those who have received more years of creative work than years of searching and waiting. Fortunate those who succeed in giving themselves genuinely and completely.

28   These favored souls must also be humble so as not to get irritated by the resistance they encounter, but to accept it as inevitable. Anyone who proposes to do good must not expect people to roll any stones out of his way, and must calmly accept his lot even if they roll a few more into it. Only force that in the face of obstacles becomes stronger can win. Force that is used only to revolt wastes itself.

29   Of all the will toward the ideal in mankind only a small part can manifest itself in public action. All the rest of this force must be content with small and obscure deeds. The sum of these, however, is a thousand times stronger than the acts of those who receive wide public recognition. The latter, compared to the former, are like the foam on the waves of a deep ocean.

30   The hidden forces of goodness are alive in those who serve humanity as a secondary pursuit, those who cannot devote their full life to it. The lot of most people is to have a job, to earn their living, and to assume

for themselves a place in society through some kind of nonfulfilling labor. They can give little or nothing of their human qualities. The problems arising from progressive specialization and mechanization of labor can only be partly resolved through the concessions society is willing to make in its economic planning. It is always essential that the individuals themselves not suffer their fate passively, but expend all their energies in affirming their own humanity through some spiritual engagement, even if the conditions are unfavorable.

31   One can save one's life as a human being, along with one's professional existence, if one seizes every opportunity, however unassuming, to act humanly toward those who need another human being. In this way we serve both the spiritual and the good. Nothing can keep us from this second job of direct human service. So many opportunities are missed because we let them pass by.

32   Everyone in his own environment must strive to practice true humanity toward others. The future of the world depends on it.

33   Great values are lost at every moment because we miss opportunities, but the values that are turned into will and action constitute a richness that must not be undervalued. Our humanity is by no means as materialistic as people claim so complacently.

34   Judging by what I have learned about men and women, I am convinced that far more idealistic aspiration exists than is ever evident. Just as the rivers we see are much less numerous than the underground streams, so the idealism that is visible is minor compared to what men and women carry in their hearts, unreleased or scarcely released. Mankind is waiting and longing for those who can accomplish the task of untying what is knotted and bringing the underground waters to the surface.

35   What to my friends seemed most irrational in my plan was that I wanted to go to Africa, not as a missionary, but as a doctor. Already thirty years of age, I would burden myself with long and laborious study. I never doubted for an instant that these studies would require an immense effort, and I anticipated the coming years with anxiety. But the reasons that made me determined to enter into the service I had chosen as a doctor weighed so heavily that other considerations were as dust in the balance and counted for nothing.

36   I wanted to be a doctor so that I might be able to work without having to talk. For years I had been giving of myself in words, and it was
with joy that I had followed the calling of theological teacher and
preacher. But this new form of activity would consist not in preaching the religion of love, but in practicing it. Medical knowledge
would make it possible for me to carry out my intention in the best
and most complete way, wherever the path of service might lead me.

37   Given my choice of equatorial Africa, acquiring this knowledge was
especially appropriate because in the district to which I planned to go
a doctor was, according to the missionaries' reports, the most urgent
of all its needs. In their reports and magazines they always regretted
that they could not provide help for the Africans who came in great
physical pain. I was greatly motivated to study medicine and
become, one day, the doctor whom these unhappy people needed.
Whenever I was tempted to feel that the years I should have to sacrifice were too long, I reminded myself that Hamilcar and Hannibal
had prepared for their march on Rome by their slow and tedious con-
quest of Spain.

38   There was still one more reason why it seemed to be my destiny to
become a doctor. From what I knew of the Paris Missionary Society,
I could not but feel very doubtful that they would accept me as a
missionary.

39   It was in pietistic and orthodox circles that at the beginning of the
nineteenth century societies were first formed for preaching the
Gospel in the pagan world. About the same time, liberal Christendom also began to comprehend the need for carrying the teaching of
Jesus to far-off lands. But when it came to action, orthodox Protestantism was first. It maintained lively and active organizations on the
fringes of the main Church, and these were able to carry out their
own independent activities. At that time the liberal Protestants were
strong, but preoccupied with inner governmental problems in their
Church. Moreover, the orthodox bodies with their pietistic ideas of
"saving souls" had a stronger motive for mission work than did liberal Protestants. For them, the Gospel signified most of all a force for
the regeneration of individual morality and for the human condition
in general.

40　Once the missionary societies inspired by pietism and orthodoxy got to work they found support in liberal circles that were friendly to missions. These believed for a long time that they would not have to found their own missionary societies, but that by joining those in existence, all Protestants would eventually work together. They were mistaken, however. Indeed, the societies accepted all the material help offered them by liberal Protestantism—how hard my father and his liberal colleagues in Alsace had worked for missionary societies that had a quite different doctrinal outlook!—but they never sent out missionaries who would not accept their own doctrinal requirements.

41　Because liberal Protestantism did not organize missionary activities for a long time, it earned the reputation for neither realizing its importance nor doing anything about it. Finally it did found its own societies, but it was too late, and the hope that there could be one mission working in the name of the Protestant Church was lost.

42　I was always interested to discover that the missionaries themselves were more liberal in their thinking than the officials of their societies. Experience had, of course, taught them that in foreign lands, especially among the native people, the problem of dogmatic constraint versus liberalism that plagued European Christianity did not exist. The important thing out there is to preach the essentials of the Gospel as given in the Sermon on the Mount and to lead people to the spiritual realm of Jesus.

43　My father had a special sympathy for the Paris Missionary Society, because he thought he could detect in it a more liberal tendency than in the others. He particularly appreciated the fact that Casalis and others among its leading missionaries wrote their reports in straightforward language of a Christian character, rather than sugar-coated devotionals.

44　But I learned, and very definitely, that orthodoxy played the same role in the committee of the Paris Society that it did in others when I offered it my services. M. Boegner, the kindly director of the mission, was greatly moved upon finding that someone had offered to join the Congo mission in answer to his appeal, but at once confided to me that serious objections would be raised by members of the committee to my theological stance and that these would have to be removed first. My assurance that I wanted to come "merely as a doctor" lifted a heavy weight from his mind, but a little later he had to inform me that some members objected even to the acceptance of a mission doctor who sub-scribed only to proper Christian love, and did not, in their opinion, adhere to the correct Christian doctrine. However, we both resolved not to worry too much about the matter so far in advance, and thought the objectors still had some years during which they might arrive at a truly Christian understanding.

45   No doubt the more liberal Allgemeine Evangelische Missionsverein (General Union of Evangelical Missions) in Switzerland would have accepted me without hesitation either as missionary or doctor. But as I felt my call to equatorial Africa had come to me through the article in the Paris Missionary Society magazine, I felt I ought at least to try to join that mission's activities in that colony. Further, I was curious to see whether a missionary society could justifiably arrogate the right to refuse the services of a doctor to the suffering people in their district because in their opinion he was not sufficiently orthodox.

46   But above and beyond all this, now that I was beginning my medical studies, my daily work and daily worries made such demands upon me that I had neither the time nor the strength to concern myself with what was to happen afterward.

and injustice. God is in charge. That is what had upheld the morale of our people, to know that in the end good will prevail. It was these higher laws that convinced me that our peaceful struggle would topple the immoral laws of apartheid.

3   Of course, there were times when you had to whistle in the dark to keep your morale up, and you wanted to whisper in God's ear: "God, we know You are in charge, but can't You make it a little more obvious?" God did make it more obvious to me once, during what we call the Feast of the Transfiguration. Apartheid was in full swing as I and other church leaders were preparing for a meeting with the prime minister to discuss one of the many controversies that erupted in those days. We met at a theological college that had closed down because of the government's racist policies. During our discussions I went into the priory garden for some quiet. There was a huge Calvary—a large wooden cross without corpus, but with protruding nails and a crown of thorns. It was a stark symbol of the Christian faith. It was winter: the grass was pale and dry and nobody would have believed that in a few weeks' time it would be lush and green and beautiful again. It would be transfigured.

4   As I sat quietly in the garden I realized the power of transfiguration—of God's transformation—in our world. The principle of transfiguration is at work when something so unlikely as the brown grass that covers our veld in winter becomes bright green again. Or when the tree with gnarled leafless branches bursts forth with the sap flowing so that the birds sit chirping in the leafy branches. Or when the once dry streams gurgle with swift-flowing water. When winter gives way to spring and nature seems to experience its own resurrection.

5   The principle of transfiguration says nothing, no one and no situation, is "untransfigurable," that the whole of creation, nature, waits expectantly for its transfiguration, when it will be released from its bondage and share in the glorious liberty of the children of God, when it will not be just dry inert matter but will be translucent with divine glory.

6   Christian history is filled with examples of transfiguration. An erstwhile persecutor like St. Paul could become the greatest missionary of the church he once persecuted. One who denied his Master not once but three times like St. Peter could become the

prince of apostles, proclaiming boldly faith in Jesus Christ when only
a short while before he was cowering in abject fear behind locked
doors.

7   I doubt, however, that we could produce a more spectacular example
of this principle of transfiguration than the Cross itself. Most people
would have been filled with revulsion had someone gone and set up
an electric chair or a gallows or the guillotine as an object of reverence. Well, look at the Cross. It was a ghastly instrument of death, of
an excruciatingly awful death reserved for the most notorious male-
factors. It was an object of dread and shame, and yet what a turn-
around has happened. This instrument of a horrendous death has
been spectacularly transfigured. Once a means of death, it is now perceived by Christians to be the source of life eternal. Far from being an
object of vilification and shame, it is an object of veneration.

8   As I sat in the priory garden I thought of our desperate political situation in the light of this principle of transfiguration, and from that
moment on, it has helped me to see with new eyes. I have witnessed
time and again the improbable redemptions that are possible in our
world. Let me give you just one example from our struggle in South
Africa, which I know best, but such transfigurations are not limited
to one country or one people. This story took place almost twenty-
five years after that first experience in the priory.

9   It was just before April 1994 and we were on the verge of disaster, literally on the brink of civil war and threatened with being overwhelmed by a bloodbath. We had witnessed the stunning release of
Nelson Mandela and other leaders in 1990 and the miraculous move
toward universal elections, but between 1990 and 1994 we had been
on a roller-coaster ride, exhilarated at one moment, in the depths of
despair the next. Thousands of people had died in massacres during
the transition, such as one at Boipatong, near Johannesburg, in which
about forty-five people were killed in one night. The province of
KwaZulu-Natal was a running sore as a result of rivalry between the
Inkatha Freedom Party and the African National Congress. Some of
us said that a sinister Third Force, including elements of the government's security forces, was behind a spate of indiscriminate killings
on trains, at taxi ranks and bus stops. We were usually pooh-poohed
by the authorities. Just before the election, there was an insurrection in
one of the so-called independent homelands, which was run by black

leaders who were prepared to work within the apartheid policy. A neo-Nazi Afrikaner group who wanted to sabotage the transition intervened in the rebellion. Inkatha, a major party in KwaZulu, was boycotting the election. Attempts were made to destabilize and intimidate the black community and to scare them away from voting. Our impending election looked like a disaster waiting to happen. We were all gritting our teeth, expecting the worst. But in the weeks leading up to the election, the insurrection failed and the neo-Nazi group was ignominiously routed. At the proverbial eleventh hour, we heaved a sigh of relief as Inkatha was persuaded to join the election.

10   Elections are usually just secular political events in most parts of the world. Our elections turned out to be a spiritual, even a religious, experience. We won't so quickly forget the images of those long queues snaking their way slowly into the polling booths. People waited a very long time. John Allen, my media secretary, said there was a new status symbol at the time in South Africa. Someone would say, "I stood for two hours before I could vote!" And someone else would say, "Oh, that's nothing—I waited four hours . . . ." There was chaos in many places, not enough ballot papers or ink or whatever. It was a catastrophe about to take place. It never did. After I had cast my vote, having waited all of sixty-two years to do so for the first time, I toured some of the voting stations. The people had come out in droves and they looked so utterly vulnerable. It would have taken just two or three people with AK-47s to sow the most awful mayhem. It did not happen. What took place can only be described as a miracle. People stood in those long lines, people of all races in South Africa that had known separation and apartheid for so long—black and white, colored and Indian, farmer, laborer, educated, unschooled, poor, rich—they stood in those lines and the scales fell from their eyes. South Africans made an earth-shattering discovery—hey, we are all fellow South Africans. We are compatriots. People shared newspapers, picnic lunches, stories—and they discovered (what a profound discovery!) that they were human together and that they actually seemed to want much the same things—a nice house in a secure and safe neighborhood, a steady job, good schools for the children, and, yes, skin color and race were indeed thoroughly irrelevant.

11   People entered the booth one person and emerged on the other side a totally different person. The black person went in burdened with all

the anguish of having had his or her dignity trampled underfoot and being treated as a nonperson—and then voted. And said, "Hey, I'm free—my dignity has been restored, my humanity has been acknowledged. I'm free!" She emerged a changed person, a transformed, a transfigured person.

12   The white person entered the booth one person, burdened by the weight of guilt for having enjoyed many privileges unjustly, voted, and emerged on the other side a new person. "Hey, I'm free, The burden has been lifted. I'm free!" She emerged a new, a different, a transformed, a transfigured person. Many white people confessed that they too were voting for the first time—for the first time as really free people. Now they realized what we had been trying to tell them for so long, that freedom was indivisible, that they would never be free until we were free.

13   Yes, our first election turned out to be a deeply spiritual event, a religious experience, a transfiguration experience, a mountaintop experience. We had won a spectacular victory over injustice, oppression, and evil. There we were—people who as a matter of public policy were deliberately tearing one another apart, declaring that human fellowship, togetherness, friendship, laughter, joy, caring, that these were impossible for us as one nation, and now here we were becoming, from all the different tribes and languages, diverse cultures, and faiths, so utterly improbably, we were becoming one nation. Now who could ever believe that that was possible? Only in 1989 police had threatened to use live ammunition to get people to disperse who were protesting against beach apartheid. In 1989 they were ready to kill to maintain apartheid and to keep the beaches just for the whites. And just a few years later there we were a nation that had elected as president Nelson Mandela. This man who languished in jail for twenty-seven years, vilified as a terrorist, and who eventually became one of the moral leaders of the world.

14   I remember sometime after the election there was a lunch he hosted for the widows of political leaders. There the widow of black consciousness activist Steve Biko was chatting with the widow of B. J. Vorster, who was the prime minister when the police killed Steve. Totally improbable, totally unlikely material for triumph, and yet it has happened. It was a transfiguration. If you had said a few years before that South Africa would be a beacon of hope, people would have taken you

to a psychiatrist. And yet it was so. Our problems are not over—poverty, unemployment, and the AIDS epidemic—because transfiguration is ongoing. But just because there is more to be done, we should not forget the miracles that have taken place in our lifetime.

15   Many of us can acknowledge that God cares about the world but can't imagine that God would care about you or me individually. But our God marvelously, miraculously cares about each and every one of us. The Bible has this incredible image of you, of me, of all of us, each one, held as something precious, fragile in the palms of God's hands. And that you and I exist only because God is forever blowing God's breath into our being. And so God says to you, "I love you. You are precious in your fragility and your vulnerability. Your being is a gift. I breathe into you and hold you as something precious."

16   But why, we ask in our disbelief and despair, would God care about *me*? The simple reason is that God loves you. God loves you as if you were the only person on earth. God, looking on us here, does not see us as a mass. God knows us each by name. God says, "Your name is engraved on the palms of My hands." You are so precious to God that the very hairs of your head are numbered. "Can a mother," God asks, "forget the child she bore?" That is a most unlikely thing, quite unnatural, but it could happen. God says, even if that most unlikely thing were to happen, God's love wouldn't allow Him to forget you or me. We are those precious things that God carries gently, God carries each one of us as if we were fragile because God knows that we are. You are precious to God. God cares for you.

17   Many people believe that they are beyond God's love—that God may love others but that what they have done has caused God to stop loving them. But Jesus by his example showed us that God loves sinners as much as saints. Jesus associated with the scum of society. And Jesus taught that he had come to seek and to find not the righteous but the lost and the sinners. He scandalized the prim and proper people of his day who believed that he was lowering standards horribly badly. Now anyone could enter heaven. He companied not with the respectable, not with the elite of society, but with those occupying the fringes of society—the prostitutes, the sinners, the ostracized ones. You see, Jesus would most probably have been seen in the red-light district of a city. Can you imagine if they saw me there walking into

a brothel to visit with what are often called the women of easy virtue. Who would say, "We're quite sure the archbishop is there for a pastoral reason"? But that's exactly what Jesus did. Someone might look like a criminal or a drug addict, but these societal outcasts remain God's children despite their desperate deeds.

18   I saw the power of this gospel when I was serving as chairperson of the Truth and Reconciliation Commission in South Africa. This was the commission that the postapartheid government, headed by our president Nelson Mandela, had established to move us beyond the cycles of retribution and violence that had plagued so many other countries during their transitions from oppression to democracy. The commission gave perpetrators of political crimes the opportunity to appeal for amnesty by telling the truth of their actions and an opportunity to ask for forgiveness, an opportunity that some took and others did not. The commission also gave victims of political crimes an opportunity to unburden themselves from the pain and suffering they had experienced.

19   As we listened to accounts of truly monstrous deeds of torture and cruelty, it would have been easy to dismiss the perpetrators as monsters because their deeds were truly monstrous. But we are reminded that God's love is not cut off from anyone. However diabolical the act, it does not turn the perpetrator into a demon. When we proclaim that someone is subhuman, we not only remove for them the possibility of change and repentance, we also remove from them moral responsibility.

20   We cannot condemn anyone to being irredeemable, as Jesus reminded us on the Cross, crucified as he was between two thieves. When one repented, Jesus promised him that he would be in paradise with him on that same day. Even the most notorious sinner and evildoer at the eleventh hour may repent and be forgiven, because our God is preeminently a God of grace. Everything that we are, that we have, is a gift from God. He does not give up on you or on anyone for God loves you now and will always love you. Whether we are good or bad, God's love is unchanging and unchangeable. Like a tireless and long-suffering parent, our God is there for us when we are ready to hear His still, small voice in our lives. (I refer to God as He in this book, but this language is offensive to many, including me, because it implies that God is more of a He than a She, and this is clearly not the

case. Fortunately, in our Bantu languages in South Africa we do not have gendered pronouns and so we do not face this problem. To avoid cumbersome usage in English, I have chosen to follow convention here, but I apologize to the reader for this grammatical necessity but spiritual inaccuracy.)

21 So why, you may ask, if God is actively working with us to transfigure and transform the world does He allow us to do evil to one another? The problem of evil is an important one and this question is not to be answered lightly. I have heard and seen many examples of the cruelty that we are able to visit on one another during my time on the commission and during my travels.

22 I was devastated as I listened to one former member of the security forces describe how he and others shot and killed a fellow human being, burned his body on a pyre, and while this cremation was going on actually enjoyed a barbecue on the side. And then he no doubt went home and kissed his wife and children. When I was serving as the president of the All Africa Conference of Churches, I went to Rwanda one year after the genocide there that claimed the lives of more than half a million people. I saw skulls that still had machetes and daggers embedded in them. I couldn't pray. I could only weep.

23 If we are capable of such acts, how can there be any hope for us, how can we have faith in goodness? There very well may be times when God has regretted creating us, but I am convinced that there are many more times that God feels vindicated by our kindness, our magnanimity; our nobility of spirit. I have also seen incredible forgiveness and compassion, like the man who after being beaten and spending more than a hundred days in solitary confinement said to me we must not become bitter, or the American couple who established a foundation in South Africa to help the children of a black township where their daughter had been brutally murdered.

24 Yes, each of us has the capacity for great evil. Not one of us can say with certainty that we would not become perpetrators if we were subject to the same conditioning as those in South Africa, Rwanda, or anywhere that hatred perverts the human spirit. This is not for one minute to excuse what was done or those who did it. It is, however, to be filled more and more with the compassion of God, looking on

and weeping that His beloved children, our beloved brothers or sisters, have come to such a sad state. But for every act of evil there are a dozen acts of goodness in our world that go unnoticed. It is only because the evil deeds are less common that they are "news." It is only because we believe that people *should* be good that we despair when they are not. Indeed, if people condoned the evil, we would be justified in losing hope. But most of the world does not. We know that we are meant for better.

25   The Bible recognizes that we are a mixture of good and bad. We must therefore not be too surprised that most human enterprises are not always wholly good or wholly bad. Our ability to do evil is part and parcel of our ability to do good. One is meaningless without the other. Empathy and compassion have no meaning unless they occur in a situation where one could be callous and indifferent to the suffering of others. To have any possibility of moral growth there has to be the possibility of becoming immoral.

26   God has given us space to be authentically human persons with autonomy. Love is something that must be given freely. If God is saying, I would like you to obey Me, then that must leave the possibility of disobeying God. Because God takes the risk of real relationships, there is the possibility that those relationships are going to splinter, and they often do.

27   This autonomy is the basis of our freedom, without which no real relationship with God—or with each other—would be possible. God created us freely, for freedom. To be human in the understanding of the Bible is to be free to choose, free to choose to love or to hate, to be kind or to be cruel. To be human is to be a morally responsible creature, and moral responsibility is a nonsense when the person is in fact not free to choose from several available options. That is how God created us. It is part of being created in the image of God, this freedom that can make us into glorious creatures or damn us into hellish ones. God took an incredible risk in creating us human beings. God has such a profound respect, nay, reverence, for this freedom He bestowed on us that He had much rather see us go freely to hell than compel us to go to heaven. As they say, hell is the greatest compliment God has paid us.

28   It is this fact that we were created to be free that is the reason that all oppression must ultimately fail. Our freedom does not come from

any human being—our freedom comes from God. This is what we mean when we say it is an inalienable right. This freedom is so much a part of the human makeup that it is not too far-fetched to say that an unfree human being is in a sense a contradiction in terms. The ideal society is one in which its members enjoy their freedom to be human freely, provided they do not thereby infringe the freedom of others unduly. We are made to have freedom of association, of expression, of movement, the freedom to choose who will rule over us and how. We are made for this. It is ineluctable. It cannot ultimately be eradicated, this yearning for freedom to be human. This is what tyrants and unjust rulers have to contend with. They cannot in the end stop their victims from being human.

29 Their unjust regimes must ultimately fall because they seek to deny something that cannot be denied. No matter how long and how repressive their unjust and undemocratic rule turns out to be, the urge for freedom remains as a subversive element threatening the overthrow of rigid repression. The tyrant is on a road to nowhere even though he may survive for an unconscionably long time and even though he may turn his country into a huge prison riddled with informers. This may go on for too long in the view of the victims, but the end cannot be in doubt. Freedom will break out. People are made for it just as plants tend toward the light and toward water.

30 If God is transfiguring the world, you may ask, why does He need our help? The answer is quite simple: we are the agents of transformation that God uses to transfigure His world.

31 In the Bible, when God wanted the children of Israel to be freed from bondage in Egypt, He could have done it on His own, but He wanted a human partner. We often forget that the patriarchs and matriarchs were flesh-and-blood humans, but the Bible reminds us of this repeatedly. These people, with all their flaws, were able to be God's heroic partners. So God went to Moses and said something along these lines.

32 "Hi, Moses."

33 "Hi, God."

34 "Moses, I want you to go to Pharaoh and tell him: 'Let my people go.'"

35   Moses was thoroughly flabbergasted: "What? Me? What have I done now? Go to Pharaoh? Please, God, no! You can't be serious!"

36   Forgetting that God knew everything, Moses pleaded: "God, you know I stammer. How can I address Pharaoh?"

37   Mercifully, God did not accept Moses' first negative reactions. If He had, the children of Israel would still be in Egypt in bondage. The God we worship is the Exodus God, the great liberator God who leads us out of all kinds of bondage.

38   Do you remember what God told Moses? He said, "I have seen the suffering of My people. I have heard their cry. I know their suffering and am come down to deliver them." Our God is a God who knows. Our God is a God who sees. Our God is a God who hears. Our God is a God who comes down to deliver. But the way that God delivers us is by using us as His partners, by calling on Moses, and on you and me.

39   But we are not alone. God does not abandon us in our moments of need. Do you remember the wonderful story in the Book of Daniel about the time God's people were being persecuted by the king, who expected them to bow down before a graven image? The king set up a golden statue and said that anyone who refused to worship it was going to become a Kentucky Fried Chicken because he was going to be thrown into the fiery furnace. Now Shadrach, Meshach, and Abednego refused to obey the royal decree. The king called the three and tried to be nice to them: "I know there are people who mislead you. You will worship the image." They said: "What? No, man." So the king said: "Do you know who I am? I am the king here. I am in charge. We are going to stoke up the fire seven times hotter than it ever was because you don't listen to me."

40   The story says the fire was so hot it burned to death the soldiers who carried the three to the furnace. But as the king looked into the fire, thinking they would be burnt to a crisp, he could not believe his eyes. For they were walking in the fire! No, there were not three! There was a fourth with them, and the king looked and said: "There is a fourth who looks like a god." The God we worship doesn't tell His people to wear fireproof suits before going into the furnace. He goes right in there with them.

41   A story from the Holocaust makes a similar point. A Nazi guard was taunting his Jewish prisoner, who had been given the filthiest job,

cleaning the toilets. The guard was standing above him looking down at him and said: "Where is your God now?" The prisoner replied: "Right here with me in the muck." And the tremendous thing that has come to me more and more is this recognition of God as Emmanuel, God with us, who does not give good advice from the sidelines. The God who is there with us in the muck. God does not take our suffering away, but He bears it with us and strengthens us to bear it.

42 At times of despair, we must learn to see with new eyes like the prophet Elisha. The Bible tells us that Elisha and his servant were surrounded by a host of enemies. But the prophet remained strangely calm and somewhat unconcerned while his servant grew ever more agitated. The prophet asked God to open the servant's eyes and the servant then saw that those who were on their side were many times more than those against them. This is not just an old story. This is a way to see that you are not alone in your struggle for justice. There are many of you who are working to feed the orphan and the widow. There are many who are working to beat swords into plowshares. There is hope that nightmares will end, hope that seemingly intractable problems will find solutions. God has some tremendous fellow workers, some outstanding partners.

43 Each of us has a capacity for great evil but also for great good, and that is what convinces God that it was worth the risk of creating us. It is awesome that God the Omnipotent One depends on us fragile and vulnerable creatures to accomplish God's will and to bring justice and healing and wholeness. God has no one but us. As the great African saint Augustine of Hippo put it, "God without us will not as we without God cannot."

44 I have often told the story of the rustic priest in Russia who was accosted by a brash young physicist who had rehearsed all the reasons for atheism and arrogantly concluded, "Therefore I do not believe in God." The little priest, not put off at all, replied quietly, "Oh, it doesn't matter. God believes in you."

45 God *does* believe in us. God relies on us to help make this world all that God has dreamed of it being.

This passage reminds Christians that we have been reconciled to God through Christ, and instructs us to carry out God's ministry of reconciliation on Earth. Paul calls us "Christ's ambassadors" who should work for Him to continue this ministry. In all aspects of vocation, it is important for Christians to implement this concept of reconciliation so that we are accomplishing God's purposes and bringing others closer to Him.

2 Corinthians 5:17–21 (NRSV)

The Ministry of Reconciliation

17 So if anyone is in Christ, there is a new creation: everything old has passed away; see, everything has become new! **18** All this is from God, who reconciled us to himself through Christ, and has given us the ministry of reconciliation; **19** that is, in Christ God was reconciling the world to himself, not counting their trespasses against them, and entrusting the message of reconciliation to us. **20** So we are ambassadors for Christ, since God is making his appeal through us; we entreat you on behalf of Christ, be reconciled to God. **21** For our sake he made him to be sin who knew no sin, so that in him we might become the righteousness of God.

Afterword

One Hundred Things to Do before Graduating from Messiah College

1. Attend Fall Convocation to see your professors in their finest regalia.

2. Play Rec-Sports with friends.

3. View the hall of Presidents in Murray Library.

4. Participate in Powderpuff Football or Cheerleading.

5. Ask a professor to tell you about his or her own college experience.

6. Enjoy Greek Food at the annual festival of the Holy Trinity Greek Orthodox Cathedral.

7. Go to a B-sides concert in Larsen.

8. Register to vote in a local/state/national or student election.

9. Play Frisbee on Bittner Beach.

10. View an exhibit at the Oakes Museum.

11. Participate in campus celebration of MLK Commemoration Week.

12. Help your floor win Deck the Halls.

13. Get to know your Academic Advisor.

14. Explore your path to meaningful work through the Career Center.

15. Serve on a College standing committee.

16. Attend a luncheon with a Chapel guest speaker.

17. Visit President Phipps at an Open Door Day.

18. Eat dinner at a professor's home.

19. Conduct research with a faculty member.

20. Study at a campus picnic table.

21. Witness the Advent Tree-Lighting Celebration in Eisenhower Circle.

22. Have family visit during Family Weekend.

23. Exercise at the Fitness Center and indoor track.

24. Get a flu shot from the Engle Center.

25. Get "mugged" at Orchard Hill.

26. Participate in a coffeehouse.

27. Make new friends in your peer group.

28. Shoot hoops on the courts at the Pit behind Naugle.

29. Make a run to a local diner for a good, late-night discussion.

30. Join a Koinonia Group.

31. Write a letter to your congressperson on an issue you care about.

32. Wear your t-shirt for the White-Out game.

33. Master a new language.

34. Audition for a play or music ensemble.

35. Take a plunge in the campus pool.

36. Go canoeing/kayaking/tubing in the Yellow Breeches.

37. Get your passport photo taken at the EpiCenter.

38. Attend Sundaes on Mondays.

39. Cheer on an athlete at Special Olympics on Service Day.

40. Spend some reflective time in the Fry Prayer Chapel.

41. Check out the memorabilia of "Ernie Boyer" in The Ernest L. Boyer Center.

42. Browse the stacks at Murray Library.

43. Write a note of encouragement and drop it in campus mail.

44. Go to Thanksgiving Dinner in Lottie.

45. Read a short story in the *Minnemingo Review*.

46. Take a walk on the Fit Trail.

47. Visit Hershey Chocolate World.

48. Visit students living in one of several Satellite Houses.

49. Participate in the finals week "Midnight Scream."

50. Apply for a grant/scholarship.

51. Bring a date to a semi-formal dance.

52. Join a student club or organization.

53. Visit the archives to see early photos of the campus.

54. Go on a service trip during Fall/Spring/J-term Break.

55. Attend Pizza with the Prez.

56. Ask a Residence Director to share his or her faith story.

57. Attend a Senior Show or Recital.

58. Tune in to WVMM 90.7 FM, Messiah's own student-run radio station.

59. Listen to a renowned guest lecturer.

60. Take in an Exhibit at the Aughinbaugh Gallery.

61. Explore Study Abroad opportunities through the EpiCenter.

62. Cheer on the Falcons!

63. Read a book by the Yellow Breeches on a quiet afternoon.

64. Compete in the Falcon Fun Run at Homecoming.

65. Take the shuttle to Harrisburg to visit the Midtown Scholar and Broad Street Market.

66. Try all the smoothie flavors at the Union Cafe.

67. Get some real work experience through an internship.

68. Enjoy the fruits (and veggies) of the Community Garden.

69. Attend a theatre performance in Miller Auditorium.

70. Take a trip to Philadelphia with Messiah's B-Line Shuttle.

71. Call a member of your family at some unexpected time to tell them you love them.

72. Attend a Finals Week Midnight Pancake Dinner.

73. Spend a semester at the Philly Campus.

74. View a Lost Film in Parmer Cinema.

75. Get coffee with an employee in at Café Diem.

76. Go worship at Powerhouse on a Thursday night.

77. Go sledding down Cemetery Hill.

78. Participate in a Heritage Month event through the MISP Office.

79. Visit a few area churches of different traditions or denominations.

80. Watch Monday Night Football at the Student Union.

81. Engage a conversation full of global perspectives during International Education Week.

82. See a Broadway show with a SAB excursion to New York City.

83. Enroll in a Cross-Cultural course.

84. Visit an art show at the Harrisburg Institute.

85. Take on the Ropes Course or Climb the Bouldering Wall at The Loft.

86. Support global development at the Mennonite Relief Sale in Harrisburg.

87. Learn a new dance (from Swing to Salsa, Jazz to Ballroom).

88. Visit Amish country and eat Shoofly Pie.

89. Challenge your RA to a game of racquetball.

90. Go night skiing at Ski Roundtop.

91. Donate blood at a campus blood drive.

92. Perfect the "Lottie Chill"—spend a whole day sitting by the windows.

93. Visit the State Capital Building in Harrisburg.

94. Support graduating seniors at Commencement.

95. Cheer on the little ones at the Early Learning Center's annual Halloween costume parade.

96. Write an article for *The Swinging Bridge*.

97. Finish a paper a week in advance—at least once (or twice)!

98. Volunteer in a local community service opportunity through the Agape Center.

99. Participate in a book chapel.

100. Create (and complete) your own Messiah "bucket list."

Acknowledgments

pp. 6–19: From *What Does the Lord Require?* by Bruce C. Birch. Copyright © 1985 by Bruce C. Birch. Reprinted by permission of Westminster John Knox Press. www.wjkbooks.com.

pp. 20–22: From *God's Trombones* by James Weldon Johnson. Copyright © 1927 by The Viking Press, Inc., renewed © 1955 by Grace Nail Johnson. Used by permission of Viking Penguin, a division of Penguin Group (USA) Inc.

pp. 23–32: From *In Search of Our Mothers' Gardens* by Alice Walker. Reprinted by permission of The Wendy Weil Agency, Inc. First published by Harcourt. Copyright © 1983 by Alice Walker.

pp. 33–51: From *Tree and Leaf* by J. R. R. Tolkien. Copyright © 1964 by George Allen & Unwin Ltd. Copyright © renewed 1992 by John F. R. Tolkien, Christopher Tolkien, and Priscilla M. A. R. Tolkien. Copyright © 1988 by The Tolkien Trust. Reprinted by permission of Houghton Mifflin Harcourt Publishing Company. All rights reserved.

pp. 52–66: From *The Rock that Is Higher: Story as Truth* by Madeleine L'Engle. Copyright © 1993, 2002 by Crosswicks, Ltd. Used by permission of WaterBrook Multnomah, an imprint of the Crown Publishing Group, a division of Random House, Inc.

pp. 67–89: From *Between Heaven and Earth: Christian Perspectives on Environmental Protection* by Fred Van Dyke. Copyright © 2010 by Fred Van Dyke. Reproduced with permission of ABC-CLIO, LLC.

pp. 90–96: From *The Care of Creation* by Ronald J. Sider. Copyright © 2000 by Inter-Varsity Press. Reprinted by permission of publisher via the Copyright Clearance Center.

pp. 107–118: From *The Anabaptist Vision* by Harold Bender. Copyright © 1944 by Herald Press. Reprinted by permission.

pp. 121–137: As appeared in *Journal of Democracy*, 6:1 (1995), pp. 65–78. Copyright © 1995 by National Endowment for Democracy and The Johns Hopkins University Press. Its argument was amplified and to some extent modified in his book *Bowling Alone: The Collapse and Revival of American Community* (Simon & Schuster, 2000).

pp. 138–147: As appeared in *Journal of Democracy*, 21:1 (2010), pp. 9–16. Copyright © 2010 by National Endowment for Democracy and The Johns Hopkins University Press. Reprinted by permission of the publisher via the Copyright Clearance Center.

pp. 150–166: Reprinted by arrangement with The Heirs to the Estate of Martin Luther King Jr., c/o Writers House as agent for the proprietor, New York, NY. Copyright © 1963 by Dr. Martin Luther King Jr.; copyright renewed 1991 by Coretta Scott King.

pp. 167–191: From *Lapse of Time* by Wang Anyi. Copyright © 1988 by China Books and Periodicals, Inc. Reprinted by permission of the publisher via the Copyright Clearance Center.

pp. 198–202: As appeared in *Christian Century*, September 20, 2011. Copyright © 2011 by The Christian Century Foundation. Reprinted by permission of the publisher via the Copyright Clearance Center.

pp. 212–218: Adapted from a speech delivered by Dr. Ernest L. Boyer Sr. on September 4, 1984, at a convocation celebrating the seventy-fifth anniversary of the founding of Messiah College.

p. 221: From *Wishful Thinking: A Theological ABC* by Frederick Buechner. Copyright © 1973 by Frederick Buechner. Reprinted by permission of HarperCollins Publishers.

pp. 222–247: From *The Will of God as a Way of Life* by Jerry Sittser. Copyright © 2000, 2004 by Zondervan.

pp. 248–262: From *Letters to a Diminished Church* by Dorothy Sayers. Copyright © 2004 by Thomas Nelson, Inc. Reprinted by permission.

pp. 272–282: From *Out of My Life and Thought: An Autobiography* by Albert Schweitzer. Copyright © 1998 by Johns Hopkins University Press. Reprinted by permission of the publisher via the Copyright Clearance Center.

pp. 283–289: As appeared in *The Other Side*, January/February, 1989. Copyright © 1989 by John McKnight. Reprinted by permission of the author.

pp. 241–252: From *God Has a Dream: A Vision of Hope for Our Time* by Desmond Tutu. Copyright © 2004. Published by Doubleday, a division of Random House, Inc.